The Italian City-Republics

The Italian City-Republics

Third edition

Daniel Waley

LONGMAN
LONDON & NEW YORK

Longman Group UK Limited,
Longman House, Burnt Mill, Harlow,
Essex CM20 2JE, England
and Associated Companies throughout the world.

Published in the United States of America
by Longman Inc., New York

First published by Weidenfeld and Nicolson in the World University Library,
1969
Second edition published by Longman Group Ltd, 1978
Third edition published by Longman Group UK Ltd, 1988
Third impression 1991

British Library Cataloguing in Publication Data
Waley, Daniel
　　The Italian city-republics. – 3rd ed.
　　1. Italy – Politics and government –
　　476–1268　2. Italy – Politics and
　　government – 1268–1559
　　I. Title
　　321.06'0945　　JN5231
　　ISBN 0-582-02510-9　CSD
　　ISBN 0-582-55388-1　PPR

Library of Congress Cataloging-in-Publication Data
Waley, Daniel Philip.
　　The Italian city-republics.

　　Bibliography: p.
　　Includes index.
　　1. Italy – History – 1268–1492.　2. Cities and towns, Medieval –
Italy – History.　3. City-states – Italy – History.　I. Title.
DG530.W34　188　　945'.05　　87-4033
ISBN 0-582-02510-9
ISBN 0-582-55388-1 (pbk.)

Set in Linotron 10/12pt Palatino
Produced by Longman Singapore Publishers Pte Ltd.
Printed in Singapore

Contents

List of plates, figures and tables

List of plates

List of figures

List of tables

Acknowledgements

Thanks are due to my mother-in-law, Mrs Phyllis Griffiths, who provided me with a quiet setting in which to write the book, and to my wife and Miss Margaret Roberts, who most kindly read the typescript and suggested alterations. Thanks are also due to Mr Philip Waley for his help in proof-reading and to Mrs R. Rubinstein, Mr M. Evans of the Warburg Institute, Professor N. Rubinstein, and especially to Mr John Hall for help with the illustrations. The friends, librarians and archivists in Italy who have helped me are too numerous for individual mention, but I think with special gratitude of some citizens of communes of today, the Beltrami and Cappelli at Cesena and the Bonelli at Orvieto. Harold Fox researched the maps. For the second edition, I wish to thank Dr Kenneth Hyde for a useful list of errata and suggestions for reading and my mother and wife, who have read and advised on the new chapter.

In preparing the third edition I have been much helped by kind colleagues in Italy who have sent me offprints, Xerox copies and even whole volumes. In particular I should like to thank Professors Enrico Artifoni, Attilio Bartoli Langeli, Paolo Cammarosano, Jean-Claude Maire Vigueur, Emilia Saracco Previdi, Giuseppe Sergi, Aldo A. Settia and Hannelore Zug Tucci. Another assistance has been the opportunity offered by conferences in Italy to keep in touch with such colleagues and their writings. For this I should like to thank the bodies which organised these conferences, in particular the Società Internazionale di Studi Francescani and the Società di Storia Patria per l'Umbria. I owe particular thanks also to Professor Quentin Skinner.

The publishers would like to thank the following for their

permission to use plates in the text: Archivi Alinari SPA (plate 2.3); the Bibliothèque Nationale, Paris (plates 6.3 and 6.4); the Mansell Collection (plate 2.2); courtesy the Museum of Fine Arts, Boston (detail from *The Mystical Marriage of Saint Catherine*, attributed to 'Barna da Siena', Italian (Sienese), active mid-14th century, tempera on panel (panel: 138.9 × 110.0 cm ($54\frac{5}{8}$ × $43\frac{3}{4}$ ins); design: 134.8 × 107.1 cm ($53\frac{1}{8}$ × $42\frac{1}{8}$ ins)), Sarah Wyman Whitman Fund) (plate 6.6); and Scala/Firenze (plates 4.1 and 7.1).

To my Mother

Preface to the third edition

This book appeared first in 1969 in Weidenfeld and Nicolson's illustrated World University Library. The second edition came from Longman in 1978; the principal change was the addition of a chapter on 'Town and country'.

In the present edition there is again a new chapter, this time on the historiography of the subject. There is also a new feature, a chronological Gazetteer briefly covering developments in some of the principal city-republics. A considerable number of textual alterations (mainly additions) have been made and the bibliography has been lengthened. The bibliographies in the first and second editions were intentionally very selective; I have decided that it would be helpful to include more titles, but naturally it is still in no way intended as a full bibliography for the subject. It now also includes more suggestions about books which contain fuller reading lists.

Introduction

This book is concerned with a social and political milieu, that of the city-state, which contrasts in almost every conceivable way with the framework within which our life is lived in the second half of the twentieth century. To convey a true picture of such a world, the purpose of this book, will not be easy in this age of the nation-state. The difference lies not so much in size itself as in the overwhelming consequences of contrasting size. In the city-state proximity gave the population a fundamental and wide community of interest. Matters that would now be of 'merely local' importance, such as water supply, were then the subject of decisions by the state and were rightly seen as significant ones for such a state. The profound dissimilarity may be illustrated in the situation of the citizen of, respectively, the city-state and the nation-state with regard to military expenditure. The former could judge this as a direct contribution to his personal security: money spent on the upkeep of the walls was likely to make his own life and that of his family safer, money spent on weapons for an aggressive campaign might provide more agricultural land, greater security of communications and better protection against retaliation by neighbouring cities. The nation-state citizen, however, finds it far more difficult to assess the value to him of such expenditure and his dilemma is all the more clearly revealed by the euphemistic extension of the word 'defence' to cover all military activity. Even if the word is confined to its strictest sense, mere geographical extent dictates that the modern taxpayer will know that the defences for which he pays serve to protect men in distant places of whom he knows little and with whom he may have little in common. The distance between 'self-defence' and 'defence' has increased immeasurably.

Nor was the sentiment within the city-state of sharing a common citizenship solely the result of having a common place of residence. The unhappy Pia dei Tolomei in Dante's *Purgatorio* (v, 134), when she says the 'Siena made me' (*Siena mi fe*), is doing more than announcing her place of birth: she is saying that the city-state of Siena provided the physical, social and political environment in which she grew up, that it moulded her outlook and personality. The modern citizen is shaped by varied forces, among which the monstrously powerful energy of the nation-state competes with international mass communications and with the diluted and disappearing strength of regional and local patriotism. The local newspaper demonstrates the survival of older loyalties and in Italy itself the spirit of *campanilismo*, of the cherished and longed-for city tower, is not yet dead. But the citizen who fought alongside his neighbours against the citizens of the neighbouring cities knew through his way of life a now vanished patriotism and *campanilismo*.

The difference of size itself is of enormous consequence. The people of most of the city-states were personally acquainted with all their fellow citizens and the nature of their politics was the product of this situation. Controversial issues were argued between such acquaintances both inside and outside council meetings, including such matters as fiscal policies and assessments which made men richer or poorer before the eyes of their neighbours. Inevitably some men had more desire and ability to influence political decisions than others and possessed more leisure. Oligarchy, which is natural to any institution comprising individuals of varying strength and ability, was a peculiarly overt phenomenon in the restricted area of a single city, while the size of the state facilitated the direct use of force by the powerful to overawe the weak.

The characteristic civic outlook and patriotism of the city-state exists in its most enlightened form in a republic. When the citizens are their own politicians, legislators and officials their loyalties are more fully involved than when their role is a subordinate one. The destiny of the town is their own work, the success or otherwise of its affairs not merely all-important for their own welfare but the outcome of their endeavours. Add the attachment that almost all people, and especially those of conventional and conservative temperaments, feel to what is familiar, the spectacle of the same daily surroundings and accustomed ways of speech. Only thus can one understand something of the intensity of that emotion which Dante conveys in a passage of the *Purgatorio* (VI, 70ff) when Virgil utters the single word 'Mantua' and a figure replies:

> 'O Mantovano, io son Sordello
> Della tua terra.' E l'un l'altro abbracciava.
> 'O Mantuan, I am Sordello
> From your town.' And they embraced.

No one could know the feeling of such a moment better than Dante. He himself had partaken to the full in the political and military duties of a Florentine citizen, coming to the fore after 1298 as a leader among the Whites, the party opposing papalist authority in Tuscany. When the Blacks triumphed in 1301 he was absent from the city on an embassy. After being sentenced to suffer the confiscation or destruction of all his property and permanent exclusion from office, he failed to appear to answer the charges brought against him and was condemned to death. He signed his letters 'a Florentine undeservedly in exile' (*florentinus et exul immeritus*), refused the offer of an amnesty and never revisited the city for which he felt both bitter hatred and an aching nostalgia. In the *Divina Commedia*, the main work of his twenty years of exile, Florence figures both as the 'fair fold' (*bello ovile*) in which he had been reared 'as a lamb' and as a 'tragic wood' (*trista selva*) of bloodstained desolation (*Par.*, XXV, 5; *Purg.*, XIV, 64).

Each of these descriptions could be applied with equal justification. The very intensity of the milieu implied strong virtues and vices, advantages and disadvantages. In this book its merits will be most apparent in chapter 5, which is concerned with civic patriotism, its faults from chapters 6 and 7, which discuss disunity within the commune and its failure to withstand the despots.

Italian writers on politics in the twelfth and thirteenth centuries approached their theme through theory rather than practice, a tradition which continued to prevail until Machiavelli and many of his contemporaries broke away from it in the early sixteenth century. Hence the special problems of the city-state received little general discussion in the heyday of the communes. But the great issues of city-state politics had already been raised, long before, by Plato and Aristotle. The state about which they wrote was the city, the *polis*, and their very definitions make clear the closeness of the Italian parallel. Few of the Italian cities (the seat of a diocese was a 'city', though places of this size would now be thought small towns or villages) counted more than 20,000 inhabitants. Plato said that all his citizens must be known to each other individually and suggested 5,040 as a possible size for this community, implying probably a total population of under 50,000. Aristotle agreed that 'if the citizens of a state are to judge and to distribute offices according to merit, then they must know each other's characters; where they do not possess this knowledge, both the election to offices and the decision of lawsuits will go wrong'; he thought 100,000 people too numerous and 'no longer a community'. Moreover, Aristotle had neatly characterised the city-republic as the state in which the citizen had to be 'able to rule and to obey in turn[1]'.

The development of the medieval Italian city, then, was not unique, for a similar drama had been played before against another background of classical scenery. Once again republican institutions were to give a quite high proportion of the male population a political education as counsellors or as officials either within their own city or its subject territory, or in other cities. Again, too, the city-state proved a dead end rather than the direct antecedent of the nation-state, even though Venice, Genoa, Florence, Parma and Modena remained states or the nuclei of states, far into the 'modern' period. This lack of direct political posterity makes it no less interesting, no less an important and instructive phenomenon in its own right. Moreover, the people of the Italian communes moved in advance of the other Europeans of their day, in wealth, in artistic and intellectual activity, as well as in the sophistication of their social and governmental institutions; and their achievement in art and thought, extending into the age of civic decline, was to prove hardly less influential than that of ancient Greece.

It remains to define more closely the theme of this book. It is concerned with the republican city-state in northern and central Italy, and in particular with its social and political life, between the late eleventh and the early fourteenth century; the despotic city-state of the Renaissance period lies outside its scope. From the Alps to the border of the kingdom of Naples (where a powerful monarchy prevented the development of fully independent municipalities) hundreds of these entities at some period achieved self-government; how many one cannot say precisely, because the frontier between autonomy and dependence is not a precise one, but at the end of the twelfth century, when many of the smaller communes had not yet been swallowed up by larger ones, some two or three hundred units existed which deserve to be described as city-states. The temptation to generalise about these extremely diverse towns is powerful and indeed the content of this book will consist of such generalisations – all of them, inevitably, misleading, since one can no more propound formulas which will hold true of scores of city-republics over a period of two centuries than one could produce them to describe accurately the modern nation-state. Exceptional cases such as Venice, the giant ruler of a maritime empire, or those largely rural centres of habitation which soon fell victim to a local lord or city, are yet more misleading. But if information is given from different types and sizes of town a picture will emerge of an 'average' republic in a city of medium size.

1 The legacy of power

It has been characteristic of much of the Mediterranean region, at least since the classical period, that a high proportion of the population has been settled in towns rather than in scattered villages and hamlets. In Italy this tradition goes back to the time of the Greek colonisers and the Etruscans; and Roman rule in the peninsula, which developed from an original agglomeration of subject cities and peoples, was essentially municipal in its institutions. Between the fifth and tenth centuries AD these institutions were shattered and the very nature of political and social authority was reshaped by a series of events which included the conquests and settlements of Goths and Lombards. The gradual but profound transformation of these centuries involved a great contraction in city life and an almost complete break in urban government. A few of the larger cities, among them Rome itself, and Milan, survived as important centres of population, but most of the ancient municipalities must have declined into sordid if picturesque decay, villages in a setting of classical ruins.

It is a sign of the weakening of central authority in the early middle ages and of the discontinuity in institutions that the principal heir to political power in the town was the bishop. From the ninth century, in the period of feudal particularism following the fission of the Carolingian dynasty, some bishops enjoyed this position by virtue of royal grant of comital powers, though these were normally held by landed families, while others exercised similar right *de facto* in the absence of any other effective local authority. The authority of the bishop, however, was compatible with the sporadic survival of skeletal civic institutions. Certain arrangements of local importance had to be made wherever an urban community of any significance existed. These included the organisation of defences and in particular the allocation of the burden of keeping the town walls in adequate repair as well as other public works, and agreements affecting the local market. Certain ecclesiastical matters also called for discussion and settlement, among them sometimes the choice of the bishop himself as well as the more routine festivities and processions.

A tantalisingly small volume of evidence exists on periodical gatherings to transact such business. An edict of the Lombard king Rotharis (643) placed this occasion, the 'gathering in front of the church' (*conventus ante ecclesiam*) under special protection. A dispute at Verona at the end of the eighth century between the citizens and judges of the city and the church of San Zeno 'about the construction of walls and ditches' illustrates the characteristic agenda of such gatherings, as does another Veronese 'meeting of citizens' (*concio civium*) which in 945 received certain powers to make decisions regarding the local currency.

The survival of three highly literary panegyrics on cities from the same period – two of which celebrate Milan and the other Verona – shows that a certain municipal patriotism existed. But the *conventus* is the real precursor of the commune only in so far as it could take decisions and exercise local authority. What evidence have we for civic activity before the eleventh century? In the main this consists of the sporadic organisation of movement of protest, often against the bishop, such as the *conspiratio populi* formed against their bishop by the citizens of Modena in 891. Analogous movements are recorded at Turin in the same decade, at Cremona in 924, and in some half dozen other cities around the middle of the tenth century. In no cases are the precise grievances of the citizens known, though we may possess a clue in a promise made later (1038) by the bishop of Brescia to 154 named men 'and to the other free men living at Brescia' not to build on the height named Monticello, near the city. Collaboration among the citizens is also evident from a mutual agreement

Plate 1.1   Orvieto, a characteristic strong site on a volcanic plateau. This city in Umbria was also typical of the communes in that its economic life was primarily dependent on an agricultural hinterland. The population at its medieval maximum (at the end of the 13th century) was probably around 15,000; then, as now, the plateau was not fully built over.

concerning currency negotiated by the inhabitants of Mantua, Brescia and Verona before 945. Border disputes over diocesan frontiers began to involve town populations (for example, those of Bologna and its neighbour Modena in 969), a theme which is developed later in chapter 5. Cautious bishops sought the approval of citizens for the foundation of monastic houses, as occurred at Treviso in 997, when the bishop made such a grant 'with the consent of all the leading men and judges and the whole people of Treviso'. There are even indications of citizens sketching out diplomatic policies, when Milan and Pavia declare themselves subject to Arnulf of Carinthia (894) and when Verona encourages Arnulf of Bavaria to undertake an Italian expedition (934). As yet there is no body of standing municipal officials and certainly no sworn commune. The leading figures are *boni homines*, who are often members of the bishop's 'court', 'law-worthy' men in standing, but not chosen for office as the consuls were to be.

Economic changes

Before discussing these men it may be well to turn to the economic developments which lie behind their assumption of authority. The eleventh and twelfth centuries probably mark the period of sharpest change, but as early as the tenth century there had begun the process which transformed northern and central Italy from a sparsely populated and under-developed region, characteristically early medieval with its vast ecclesiastical estates and its huge areas of swamp, marsh and forest, into the crowded and economically evolved Italy of the Renaissance. The most fundamental change was in the size of population, which is estimated to have doubled between the tenth and fourteeth centuries. The town-dwelling population certainly increased in an infinitely greater proportion, as the absolute demographic growth was accompanied by a whole sale movement townwards from the countryside. One effect of the population rise was a great work of clearing. Large areas of marshy and flooded land, particularly in the valley of the Po, were claimed for farming by the laborious construction of drains and embankments, dykes and irrigation canals. Elsewhere reclamation took the form of deforestation and, on the hillsides, of terracing. New villages and (more rarely) towns came into being, sometimes through the highly-organised schemes of the authorities of the greater towns. As the population rose, land became expensive; isolated evidence suggests that around Milan it doubled in price between the late tenth and early eleventh centuries, and the long-term increase in the cost of both land and agrarian produce was revolutionary.

Meanwhile a connected (and better-known) revolution was taking place in commerce. Much Italian trade was concerned with the interchange by land of grain, oil, wine, salt and other food-stuffs and of the cheaper textiles and products of local artisans. Such commerce, however great its bulk and value, is liable to leave less mark in the written records than the long-distance exchange, particularly by sea, of valuable commodities, such as spices, dyes and high-quality textiles. This is in part the expla-nation of the tendency of many writers on this period to over-emphasise the latter, more spectacular, forms of trade and their accompanying financial phenomenon, the evolution of banking and credit arrangements. Ultimately, of course, the wealth and way of life of most of the largest cities came to be bound up with 'international' trade and finance, and if these are not much discussed here (they can be studied elsewhere in a number of admirable books), this is because they are less characteristic of the medium-sized town.

Long-distance trade was not in itself, of course, an innovation. Italy's geographical situation made the peninsula the logical halfway-house between north-western Europe and the Levant. The Po and its connected waterways facilitated the interchange of the sea-salt of the Venetian lagoon and the grain of the western Po plain at least as early as the seventh century and probably before. A curious document from the early eleventh century, the *Honorantiae civitatis Papiae*, reveals Pavia's merchants and finan-ciers dealing with traders from beyond the Alps as far afield as England; woollen and other textiles, slaves (or serfs), tin, swords and horses are mentioned among the commodities on which such traders have to pay customs dues. Pavia also expected 'many wealthy Venetian merchants', the nature of whose wares is indicated by the demand that their regular payment to the master of the treasury should include certain quantities of pepper, cinnamon and ginger. Other maritime traders mentioned here are those of southern Italy, from Amalfi, Salerno and Gaeta. More-over, Pavia, which lies on the Ticino near its confluence with the Po, was only one of a number of north Italian towns committed to the routine of long-distance trading. Others in Lombardy were

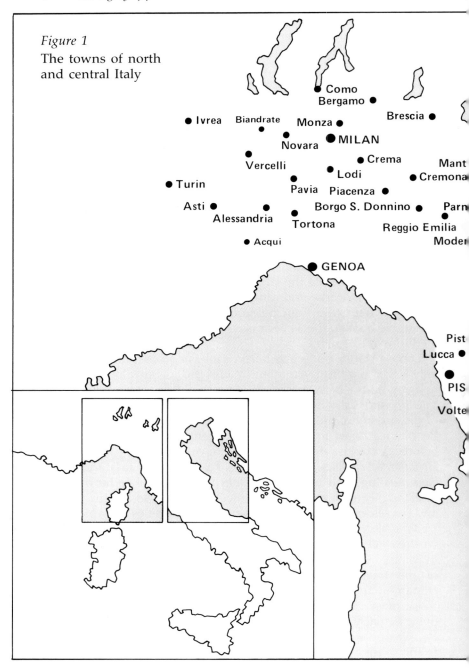

Figure 1
The towns of north
and central Italy

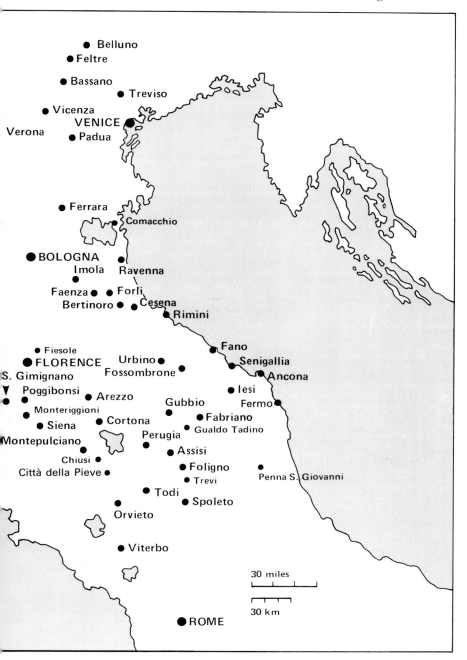

Cremona (on the Po itself) and Milan, in Piedmont there were Asti and Vercelli, close to more westerly tributaries of the same river. The main route from France had also brought to life Piacenza, at the Po crossing, and Lucca, at the southern gateway of the Apennine pass. The role and triumphs of the three main centres of maritime commerce need no emphasis. In the ninth and tenth centuries Venice was already the main point of economic contact with Byzantium and the Levant. Genoa too possessed shipping in the Carolingian period but, like Pisa, suffered later from the naval assaults of Islam. In the eleventh century both these ports had fleets capable of striking back at the Muslims; they combined commercial expansion with a naval role in support of the Normans, who drove the Arabs from Sicily, and with raiding against the north African coast. By 1100, after a cautious wait to determine the direction of prevailing politico-religious winds, these three maritime cities all committed themselves to support of the crusaders and thereby gained a yet firmer foothold in the eastern Mediterranean. Their concessions on the Syrian littoral, together with Constantinople and Alexandria, became the greatest centres of transit in the Italian trade with the Levant and beyond.

The nascent commune

In Italy as a whole, however, the greatest beneficiaries of tenth- and eleventh-century economic developments were probably the minor feudal nobility, who had become *de facto* owners of much of the land. Slowly the great ecclesiastical estates accumulated in Lombard and Carolingian times had broken up, leaving lay vassals to enjoy the actual possession of the now valuable land and its produce. In the smaller towns the only prominent class in the eleventh century is that of the landowners, the *maiores*, so named in contrast with the craftsmen and town-dwelling peasantry, the *minores*. As for the larger cities, a document from Pavia (1084) sets out conveniently the range of classes composing the *populus*; it records the hearing of a lawsuit between two monasteries by the captains, valvassors, and the major and minor citizens. Of these, the 'captains' seem to have included the principal episcopal tenants and officials (the *curia*), while the valvassors were minor feudal tenants. Alongside these would normally be representatives of minor feudal lines, among them the 'Visconti' and 'Visdomini' whose surname recurs monotonously in most of the cities, together with some members of great dynasties, such as the Obertenghi (at Pisa) or the Malaspina and the palatine Counts of Lomello (at Piacenza).

Political action by these citizens continued to be essentially spasmodic throughout the eleventh century. Only the precocious and untypical Milanese provide a partial exception. They rose in revolt against Archbishop Landulf in 979 and against Archbishop Aribert in 1035, the latter movement merging into a widespread war when the captains aligned themselves with the archbishop against the valvassors, who turned for support to the Emperor Conrad II. But even here co-operation among the population was lacking until the knightly classes allied with the 'citizens' in 1045 and after this it was at least thirty years before firm communal institutions emerged.

In this formative period, grants of imperial privileges to certain cities perhaps provide firmer evidence of the evolution of a rudimentary commune. As early as 958 the 'true men and residents' (*fideles et habitatores*) of Genoa received privileges concerning land and in 1056 a more important grant to its citizens confirmed their customary rights over the market. A diploma of 998 in favour of the bishop of Cremona mentions what appears to be a municipal building (*domus civitatis*). Privileges were conferred on the population of Mantua (1014) and Ferrara (1055), but the first substantial grants were those made by Henry IV in Tuscany. In 1081 he engaged himself to build no place in Lucca and no castle within six miles of the city; he also renounced jurisdiction within the city of Pisa and promised to name no new marquis in Tuscany without the consent of the Pisans. From the imperial point of view such concessions, significant though they may seem in the light of later developments, were preferable to the periodic violence of Pavia, where the first half of the eleventh century had seen two anti-imperialist insurrections, in one of which the royal palace was destroyed; the order to rebuild seems to have been neglected. Such defiance and the tacit recognition of municipal rights in Milan and some other cities mark as clearly as do the diplomas the ascent of the cities at the emperor's expense. An essential part of this ascent was the weakening of imperial authority in appointing to bishoprics; in this respect the claims of the townsmen were connected with the wider 'Church and State' disputes of the time, just as their political independence was forwarded by local anti-episcopal movements which were involved in the greater cause of religious reform. The role of ecclesiastical disputes (sometimes labelled as 'the Investiture Controversy') was to serve as the occasion rather than the cause of political motivation. The 'new' social elements would seek a sharing of power with the bishop even where they were not his religious critics.

The second half of the eleventh century, the period which saw these civic gains at the expense of imperial and episcopal authority, brought also the installation of Norman rule in southern Italy. This was the decisive stage in the foundation of a powerful monarchy which firmly inhibited the evolution of city-republics in the southern mainland and Sicily. Even after the middle of this century the cities of the north and centre had evolved no fixed political institutions. The essential role of the binding oath meant that the advent of the commune had a precise date, yet such an institution would not necessarily endure. The independence which was noted in the following century by the German chronicler Otto, Bishop of Freising ('They are governed by the will of consuls rather than rulers') and by a Jewish traveller, Benjamin of Tudela ('They possess neither king nor prince to govern them, but only the judges oppointed by themselves[1]') was essentially that of communities now continuously exercising the power to appoint their own political officials. When the earliest form of this authority, called (with a classical reminiscence) the consulate, had come into being, in the late eleventh and early twelfth centuries, the commune or city-republic was present. But before describing its institutions it is logical to turn again to the people who brought these into being.

2 The population

Status and occupation

A recent writer has described the medieval Italian towns as 'mixed societies of noblemen and rentiers (*milites*), of shopkeepers and artisans, notaries and peasants (*pedites*)[1]'. This admirable definition requires a rider and it is an important one. Many of the inhabitants do not belong clearly to any one of these categories because they were engaged to a significant degree in more than one type of activity. It was common to combine the profession of notary with a craft or trade, but even more it was usual for landownership to be combined with all other kinds of activity, so that a very high proportion – often, one suspects, the absolute majority – of the population was vitally committed to both agrarian production and other forms of commercial or industrial activity. To have both a warehouse or shop and a holding in land, so being by income and outlook neither fully rentier or peasant nor artisan-shopkeeper, was thus extremely common and any census which placed men in one category alone would be very seriously misleading. Not only is classification by economic activity more than usually fallacious in this context, since so many belonged to two or more categories, but naturally the classes shaded into one another – flourishing peasantry into minor rentiers, thriving shopkeepers into merchants, part-time money-lenders (most obviously) into bankers and financiers.

We may start by returning to the knightly *maiores* already referred to as the most prominent class in the nascent commune. Certainly they are an omnipresent feature. In 1180 the council at Piacenza was attended by 130 'nobles'. The councillors of Mantua

Figure 2
Regions and relief
in north and central Italy

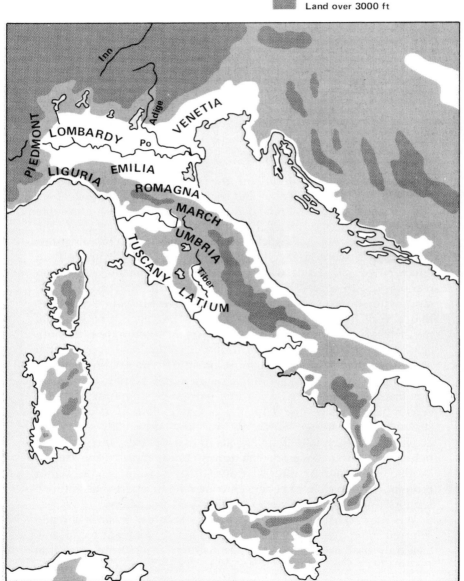

in 1199 numbered about a hundred, some eighty of whom descended from noble (including knightly) families; against these one can set only two butchers and a money-changer. The Pisan consuls and other officials during the second half of the twelfth century included representatives of thirty different 'noble' families, that is, of families whose ancestors had ranked among the feudal aristocracy. On the other hand there were certainly some towns where the noble element was in a minority even in this early phase; San Gimignano, where only two noble families of rural origin are recorded, was one, and probably Florence was another. And it is important to emphasise that there was no stage at which noble descent was incompatible with trading. Verona provides a number of examples from the very early twelfth century of wealthy holders of castles and land who traded on the Adige and in the Trentino, or sometimes further afield in Germany, and who also bought up land as well as having their own property in Verona. Later in the same century the chief official of the merchants' organisation (*consul mercatorum*) was himself a noble, both at Modena (Guglielmo de Atto, 1182) and at Florence (Giovanni di Cavalcante, 1192–3). Landholding was the normal accompaniment of other economic activities, as may be seen from the earliest tax records (in the second half of the thirteenth century) which suggest that normally about two-thirds of the heads of urban households owned land. Table 1 shows the distribution of landownership in a characteristic inland town[2]. It is interesting, incidentally, how these towns contradict Aristotle's belief that a high proportion of landowning citizens makes for political stability.

In contrast with the merchant-noble, the 'pure' merchant only requires brief treatment here. In the early period he is likely to travel with his own wares and should he be engaged in long-distance commerce with the Levant or north Africa, he will probably be an exporter of European cloth, an importer of spices and gold. He will be more typical if he is mainly concerned in local or regional exchange of commodities. He is likely to be involved in one of the many forms of trading partnership. If his base is an inland city, and particularly if it lies on an important trading route, he may well be a financier, banker or money-changer rather than a dealer in commodities; this is true in particular of bases such as Piacenza, Pistoia and Siena, but also of Asti and elsewhere in Piedmont. Such activity varies in scale from partnership in a great banking firm with branches (by the later thir-

Table 1   Tax assessment of land owned by residents of Orvieto in 1292

Total number of property-owners assessed: 2,863

	number of owners	per cent of total (approx.)
Property assessed at less than 10 L	74	3
Between 10 L and 50 L	454	16
Between 50 L and 100 L	484	17
Between 100 L and 500 L	1,031	36
Between 500 L and 1,000 L	371	13
Between 1,000 L and 2,000 L	244	9
At more than 2,000 L	205	7

teenth century) in other Italian cities, which might do business at the Champagne fairs (or elsewhere in France) and with the papacy, down to the man who lends money to peasants to tide them over until the harvest. The number of people involved could be considerable; fifty-seven bankers from Piacenza were among those who financed St. Louis's immensely expensive Crusade (1248-54). Again versatility would apply. No bankers were such specialists that they disdained to trade in commodities.

Another very prominent figure in the town, particularly so in its early phase, is the lawyer or 'judge'. The acquisition of a legal education being a long and expensive process, it is evident that these judges came, for the most part, from the very same families as the knightly *maiores*; presumably they were merely the members of this class who had received a training in secular book-learning, as opposed to those whose upbringing had been primarily military or ecclesiastical. They seem often to have been treated as *prima facie* nobles; at Pistoia, for example, there was a joint *pars iudicum et militum*. The combination of birth and education makes their early prominence no surprise. At Padua in 1138 five of the seventeen consuls were judges, while at Mantua in 1164 they constituted four of the council of forty, and at Bergamo in 1219 seven of the council of 104. Of these four Mantuan judges, two were definitely of noble descent, another had inherited much land, the fourth was a councillor of the bishop. The judge-landowner was of course as common a hybrid as the merchant-landowner; one is to be met in Boccaccio's Riccardo di Chinzica whose neglected wife thought her sex-life impoverished by his punctilious observance of feast days: 'And I tell you that if you had allowed the labourers who till your lands to keep as many holidays as you allowed him who had the tilling of my little field, you would never have reaped a grain of corn' (*Decameron*, ii, 10).

Although in some cities the notaries were included in the same gild as the judges, their rank was normally a humbler one and they were rarely if ever of noble descent, though a successful notary might elevate his own family in the social scale. Their work was to record all transactions, commercial and others, of which a written record might be required, and this involved a considerable share in the paper work of government. Almost all officials employed notaries as assistants, some of them a good many; the statutes of Modena required the third judge of the city to choose twenty notaries *de melioribus civitatis*, who were to enquire into the legality of the elections of the commune's officers. Manuals of instruction written for notaries included advice concerning communal deeds; clearly the notaries did much to decide how the commune functioned as an administrative organisation. As literate laymen on a large scale, these men represented an extremely important and distinctive element in the towns' precocity, their presence being incompatible with the conventional picture of a medieval society comprising literate clergy and illiterate laity. In the larger towns by the late thirteenth century their total numbers were enormous: Bologna may have had as many as 2,000, Milan 1,500 and Padua 600. One wonders how the members of this inflated profession were all able to make a living. To some extent the explanation must be that, as with so many occupations, this was often a part-time activity, compatible with trade, with medicine and hotel-keeping, and even with such crafts as weaving, milling and smithery. The political role in the commune of both judges and notaries was very considerable. Not only did they occupy a quite disproportionate share of offices, they attended tirelessly at council meetings – thus, a meeting of 353 councillors at Modena in 1220 included twenty-three notaries and four judges, and one of 247 councillors at Arezzo some thirty years later eighteen notaries and ten judges – and they were there not merely to vote but to *give* counsel: the minutes record speech after speech by lawyers and notaries.

The artisan element in most of the towns must have been considerable from an early period – any nucleus of population will require certain services for keeping its members tolerably fed,

Plate 2.1 Detail from Ambrogio Lorenzetti's fresco portraying the effects of good government in a city (Palazzo Pubblico, Siena, *c.* 1338–9). Shops in foreground, with an academic lecture, probably in law, in the background. A good selection of shoes is on sale at the stall on the left; shoemaking was one of the most flourishing crafts at Siena, as in several other Italian cities.

clothed and housed – and with increasing specialisation the proportion of the population mainly employed in this way must normally have greatly increased. As early as the tenth century Verona could boast at least six tailors, six bakers, four millers, three hosiers and two smiths, and 200 years later the much less precocious city of Florence counted three smiths, a tailor and a bell-founder among its *boni homines*. The artisan element in the councils was generally small in the early commune, tending by the early thirteenth century to increase greatly. It is probably typical that the 'secret' council of Cremona in 1188 only included one clearly identifiable craftsman, a dyer (there was also a money-changer), whereas Modena's admittedly larger council in 1220 included many artisans and shopkeepers, among the fish-mongers, smiths, and even clothes-repairers (*strazaroli*); the political ascent of the gildsmen is, however, a topic to which we shall return in a later chapter.

The size of the artisan population can perhaps be best judged from surviving early lists of jurors. It was quite usual for communes to bind themselves to the terms of diplomatic contracts by agreeing that the entire adult male population should take an oath to obey the treaty. These lists by no means always recorded a man's occupation, in fact they often did so only to avoid confusion between men with the same name: therefore they cannot help us much about the proportion of craftsmen in the population. The fact that, for instance, two per cent of Pistoia's jurors in 1219 are named by their trade, whereas twenty-five per cent of Pisa's in 1228 have this addition, cannot possibly indicate the respective proportions of the population in these two cities engaged in a craft. But they do give some indication of which crafts were early practised on a considerable scale, and in particular one notes the ubiquity of the iron-worker or smith. Bergamo's 1,000 jurors in 1156 include a number of identified tradesmen, but only smiths (four) appear more than once on the list. Many crafts-men are among Borgo San Donnino's jurors in 1191; again the smiths are in the lead with seven, followed by four muleteers. Among Poggibonsi's jurors in 1221, the smiths (who are leaders also at Pisa and Pistoia in the documents mentioned above) are followed by millers, flax-weavers, inn-keepers, tailors, barbers, pork butchers and 'jugglers'. But the main impression derived from these lists is of the variety of trades. At Poggibonsi are also found a saddler, a baker and a cloth-beater and this list of crafts is extended by Orvieto's jurors in 1221: coopers, tanners, clothiers, shield-makers and sword-makers, manufacturers of rope, bells, clogs and pots, as well as a dealer in salt, are present.

By this date another indication of economic activity is the existence of craft gilds, most towns possessing gilds of clothiers (the textile industry being the most ubiquitous of all), tanners, smiths, masons, butchers, vintners, fishmongers, millers, tavern-keepers, as well as associations of 'merchants' and money-changers. Soon these gilds began to splinter and to proliferate; the dozen or so gilds of the early thirteenth century might become forty or fifty or even, at Venice, 142. Naturally some of these trades were infinitely more important than others. Pisa's jurors in 1228 included 125 smiths, 112 shoemakers and 85 tanners (as well as more than 70 other leatherworkers) and 64 furriers. We may perhaps get some idea of the strength of various crafts at Cremona from the list compiled in 1283 of the nearly 8,000 gild members of that city. A trade is only given for a minority of these, but once again the smiths (100) are much the largest group, followed by porters (54), bakers (53), millers (38), tailors (24) and barbers (21). Pisa may have been more typical than Cremona in the high numbers of leather workers; at Bologna in 1294 over 2,000 of the city's 9,000 gild members were involved in the leather crafts.

These craftsmen very commonly combined their trade with landholding. In 1292 some 3,000 residents of Orvieto owned land, of whom at least 250 were artisans. Boccaccio's ingenuous painter, Calandrino, was doing the conventional thing when he decided to use his aunt's legacy of 200 L 'to buy a bit of land' (*Decameron*, IX, 3) and Giotto himself combined painting and architecture with the ownership of agricultural property and hiring out looms to textile workers. Finally there was a class, probably a very considerable one in all but the largest towns, whose sole occupation was agriculture. These small-holders and agricultural labourers often tilled the soil or tended animals at a considerable distance from the town. The petitioners at Orvieto who claimed to be 'weak and impotent and common men' (*populares*) owning land in the city's subject territory spoke for many thousands of residents of the Italian republics.

Growth of the town

The essential function of the great majority of towns was as the principal market centre for local commodities. Most towns were

Figure 3
Florence:
the expanding city walls

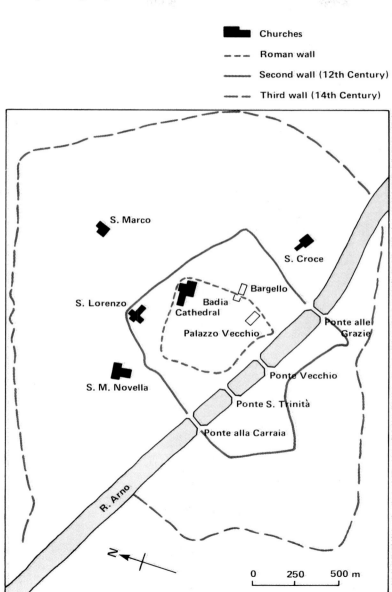

■ Churches
--- Roman wall
—— Second wall (12th Century)
—-— Third wall (14th Century)

S. Marco

S. Croce

S. Lorenzo

Bargello
Badia
Cathedral
Palazzo Vecchio

Ponte alle
Grazie

S. M. Novella

Ponte Vecchio

Ponte S. Trinità

Ponte alla Carraia

R. Arno

N

0   250   500 m

probably mainly dependent on their own rural territory for grain, wine, meat, cheese, vegetables and fruit, a majority even for their hides and wool, a great many too for their oil and fish. Those cities, such as Genoa and Florence, which became so large that they could not find sufficient cereals in their own vicinity, were quite exceptional. And the commodities that most towns had to import from further afield – salt, iron, perhaps building-stone – were also the exceptional ones. Its position as a centre of roads and often waterways for receiving and marketing wares is the key to the economic life of almost every city except the greatest nuclei of international commerce.

It is a great obstacle to generalising accurately about the Italian republics that most of them grew very considerably during the twelfth and thirteenth centuries, inevitably changing their nature as communities. For the earlier period it is quite impossible to give estimates of population. These can be attempted for few cities of the thirteenth century and even then must be regarded as very approximate indeed. It seems likely that Padua had some 15,000 inhabitants three-quarters of the way through the twelfth century and at least 35,000 by about 1320. Florence, which became one of the largest cities, had perhaps 50,000 inhabitants at the start of the thirteenth century and nearly double that number at its close. The tremendous growth of Florence can also be estimated from the need to build new circles of town walls; the walls begun in 1172 enclosed an area of only about 80 hectares (197 acres), whereas the circle projected in 1284 and completed some fifty years later enclosed 620 hectares (1,556 acres). Pisa's walls tell a story of earlier but less spectacular development; the area of early medieval Pisa was about 30 hectares (74 acres), the wall completed north of the Arno in 1162 (when Florence had not yet caught up on the population of Pisa) enclosed 114 (282 acres), and the wall completed about the end of the thirteenth century 185 (456 acres). Elsewhere more direct indications of economic growth confirm the evidence for demographic growth. At Genoa the value of goods passing through the port is said to have doubled

Plate 2.2   An illumination of a cloth market from the statutes of the Bolognese drapers' gild (Bologna, Museo Civico). Bologna was an important centre for both the wool and leather industries. A textile industry was to be found in all the cities of considerable size, though in many production was limited to low-quality cloth for local use.

between 1214 and 1274, and then quadrupled between 1274 and 1293, though these statistics must be regarded with suspicion. Again, these are exceptional figures. A recent estimate suggests that only twenty-three cities of northern and central Italy had attained a population of 20,000 by the end of the thirteenth century, and it is not likely that this list would be much increased in the late middle ages or the 'Renaissance'; few towns grew greatly in the half century before the Black Death (1348), and few of them surpassed their medieval population until the nineteenth century. But the list of twenty-three would be much longer if a population of 10,000 were taken as the criterion of a fair-sized town; and many enjoyed genuine municipal independence with a population of as little as 5–10,000.

The attitude of the town authorities towards immigration from the *contado* and further afield changed radically from time to time in accordance with what the governing class believed to be its own interest, just as the prescriptions of economists have changed in more sophisticated times. Bologna sought with success to attract textile-workers in the 1230s, but in 1246 and again in 1259 tried to return all immigrants from the *contado* to their original homes. In the latter year the trouble was famine and an attempt was made to expel all the city's poor as 'unproductive'. However, the massive scale of political expulsions from Bologna in 1274 (the exiles may have numbered as many as 12,000) led to new measures aimed at increasing the city's population. The essential mobility of the population was assumed; compulsory transfers of population to strategically important fortified places (*castra*) or from abandoned or vulnerable ones into the main town were a matter of routine. There was nothing exceptional about the oath taken by the entire population of Castel Imolese that they would move into Imola (1210) – and probably nothing exceptional either about the need to repeat both the 'destruction' of Castel Imolese and the transfer of its population after only eleven years. In the late thirteenth century Parma issued a list of no less than forty-two *castra* which the city had destroyed and were henceforth not to be inhabited.[3] The Bolognese policy of founding new *burgi* for strategic and agrarian purposes also led to characteristic struggles to prevent the drainage of population from these. Initial grants of fiscal exemption were sometimes succeeded by heavy taxation, hence – for instance – the desertion of many of the inhabitants of Bologna's Castelfranco in 1295; these moved into Modenese territory, 'taking their houses with them'.

It would be misleading to emphasise the growth of the towns without mentioning that the population was certainly not rooted to its home city. In the case of the larger cities much involved in long-distance trade – and even more perhaps with those specialising in finance – a quite sizeable proportion of the adult male citizens must have been away on business. A thirteenth-century book of advice for men taking office, the *Oculus Pastoralis*, provides a number of set speeches appropriate for certain circumstances; one is a funeral speech for a citizen 'who has recently died in France'. This was part of the everyday order of things. St Francis, the son of a merchant of Assisi, was called 'Francis' because his father was away at the French fairs at the time of his birth (1182). Giovanni Boccaccio was the illegitimate son of a Tuscan merchant frequently resident at Paris; and a great many stories in the *Decameron* depend for their plot on the itinerant life of the merchant community. The merchant of the pioneering days, in the twelfth century and in the early thirteenth, was likely to travel with his own wares, but this had ceased to be true before 1300, by which time the sedentary merchant was the rule. By then he had his own representatives resident abroad and it must have been common for young men to serve as agents in the eastern Mediterranean and elsewhere before returning home to marry and settle down. The resident Venetian colony at Constantinople numbered as many as ten thousand before the Fourth Crusade (1204). Rather later, communities of Italian traders and financiers could be found in all the Syrian and north African ports, in France, the Low Countries, England, in central and eastern Europe. The greater Florentine banking houses employed scores of men in their various branches, and small settlements of enterprising Florentine and Venetian financiers were scattered throughout the relatively unadvanced regions of southern and central Italy. Nor were all overseas residents merchants; Pisa early acquired Sardinia and Corsica (later both lost to the Genoese), while in the thirteenth century Venice and then Genoa gained empires in the Levant, in which many served as colonial administrators. Moreover, many Venetians settled as landowners in Crete, in mainland Greece and in the Ionian islands. Within the peninsula, of course, commerce was merely one of many motives for travel. Men also journeyed to other cities to hold office and on ecclesiastical business. It is significant that Viterbo, the last considerable town on the road south to Rome, helped to defray its military budget by decreeing that 'if any pilgrim or stranger or foreign merchant dies in the city of Viterbo, two-thirds of his property is to go to the fund for paying compensation for the [killed or maimed] horses of the Viterbese cavalry'. The remaining third (a curiously trustful provision, this) went to the dead man's host or innkeeper[4].

It was likely, then, that at any time a quite high proportion of the town's population would be newcomers or the descendants of recent immigrants; analyses of Pisa's residents in the late thirteenth century suggest that well over half of them were immigrants from the *contado*. Moreover, many of these new arrivals would have been among the wealthier elements. The attitude of the older citizen families towards the immigrants is therefore important.

New categories and class feeling

Conventional twelfth-century categorisations of the citizens as *maiores* and *minores* (and a class of *mediocres* between them) became quite inadequate as the result of immigration and social mobility. The noble class itself received additions when the commune began to create knights or (more usually and correctly) to nominate men to be dubbed as knights by nobles. Soon after the middle of the twelfth century this development was mentioned by Bishop Otto of Freising: 'That they may not lack the means of subduing their neighbours, they do not disdain to give the girdle of knighthood or the grades of distinction to young men of inferior station and even some workers of the low mechanical crafts, whom other people bar like the plague from the more respected and honourable pursuits'[5]. The bishop was perfectly correct in attributing this development to the need to create a larger class of men owing the commune cavalry service. The Genoese consuls concluded in 1173 that wars conducted by

Plate 2.3   Enrico Scrovegni (d.1336) was the donor of the Arena chapel at Padua, which contains Giotto's greatest cycle of fresco paintings; the foundation stone was laid in 1303. Enrico was a typical second-generation figure in a successful landed family connected with the bishops of Padua. He inherited a fortune from his father, a financier and merchant, continued the business, was himself knighted, and married into the aristocratic families of Carrara and d'Este. He also endowed the convent of S. Orsola.

paid feudal allies were too costly and had brought the city into debt. They decided, as the chronicler Caffaro records:

Our city, thanks to God, outshines others in strength, wealth and agreeable qualities. If therefore we wish to preserve praise, nobility and quiet and to destroy utterly our hostile neighbours, it would be wise and most useful to begin to create native-born knights in our city . . .

And so the consuls, 'despite the labour and expense involved, created more than a hundred knights from within Genoa and outside[6]'. The experiment was a success and was repeated in 1211 when 200 citizens were knighted to serve with the cavalry in a campaign against the Malaspina.

It also became necessary to make finer distinctions among the non-nobles (*popolani*) and in particular to invent terms to describe the wealthier among them. Hence the appearance of phrases like *boni homines de populo, convenienter divites* (wealthy *popolani* of good family), *grandi e possenti popolani* and even, most paradoxically, *antico e nobile popolano e ricco e possente, grandi e nobili popolani* or *nobiles populares*[7].

A term was also coined to describe those who had recently started to play a part in city politics: they were *gente nuova*, new men. This phrase was, however, used, confusingly, to describe two categories of people which overlapped but did not coincide: it was used for the *nouveau riche* as well as for the *nouveau venu*. The 'older' elements in the cities tended to share a generally felt prejudice against these men. In every age in which a capable or fortunate businessman has been able to amass a lot of money quickly and taxation has been light the *nouveau riche* has been a familiar figure and a favourite of the satirists. Dickens introduces us to a couple in *Our Mutual Friend*:

Mr and Mrs Veneering were bran-new people in a bran-new house in a bran-new quarter of London. Everything about the Veneerings was spick and span new. All their furniture was new, all their friends were new, all their servants were new, their plate was new, their carriage was new, their harness was new, their horses were new, their pictures were new . . .

The Veneerings must have been as numerous in the Italy of the twelfth and thirteenth centuries – when a profit of 150 per cent seems to have been a not strikingly exceptional return on a trading venture – as in Dickens' England. The prejudice against them is well illustrated by Sacchetti's presumably apocryphal story (*Il Trecentonovelle*, LXII) about Giotto's reaction to an invitation to paint a coat of arms on the shield of a 'boorish craftsman' (*grossolano artefice*); the 'arms' that the great man painted were a helmet, a gorget, pairs of arm- and leg-armour, a sword, a knife and a lance.

To despise the upstart was natural and easy for the nobly-born, such as the Paduan Giovanni de Nono whose elaborate treatise on more than a hundred families of his native city is a diatribe against upstarts. De Nono's particular *bêtes noires* were the Scrovegni, those successful financiers who were the donors of the church whose decoration is Giotto's masterpiece. For others this sentiment involved the need to discover an aristocratic genealogy for themselves; such a one was Dante, whose father was in fact a money-lender, but who fabricated a more satisfactory ancestry including a crusading great-grandfather who was of Roman descent and had been knighted by the Emperor Conrad III. Ingenuous snobbery, which after all (despite occasional outbreaks of inversion) is one of the great unchangeables of social life, was a commonplace. Story after story in the *Decameron* centres round class differences, around people who have married above or below their rank and so on. And the argument reported in one of the tales (VI, 6) about 'which is the oldest and most *gentile*' [noble] family in Florence must echo a favourite topic of discussion. We meet this attitude in the thirteenth-century Ferrarese chronicler who reports nostalgically: 'I have heard our ancestors enumerate thirty-four noble families, of which many have failed (*defecerunt*) and ten have no living descendant'[8].

Although so many 'noble' families were themselves involved in commerce and finance, the ethos which pronounced such occupations sordid was immensely influential. Nobles who had come down in the world – like the Count of Rocca di Tintannano to whom the Sienese voted a cloak and boots 'on account of his poverty' – were certainly not the only people to proclaim the values of a vanished dream-world of feudal chivalry. French literature and especially chivalric writings contributed greatly to this. The Carolingian and Arthurian epics, the verse of the troubadours, the *Roman de la Rose* and other French romances, all enjoyed an immense vogue in the Italian towns, leaving their mark on iconography, personal names and, above all, people's outlook on life. The names 'Orlando', 'Oliviero', 'Rinieri', 'Artù' – all derived from the epic cycles – became quite common, while 'Cavalleresco', 'Biancafiore' and others bear witness to the taste for French romances. St Francis of Assisi was a typical merchant's son in his enthusiasm for Provençal songs and French literature. He once rebuked a friar who wanted a psalter by explaining that merely reading about saints ranked a long way below performing saintly deeds:

Charles the Emperor, Roland and Oliver, and all the Paladins and strong men, being mighty in war, chasing the infidels with much travail and sweat to the death, had notable victory over them, and at the last themselves died in battle, holy martyrs for the faith of Christ; but now there are many who would fain receive honours and human praise for merely telling of the things which those others did. So also amongst ourselves are many who would fain receive honours and praise by reciting and preaching the works which the saints did[9].

A passion for jousting and indeed for all the outward forms of chivalry extended throughout Italy and was not confined to the knightly class. A typical occasion for chivalrous dressing-up was the procession to celebrate the election of a new Venetian doge, Lorenzo Tiepolo, in 1268. The representatives of each gild chose their own costume, and the barbers appeared as knights errant, making a speech to the doge in which they declared: 'Sire, we are two knights errant who have ridden on horseback to search for adventure; we have suffered and laboured and we have now won these four ladies', whom they offered to defend in battle against all comers[10]. Three whole centuries before Don Quixote's friend the barber discussed with him the feats of Amadis of Gaul, Venice's barbers nourished their imagination on knightly deeds. And so popular were public recitations of the French epics that Bologna had to legislate against 'singers of French themes' (*cantatores Francigenorum*) performing in the Piazza del Comune.

The enthusiasm of Italian town-dwellers for chivalry was not just a matter of escapism, the snobbish nostalgia of the bourgeois for an unattainable and romantic universe of the imagination. The courtly love of the sonnets and the knightly deeds of the epics did not represent a world which was entirely alien to the townsmen. There was no sharp contrast between the way of life of the city and that of the countryside. The man of affairs could enjoy the stories, such as Boccaccio's, in which his own commercial milieu was portrayed with cynical accuracy, and at the same time could be directly acquainted with much of the stage property of chivalry, such as fortified castles and the ceremonial dubbing of knights, both matters of everyday reality to the men of the Italian communes.

'Knights' names should always be put before merchants', says a thirteenth-century Bolognese writer, 'but people sometimes put merchants' names before barons', because the latter go barefoot or in sandals, whereas the former go by coach or on horseback: for the majesty of riches is most holy in our day.'[11] Envy of the wealthy is an understandable feeling, the more so as the wealthy usually derived full and open enjoyment from their riches. The great spenders were like the three brothers whom Boccaccio describes:

They found they had been left extremely wealthy, both in money and land, and they had nothing to guide them but their own pleasure, so they began to spend without any brake or restraint; they kept a great household, with many fine horses and dogs and hawks, and continually held court, gave alms, jousted, and did not merely what is becoming to gentlefolk but whatever appealed to their youthful tastes.

To adopt again the vocabulary of Boccaccio, the three brothers were 'pursuing a chivalrous way of life' (*vita cavalleresca tenendo*) and there was a fairly firm distinction between this and 'living as a citizen' (*cittadinescamente viveasi*) (*Decameron*, II, 3; VI, 4; VIII, 7). Life was lived so much in the open air that there could never be much doubt about who was spending money and who was short of it. Nor was there any of the anonymity that prevails in the vaster cities of today. When relatives quarrelled about Genoese foreign policy they did so, as the chronicler says, in the squares and the streets (*in plateis et vicis*).[12] Even in some of the largest cities everyone knew everyone, quite literally. Opicino de Canistris, the author of a work in praise of Pavia (the *Liber de Laudibus civitatis Ticinensis* of *circa* 1330) explains that in this city of some 50,000 people 'they know each other so well that if anybody enquires for an address he will be told it at once, even if the person he asks lives in a quite distant part of the city; this is because they all gather twice a day, either in the "court" of the commune or in the (adjoining) cathedral piazza'.

The extremely influential idea that the newer elements in the population represented an unworthy falling-away from the nobility of earlier days was not merely the product of large-scale migration into the towns, combined with snobbery. It was connected with the common and strongly-felt notion that human history is the story of a decline from a primitive Golden Age of austerity and moral virtue. This nostalgia was no invention of medieval Italy, but seems rather to be a deep-seated human illusion. It runs right through Greek literature, from Homer and Hesiod to Aristophanes and Demosthenes; 'Fair Argument' in the *Clouds* recalls education

. . . in days gone by
When Sobriety was its goal, and truth like mine was rated high.
Children then had no licence to chatter; gravely they marched to school,
The boys of a village all in a body, simplicity was the rule,
Not muffled in wraps though it snowed a blizzard, striding with legs apart,
Singing some old and martial strain just as their elders had taught.

(trans. M. Hadas)

In medieval Italy the same myth is to be found in an extreme form in Dante's *Paradiso* (cantos XV–XVI). Through his great-grandfather the poet recalls the primitive austerity of twelfth-century Florence, 'at peace, sober and pure'. Its houses then were smaller and more simply furnished. The women wore no jewellery or ornaments and used no cosmetics. They tended their babies in the cradle, chanting the traditional lullabies, or worked at their spinning and told the old tales of Troy, Fiesole and Rome. The origin of civic ills always lies in what is now called 'social mobility' (*la confusion delle persone*) and the cause of Florence's moral decline is immigration. Now 'the citizens are intermingled with Campi, Certaldo and Figline' [places in the *contado*]; how much better it would have been if the boundary had remained closer to the city, rather than the Florentines having to endure the stink of the rapacious immigrants. Dante's attitude was shared by other articulate Florentines of his day. Giovanni Villani (VI, 70) looked back with longing to the mid thirteenth century when the Florentines 'with their simple life and poverty did greater and more virtuous things than are done in our times with more luxury and riches'. In some writers this outlook is an expression of puritanical indignation, as in Giovanni dei Mussi of Piacenza, who raged against the wine-drinking habits and décolleté dresses of his day. In others it comes closer to the classical belief in a past Golden Age, as with Rolandino of Padua who thought that 'Ovid's prophecy is fulfilled; he says the world began with gold, yet now such wickedness prevails that there can be no trust even between guest and host, brother and brother, father and son'. Occasionally a more genuine economic basis could be adduced, as when a writer explained Milan's military decline: 'they spend everything on foreign clothes, so they cannot afford horses'[13].

In this lament over past achievements and present decadence one hears the voice of the elderly: 'I heard this as a boy from my father, talking by the hearth on a winter's night', says a Ferrarese concerning the now-destroyed towers of his city[14]. But it is an important element in the population's psychology that while some strove to acquire wealth and looked to the future, others looked to the past and deplored corruption, luxury and licence, the consequences of wealth. The wealth that they particularly lamented was of course that of 'the others' (*gente nuova*), for no writer would himself admit to being a new man.

The extremely important effects of social mobility on the political life of the commune will be discussed in a later chapter.

3 Government

Origins of the commune

Because the material for the formative period is very scanty, the crucial process whereby a 'commune' came into being and acquired supreme juridical authority within the cities unfortunately cannot be shown in satisfactory detail.

The process involved three essential elements. In the first place the role of the 'law-worthy' men, the *boni homines*, had to be transformed by the setting-up of a regularly instituted and permanent body among them as an executive for the citizens. When the *boni homines* no longer appoint some of their number to act for them on a particular occasion, such arrangements having been superseded by the choice of consuls, above all when the consulate becomes a permanent institution, then the commune is present. No contemporary source describes this momentous change, though it is sometimes possible to date it to within a few years. Pisa, for example, probably had no consuls in 1081 when Henry IV's privilege (see p. 9) provided that any future nomination of a marquis of Tuscany would require the assent of twelve Pisans to be elected in the *commune colloquium*; by 1085 it certainly possessed consuls, the earliest recorded for any Italian city. At Siena too the change can be accurately dated, for this city was represented in an ecclesiastical dispute by *boni homines* in 1124 and in the following year had consuls.

The second element in the process was the gradual replacement of episcopal and other authority by the commune as the most important jurisdictional power within the city. The stages of this relationship with a bishop or lay lord, with whom consuls first co-operated, and whom they then overshadowed, are much better documented. At Pavia, for instance, the consuls heard a case in 1112 involving a dispute between two citizens and a monastic house, but the judicial duel to settle the matter had to be staged in the presence of the Count (of Lomello), who indeed continued to hear some suits for the next forty years. A compromise stage might involve joint jurisdiction or arbitration: this may be seen in action at Verona, where in 1181 a case concerning the *contado* was heard 'in the house where the consuls hold the pleas' by the bishop, the Count and the consuls. Evolution in this sort of matter must normally have been a quite slow process of argument and precedent, as the more powerful authority dispossessed one which had a better legal claim. At Ivrea commune and bishop came to terms in 1200 over such disputed matters as the bishop's share of expenses in war and of revenues from mills and other 'rights', but ten years after this the bishop was still investing the city's consuls with 'their right fief (office) and all their good customs[1]'.

An important stage in the winning of juridical supremacy was of course recognition by the western emperor. A suzerain who was normally fully occupied north of the Alps and whose Italian plans were dependent on much support from the cities – particularly those possessing ships or in vital strategic situations – was inclined to favour terms with communes, even if they derogated from his rights and conflicted with his ideas concerning the place of towns in the scheme of things. Hence *de facto* gains by the cities tended to win *de jure* acceptance whenever emperors met with defeats in the peninsula, sought allies among their 'subjects' there, or merely strove to evolve from the muddled reality a *modus vivendi* which would preserve their fiscal and military position. This story, which is too involved for narration here, will also require some discussion below in connection with the role of diplomacy and leagues of towns in the formation of the republics. A characteristic early instance of imperial recognition is Bologna's reception (1116) of the right to keep half the sum received in fines for infringing imperial orders. The process had advanced much further when Genoa (in 1162) received the right to choose its own consuls, together with full powers over justice and of making war, peace and alliances, and exemption from imperial taxation. Two years later Pavia also gained powers of higher and lower jurisdiction and the right to name its consuls, while the terms of the Peace of Constance (1183) further weakened the standing of the Lombard bishops by recognising the jurisdiction of the consuls 'in both criminal and financial suits'.

The third element in the formation of a republican city-state was the acquisition of rights outside the city and the development of relations with other communes. This process, which gave momentum to the others, involved the formation of new institutions, administrative, military and diplomatic, and conferred on the city an awareness of its individuality. Patriotism was above all the product of conflict. This third strand in the making of the commune as a state was interwoven with the second and was contemporaneous with it. Just as the judicial take-over from the bishop was a gradual process, so too was the winning of autonomy by the commune in its relations with the subject territory. The early 'submissions' by feudatories and rural or village communes were often made to the bishop as the recognised civic authority. Then there often followed a phase during which submissions were received jointly by bishop and consuls. Ultimately the bishop was eliminated and the consuls then acted on their own.

By that time the word *commune* was no longer merely an attributive, as in 'common counsel' or in deliberations 'in common', but a substantive in its own right, signifying the citizens or their assembly. This was the situation described by outside observers such as Otto of Freising and Benjamin of Tudela soon after the middle of the twelfth century. Both of these noted that the north Italian towns, under their consuls, were autonomous. 'The entire land is divided among the cities', wrote Otto, with some exaggeration; 'scarcely any noble or great man can be found in all the surrounding territory who does not acknowledge the authority of his city . . . They are aided . . . by the absence of their princes, who are accustomed to remain on the far side of the Alps'[2]. So complete was the practical autonomy of the republics in normal circumstances and so accustomed did their authorities become to this that Asti and Alba in Piedmont negotiated in 1223–4 a *coniunctio et unitas* and some years later Iesi and Senigallia in the March of Ancona agreed on a similar union and merger without the parties involved troubling to consult the relevant imperial and papal overlords.[3]

Institutions

The chronology of the consulate is most conveniently established by giving a short list[4] of the earliest surviving references to this institution in some of the more precocious cities.

Before 1100:	*Between* 1100 *and* 1125:
Pisa 1081–5	Pistoia 1105
Biandrate 1093	Ravenna 1109
Asti 1095	Pavia 1112
Milan 1097	Cremona 1112–16
Arezzo 1098	Bergamo 1117
Genoa 1099	Bologna 1123
	Siena 1125

A number of other large towns (Piacenza, Mantua, Modena, Verona, Lucca, Florence and Parma) are known to have had consuls before the middle of the twelfth century, but the entire list is subject to the proviso that the evidence from this period is fragmentary and towns may well have had consuls for some years before the earliest surviving document records their existence.

Since the early history of the consuls is the history of an experiment or, rather, of a number of experiments, it is natural that there should have been no fixed size for the consulate. Thus Milan seems to have had at least twenty-three consuls in 1130, but only four in 1138, eight in 1140 and six in 1141. Elsewhere too it was common for the numbers to fluctuate from year to year; Verona had four in 1136, seven or eight in 1140 and, at different times in the second half of the century, eight, nine, ten and thirteen. In some cities it was the practice to name a proportion of the consuls from the various 'orders' in the population or else to allot a certain share to the non-noble element. Otto of Freising says that 'the consuls are chosen from each of these classes' (captains, vavassors and commoners) and the Milanese certainly made a division of this sort. It also became customary, as the judicial work of the consuls increased, to appoint 'judicial consuls', whose functions were distinct from the general executive powers of the ordinary consulate; this institution is to be found at Pavia in 1145, at Milan from about 1153.

Little is known of how the consuls were chosen. The Pisan consuls in 1162 derived their authority from the acclamation of the general assembly, but were not elected in it; there was already a form of indirect election. The precise powers of the consuls as supreme executive and judicial officials of the commune are not easy to ascertain; they certainly came to be circumscribed by conciliar authority, but this may not have been the situation in the very first period of the commune. By the early thirteenth century the consuls of Volterra had to take an oath binding them to follow the advice of the majority of the council on questions of war and peace, alliances and taxation. Already before this the Pisan consuls were similarly circumscribed in matters of 'war and peace'. In 1219 the consuls of Piacenza had to disown a truce with Parma and Cremona on the grounds that they had lacked a mandate; the truce had been made 'without the consent of the people and of many nobles[5]'.

The characteristic conciliar body of the nascent commune, it is usually suggested, was the assembly of all the citizens, the parliament (*arengo*). As notions of voting and majorities were still primitive, it is argued, decisions required the approval by acclamation of this body, whose way of proceeding is illustrated by the claim of the Pisan consuls to authority 'granted by the entire people of Pisa in public gathering, by a cry of *Fiat, fiat*'. The general assembly is also to be met in other contexts, for example at Cremona where, in 1118 and 1120, certain knights were invested with lands and took an oath in the presence of the people 'and the whole *arengo*[6]'. In small towns it continued to be feasible to hold meetings of all the citizens, and the general assembly still met after the mid thirteenth century at such places as Gualdo Tadino, Bassano and Comacchio, long after it could play any part in the government of the larger cities.

But so little is known about the earliest phase of communal history that it must remain a matter of conjecture whether in fact there were cities where for a time the sole institution accompanying the consulate was the *arengo* and where decisions were considered in this general assembly. A meeting in which decisions were approved by acclaim was obviously ill-suited to controversial discussion and the statement of dissentient opinions and it would probably be unrealistic to assign to it an important practical constitutional role. At least as early as 1164 the Pisan consuls were working in harness not with the assembly but with a council – this was 'the senators and the 24', the latter being composed of six men from each of the city's 'quarters'. In fact most of the cities soon evolved a conciliar structure consisting of a large council and a small, inner 'secret' council. Occasionally there was an intermediate one as well. In places of some size these councils must quickly have superseded the parliament.

The size and nature of these councils were the subject of constant experiment. It may give some general indication of the order of numbers involved in each of these types of council if a few figures are given by way of example. The 'great council' quite commonly counted 400 members, though other round numbers, including 200, 300, 800, 900, 1,000 and even 4,000 are to be found. It was certainly not rare for such a council to include more than 600 members; in 1254 at Verona 1,285 men were eligible to attend the great council and the council of Modena in 1306 had no less than 1,600 members. Naturally numbers did not rise so high in the lesser communes; Bassano had councils of 100 and 40 members respectively. Forty was about the ordinary size for an inner council, though quite often they were smaller still, numbering (say) twenty-four or sixteen.

Methods of election to councils and to other offices were frequently complicated and were also the subject of constant experiment: a meeting of the major gilds at Florence in 1292 considered as many as twenty-four different methods of electing the priors. This topic could well be the theme of a book; curiously enough it has not been yet. Three quite different principles play an important part in these arrangements. One is indirect election, that is, the system whereby election takes place in two distinct phases, the first election determining the personnel of the electors who make the final choice. Another is election by the outgoing councilors or officials at the end of their term of service. The third is election by lot or 'sortition'. The intention both of indirect election and of the lot was to hinder the domination of city politics by cliques, who might prolong their control by securing the choice of members of their own faction. It was very common to combine these different techniques of election. This rather difficult point can only be made clearly by illustrating it. At Lucca a meeting was held in each region (*contrada*) of the city at which lots were drawn; each of the 550 men who drew slips inscribed *elector consiliarii* then had the duty of naming one man from his own *contrada* as a councillor. The podestà of Vicenza was chosen in this way (1264), after the first phase in which the Major Council determined from which city the podestà was to come. Twenty electors were drawn by lot, and of these twelve were eliminated by voting; the eight remaining electors then proposed three names, from which the final choice was made by a further vote of the Major Council.

Councils could only reach decisions if a quorum was present; very often this was two-thirds of the members. Fines for absence were decreed by some cities. At Parma absentees from the General Council normally had to pay four *imperiali*; on Fridays the fine was five *soldi* and for unauthorised absence from part of a meeting it was three *soldi*. Though a simple majority' was often sufficient for normal business, a majority of two-thirds was frequently needed for important resolutions, and it was quite common to safeguard against rashness by demanding a larger quorum and a larger majority for certain types of decision, extending not only to a favourable vote of 3/4 or 4/5 of those present, but even to 10/11 or 16/17. Thus Parma had four distinct categories of business requiring different quorums and majorities to take effect[7]. Voting, particularly in the smaller councils, was most often by a secret ballot, the voters placing counters or beans in a bag; the choice was indicated in some communes by the colour of the bean (black being the normal colour for 'no'), whereas in others there was only one type of bean but two bags. Precautions to secure secrecy included lining the voting-bag, to make it silent, and insisting that voters should put a hand in each bag. Individual voting by word of mouth to a neutral scrutineer is recorded, but the most common alternative to the ballot, particularly in larger councils, was the vote 'by sitting and standing', supporters and opponents of the motion standing in turn to be counted. Minutes were kept of the proceedings of council meetings by an official notary and these *riformanze* provide the best picture of city-republican government in action. Those that have survived vary a great deal in the completeness with which speeches are recorded; there could be many ways of interpreting the podestà's instructions (suggested by Brunetto Latini in *Li Livres dou Tresor*, Bk. III, pt. 2) to his notary 'to write down diligently what the speakers say, not everything they say, but what is most to the point of the discussion'. Parma required the notary of the *riformanze* to read out his summary of the speeches before the conclusion of the meeting. Latini also advised the podestà not to permit too many councillors to speak and some cities, probably with little effect, attempted to place a legislative curb on the eloquent; Pistoia determined in 1294 to ration each councillor to a maximum of one speech per week. Some other rules of debate must have been even more difficult to observe, particularly the statute of Parma forbidding any speaker 'to mention what has been said by any previous speaker'[8].

'Where there are many councils, there is safety' (*ubi multa*

Plate 3.1 Oldrado da Tresseno, podestà of Milan in 1233. Sculptural relief in the Palazzo della Ragione, Milan, attributed to Benedetto Antelami. The Patarine movement was strong in Milan in the early 13th century but its development was checked by the Dominican inquisitor Peter (later martyred) who launched a campaign against these heretics, with the support of Oldrado. The inscription records that 'he burned Cathars as he should' (*catharos ut debuit uxit*).

consilia, ibi salus) says the sententious author of the *Oculus Pastoralis*, and whatever the danger of Italian republics, lack of counsel was not among them. The city was indeed the paradise of the committee-man, particularly from the time when the already luxuriant forest of conciliar growths was thickened by the new timber of 'popular' institutions (see pages 133 to 143). 'When in doubt appoint a committee' was the accepted doctrine, and a particularly important institution was the *ad hoc* commission or *balia*. 'In cases in which quick action must be taken, this can be done better and more efficiently by a few than by many', the Sienese decided when appointing a *balia*. The most common occasion for recourse to such a body was a military or fiscal crisis: a *balia* was often appointed to advise on the conduct of a campaign. Small commissions of *savi* (*sapientes* = wise men) are an analogous and highly characteristic institution. A typical example is provided by the eight *savi* appointed in 1285 'to find out ways and means whereby money may come in to the commune to pay the debts of the commune of Arezzo[9]'. Ideally these *savi* and members of *balie* were experts, often in military, financial or diplomatic affairs, sometimes in the even more difficult arts of arranging internal truces between hostile factions or recommending measures to repress the magnates. The attraction of the *balia* was its comparative informality; however closely its authority was defined, it enjoyed a certain exemption from the rules of the routine institutions of government. Since it could receive normally unconstitutional powers, it was the ideal means of penetration for the would-be dictator, and in fact this was a common manoeuvre: many a *signore* took over his 'special' powers from a favourable *balia*.

The podestà

In the period when the commune was struggling to claim a place at the expense of the older authorities in the political scheme of things, it was logical that its executive should be the consulate, representing a continuation or formalisation of an already-existing institution, the *boni homines*. Nevertheless, such an executive alliance of leading elements had the disadvantage that disputes within this governing class were reflected in fissures in the consulate itself. The more the commune succeeded in asserting its autonomy, the harder it became to hold rival families together in office. The Genoese chronicler reports under the year-heading 1190:

Civil discords and hateful conspiracies and divisions had arisen in the city on account of the mutual envy of the many men who greatly wished to hold office as consuls of the commune. So the *sapientes* and councillors of the city met and decided that from the following year the consulate of the commune should come to an end and they almost all agreed that they should have a podestà[10].

Even if the chronicler oversimplifies the matter, he gives us the fundamental explanation of the Genoese decision to transfer the principal executive power to a single individual, who had himself to come from outside the city and hence to be neutral in its 'discords and conspiracies'. The man they chose was in fact a Lombard, from Brescia.

The development of this interesting and characteristic institution, the *podesteria*, cannot be attributed solely to the need for an outsider who would transcend local rivalries. The Emperor Frederick Barbarossa had set a precedent by appointing or recognising such officials in a number of towns of Lombardy and Emilia after 1160; thus Milan agreed in 1162 to 'receive the podestà whom the Emperor wishes, whether he be a German or a Lombard'. The word itself merely means 'a power' (from the Latin *potestas*) and has a medieval French equivalent in *poestatz*, which was used of feudal magnates. A single executive official was also found convenient by the communes in their dealings with outside authority, in particular in negotiating with the Emperor at the time of the treaties of Venice and Constance (1177 and 1183). Moreover, at a time when the organs of the commune were not yet fully institutionalised, resort to a temporary substitute for consuls was frequent in periods of crisis. Sporadic experiments with a single *rector, gubernator, dominus* or *potestas* were made by a number of cities soon after the middle of the twelfth century. Many of these early officials were feudatories: thus the Count of San Bonifacio was podestà of Verona in 1169 and Mantua appointed podestà almost all of whom were lords from the surrounding lands. Indeed, it was the rule rather than the exception that a commune's first podestà should be recruited from the city or nearby.

But in his most characteristic guise the podestà was a citizen-noble from another (not a neighbouring) commune trained in the law and holding his office only for six months or a year. Gradually he supplanted the local consuls, the two forms of office alternating in many cities for a considerable period. Before Genoa made the change in 1191 a number of Lombard and other northern cities had experimented with podestà (Bergamo, Lodi, Parma and Padua, for example, by 1175, and Cremona, Milan and Piacenza in the 1180s). By the first decade of the thirteenth century the podestà had become the rule rather than the exception.

The example of Modena will serve to illustrate the *podesteria* in its fully evolved form[11], when both pay and retinue had increased considerably. There the podestà in the early fourteenth century served for a period of six months (a one-year period of office became rare after the mid thirteenth century) for a salary of 1,200 L, one-third of which was paid every two months, the last instalment, however, being retained until he had undergone the *sindicatus*, the routine investigation of his tenure which took place at the end of his term of office. He also received certain extra payments when travelling in the service of the commune. He had to bring with him four judges and a household of twenty-four cavalrymen, serjeants and stable-boys. He and all his accompanying household had to be aged at least thirty, to have no relatives at Modena and none who had held office there within the previous three years. He was not to leave the city during his time of office without the consent of the General Council nor was he to eat or drink in the company of any citizen. On assuming office he took an oath to give justice according to the city's laws and to be present in the Palazzo Comunale during the appropriate hours on at least three days in each week. He had to be prepared to remain for at least five days, and possibly ten, after his period of office, for the *sindicatus*, and to give pledges that he would restore any money which he was found by the syndics or 'investigators' to have received illegally. The institution of the *sindacatus*, which was based on a juridical analogy with the protection of minors in Roman law, was aimed at detecting the illicit appropriation or occupation of the commune's property as well as corruption as such. In some cities even the syndics themselves had to undergo a *sindicatus*. The podestà could not engage in trade when in office. He was not immediately re-eligible for appointment as podestà in the same city, though occasionally communes attempted to revoke such statutes when they wanted to keep a man on for a second term. Siena required each of its podestà to reside in turn in the three 'regions' of the city, an extreme measure to ensure his neutrality.

It was the very essence of the podestà's standing that he was an official, an executive administrator, above all the head of the judiciary; he was not a ruler, but rather he stood for the rule of law. He had police powers and might serve as the commune's military commander, but it was not for him to take the initiative in political decisions. 'The podestà is not to act against the brief given him by the Council', say the statutes of Viterbo (1251)[12] and the true heirs of the consular power are these ever-proliferating councils, rather than the podestà himself. In practice the podestà's authority varied greatly. At time of crisis he might take the initiative in exiling factional leaders (as at Modena in 1225 and Verona in 1230) or in persuading the commune to enter a war (Genoa, 1227). The Genoese chronicler makes the interesting comment that a podestà often got his own way early in his period of office[13]. But the powers of the podestà dwindled with the rise of the Popolo in the second half of the thirteenth century (see pages 130 to 143). The podestà of Pistoia (1284) was not permitted to open official correspondence except in the presence of the local prior of the *anziani* and such letters had to be read aloud before these elders[14]; similar provisions existed elsewhere. By the fourteenth century the podestà was normally no more than a sort of chief justice with police powers.

In the course of the thirteenth century the *podesteria* became virtually a regular profession for able administrators with legal training who took to the work. Some of these men came to specialise in the office and moved on regularly from city to city; Guglielmo Pusterla, a Milanese, had at least seventeen periods of office as podestà. In the thirteenth century Lombardy and Emilia seem to have furnished a very high proportion of podestà, though later an equal share came to be provided by other regions. Certain families also, such as the Mandelli of Milan, the Rossi of Parma and the Visconti of Piacenza built up a tradition and produced many podestà. Moreover, several manuals of advice were composed for podestà, notably the *Oculus Pastoralis* (which probably dates from before the middle of the thirteenth century) and John of Viterbo's *Liber de Regimine Civitatum* (written perhaps in the 1260s). Apart from advice on his administrative duties, both these works give him assistance with speech-making, providing formulas for occasions which are likely to arise, such as when another city is to be accused of wrecking a ship and looting corpses, or when the podestà's own city has to deny a similar accusation. The podestà should never take a citizen with him when he goes for a walk, advises John of Viterbo, and he proceeds to the time-honoured enquiry (later to appear in Machiavelli's *Prince*) 'whether it is better to be feared or to be loved'. He also gives the podestà a good deal of military advice, assuming that he will act as commander of the commune's forces, though he is advised 'not to fight in the real battle himself, but to send forward others to fight'.

Whether or not he fought in 'the real battle', the task of the podestà was neither safe nor easy. Even to take up office was not necessarily easy; in 1240 a Bolognese noble on his way to become podestà of Milan was apparently imprisoned by the commune of Reggio, though the Reggians denied this and claimed that they had merely liberated the man from the Cremonese! But it was after a man had taken up the job that his dangers really began, and to travel to – rather than from – Bologna seems to have been peculiarly dangerous. In 1195 Guidottino of Pistoia, the podestà of Bologna, was attacked by various nobles he had fined, who fitted a new crime to his punishment by extracting his teeth; not unnaturally, he fled the city. In 1231 a powerful merchant Giuseppe de' Toschi together with the rectors of the gilds approached the podestà in his palazzo, asking for 'counsel'; when the podestà demurred, a mob attacked the building, destroying part of it along with all the city's legislative and judicial records. Bologna's tradition of violence was still lively in 1269, when the gild of hosiers set fire to the palazzo because the podestà had refused bail to one of their members; this time the unfortunate official was driven from the city and five years later was still attempting to secure payment of the balance of his salary and claiming 10,000 L compensation for injuries suffered by his horses in the disturbances and other damages.

Many cases are recorded of podestà who became involved in civil disputes and were thrown out of office before their term had expired; inevitably these circumstances led to claims for unpaid salaries and equally inevitably such claims were not met promptly. Sometimes podestà also put in claims for compensation for excommunication incurred in the performance of their functions. Occasionally trouble arose because unsuitable choices were made. Tobias de' Rangoni of Modena was elected podestà of Reggio in 1284 but had to be dismissed because he was inexperienced, because he became entangled in the city's factional disputes and – most serious of all – he had a speech defect which made the citizens laugh at him. On other occasions the fault lay squarely with the podestà; in 1305 the Paduan Pantaleone de Buzzacarini, then podestà of Modena, took advantage of the death of a merchant whose warehouse was near his palazzo to steal the merchant's entire stock of cloth. The *sindicatus* was not, of course, a mere formality. Ravenna accused its podestà in 1198 of having abandoned a military campaign without due cause, and three times within five years (1271–5) Padua condemned its podestà and declared him ineligible for re-employment there. All in all it is not surprising that at times it was difficult to find men willing and able to serve. Fabriano had to try four times in 1285. Its first choice was in prison, its second already committed to another city, Lodi. Its fourth choice agreed either to come himself or send his son.

Other officials

By the end of the twelfth century, if not before, every commune must have had at least one paid financial official, generally known as the chamberlain (*camerarius*) or occasionally as the administrator (*massarius*). Sometimes two men did this work together, but it became normal to appoint a single chamberlain, who was a local man, though not necessarily a layman; many communes preferred to employ monks in this office. The chamberlain usually served for a period of six months. There might be a property qualification, presumably to increase the commune's chances of recouping in case of default, or the chamberlain might be required to offer financial pledges, as at Modena where eight citizens had to stand surety for a total of 2,000 L. The principal duty of the chamberlain, with the assistance of his notaries, was to keep accounts; naturally these had to undergo scrutiny at intervals of one or two months, usually by specially appointed *savi*.

The chancery (letter-writing) aspect of administration was divided among the numerous notaries in the pay of the commune (see chapter 2) and in the period covered by this book no city appointed a chancellor as head of a separate office conducting correspondence. By the mid twelfth century, however, a number of leading cities had one or more official notary-scribes and the Pisans seem to have called theirs a 'chancellor'. The Paduan 'notaries of the seal' (mentioned in 1256) probably occupied a similar position.

Many other officers held part-time posts for which there was normally some remuneration. Such were the many 'valuers' (*estimatori*) involved in fiscal assessments and the commissions appointed to 'syndicate' podestà or to revise statutes. 'Bailiffs' in charge of the repair of roads and the water supply might (as at Viterbo, 1251) be paid one soldo a day while work was in progress, but the same officials were also liable to a 10L fine if the fountains and water troughs were not cleaned out monthly. Modena recompensed its 'judge or official overseeing municipal works' (1327) by ordering that he should be paid by those deriving advantage from the 'wells, fountains, streets, conduits, canals and bridges' with which he was concerned. The same city employed two notaries as municipal archivists; all accounts and judicial and other records were stored in the 'chamber of deeds' and could be consulted and copied. In daytime the statutes and other legislation were kept 'in public outside the chamber', so that whoever wished could copy from them without any difficulty[15].

This by no means exhausts the lists of officials – thirteenth-century Pisa had an officer 'for strayed children and animals and other lost property[16]' – but this is a topic to which we shall return when discussing the involvement of the citizens in communal government (see pages 66–8).

Administration

A characteristic of the government and administration of the Italian republics is the extent to which these were undertaken by the citizens themselves in the time left free from professional and other preoccupations. This is all the more striking when one remembers that the energy and time spent on legislating, giving and hearing counsel, administering and superintending finance, governing subject territory, engaging in diplomatic negotiations, organising and conducting war, was stupendous.

To issue a legislative code is necessarily a lengthy business, requiring much technical knowledge as well as time and industry. At first the communes seem to have been content with a few laws and a constitution defined by the oath taken by their consuls and other officials, but already in the twelfth century some cities issued quite elaborate codes and, by the mid thirteenth, John of

Viterbo, after quoting from the Roman law, could add with justice 'but now the cities live by the laws that they make themselves'. The citizens in no way spared themselves, but put out a truly Platonic stream of statutes and decrees (*riformanze*) concerned with every aspect of life, unimpeded by any barricade of laissez-faire principle. This legislation provides the information on which most of the first part of this chapter is based. The extraordinary zeal with which the communes tinkered with their constitutional arrangements, ever in pursuit of perfection, is immortalised in Dante's sarcastic outburst against the Florentines:

> *Atene e Lacedemone, che fenno*
> *L'antiche leggi, e furon sì civili,*
> *Fecero al viver bene un picciol cenno*
> *Verso di te, che fai tanto sottili*
> *Provvedimenti, che a mezzo novembre*
> *Non giunge quel che tu d'ottobre fili.*
> *Quante volte del tempo che rimembre,*
> *Legge, moneta, offizio, e costume*
> *Hai tu mutato, e rinnovato membre!*
> *E se ben ti ricordi, e vedi lume,*
> *Vedrai te simigliante a quella inferma,*
> *Che non può trovar posa in sulle piume,*
> *Ma con dar volta suo dolore scherma.*

> (Athens and Lacedemon, that did frame
> The ancient laws and were so civilised,
> Made but a feeble feint of living well
> Compared with thee, who dost so subtilly
> Provision make, not to November's midst
> Will reach what in October thou dost spin.
> How often in the time thy memory holds,
> Laws, coinage, offices and customs thou
> Hast changed and all thy members hast renewed!
> If we thou call to mind, with vision clear,
> Like a sick woman thou wilt see thyself,
> Who on her bed of down can find no rest,
> But by her tossing tries to ease her pain.)
>
> (*Purg.* vi 139–51, tr. A.L. Money)

The financial arrangements of the communes present the same picture of rapid development. Revenue was required essentially to cover two things: the payment of officials' salaries and the cost of war. The former of these, the less important, had the advantage of fluctuating little. It tended of course to grow as the towns

built up their bureaucracies; by 1228 Verona was expending the considerable sum of 9,435 L per annum on salaries. Military expenditure was the crucial aspect of finance and in wartime (a very common condition) the commune's budget would be many times greater than in a year of complete peace. In these rather rare years the city could get by with very little taxation. Siena, the only city of which the thirteenth-century budgets are well documented, illustrates how warfare multiplied expenditure, hence revenue, and was the main force which matured the cities' fiscal institutions. While Siena was locked in a bitter struggle with Florence in 1230–1 the expenditure of the commune ran at a figure of above 50,000 L or 55,000 L per annum. The following years, up to the mid century, were comparatively peaceful and at that time annual expenditure normally fluctuated at between 10,000 L and 20,000 L. Another period of military crisis, between 1257 and 1268, raised outgoings to a level of around 60,000 L per annum; in the latter year a single forced loan produced over 6,000 L and one payment to German troops cost 12,000 L. Later in the century normal expenditure – both for an 'average' year of peace and for one of war – continued to rise. Siena's budgets (see table 2)[17] were fairly typical, as is confirmed by the few isolated figures for the thirteenth century available for Pisa, Genoa, Cremona and Venice, which record comparable sums and suggest a similar tendency to increase. Genoa's revenue for the year 1162–3 is recorded by the city's chronicler[18] as 6,850 L; half a century later the annual farm of the toll on the port was worth about the same sum. These increases were due in part to inflation and to the growth of officialdom, but the main cause was the ability and willingness of the citizens to conduct costlier forms of warfare, fighting longer campaigns and making more use of highly-paid troops.

Plate 3.2 Biccherna cover, 1388. The 'Biccherna' (the derivation of the word is unclear) was the central financial office of the Sienese commune. The Biccherna preserved two copies of the complete records of the commune's revenues and expenditure, most of which (from the year 1226) are still extant. The volumes were bound and the covers painted. This cover probably portrays the main financial official (the chamberlain) with his clerk: it is the work of a Sienese painter, possibly Paolo di Giovanni Fei.

Table 2   Annual expenditure by the commune of Siena,
1226–1328 (to the nearest 100 L)

1226	6,300	1272	17,100
1231	61,100	1273	21,100
1236 (6 months)	6,300	1276	43,800
1246 (6 months)	6,000	1278	28,700
1247	8,400	1288	140,100
1248 (6 months)	12,500	1292	105,900
1251	67,400	1295	76,300
1252 (6 months)	120,400	1302	119,500
1254	68,700	1310	135,500
1255 (6 months)	30,000	1317	337,400
1261 (6 months)	30,600	1322	149,700
		1328	347,300

Most expenditure had to be met from taxation and loans. Revenue from communal lands and the leases of market booths and from the profits of justice were not inconsiderable – at times confiscations from political 'rebels' constituted a significant windfall – but these sources could not normally go far to cover the costs of war and salaries. The form of direct taxation already familiar from imperial practice was the hearth tax. The number of hearths was used as a basis to determine the total amount due from a given area, the actual sum levied from each household varying 'according to the rich and the poor'; thus this was not inequitable in principle (as was a poll tax demanding the same amount from every inhabitant). The disadvantage of the hearth tax was that it implied a very rough and ready way of determining the ability to pay both of regions and individuals. The *allibramentum*, a tax based on a census (*estimo* or *catasto*) of property, was a much more sophisticated fiscal instrument. It existed at Pisa by 1162, in a number of other cities before the end of the

Plate 3.3   Folio from a volume of Biccherna records. Siena, Archivio di Stato, Biccherna, Entrata e Uscita, n. 95, fo. 94v. The entries relate to expenditure in August 1287. The two main items concern military expenditure (23 *lire*, 5 *soldi*, 4 *denari* was the cost for 17 days of the small garrison at Roccalbegna in the southern *contado* of Siena). Some judicial, fiscal and notarial expenses are also noted. The total recorded in the folio shown is 42 *lire*, 9 *s.*, 4 *d.* (Sienese currency).

twelfth century, and by the middle of the following century it had taken the place of the hearth tax in most of the communes. Milan's first *catasto* was compiled in the 1240s by twelve groups (later increased to eighteen), each of which comprised four officials, two of them surveyors and two notaries. Surveyors and notaries were paid by the men being assessed, who made an initial declaration of the value of their property and were liable to fines in the event of under-valuing. The officials had to note the condition of houses and the use made of land. A special judge was named to hear suits arising from disputed assessments. At Florence the assessment was arrived at by calculating the average of the three middle estimates from those made by five *allibratores*. All in all the *estimo* implied a considerable output of administrative energy and one that had to be repeated at fairly frequent intervals if it was to remain an efficient basis for taxation.

Direct taxes were naturally supplemented by many forms of indirect taxation, themselves also familiar from an earlier period. These included tolls and customs duties, levies on sales and other commercial transactions and the very profitable monopoly of the distribution of salt, which was usually farmed out to a merchant. In some Tuscan cities, and perhaps elsewhere, these 'expenditure taxes' tended to gain in importance at the expense of the *allibramentum* during the fourteenth century. The poorer elements opposed this, realising that 'level' taxes on food hit them much more heavily than they did the wealthier classes, and a return to the *estimo* figured among the demands of the democratic rebels at Florence in 1378. But such was the convenience of indirect fiscality – easy to levy, to farm and to mortgage – that when the rebellious Ciompi did gain power for a time they too preferred it to the *estimo*.

Like all governments the communes also had recourse to loans. Genoa, later to be a pioneer of the funded state debt, had already become indebted to its citizens to the tune of 15,000 L as early as 1154. The forced loan – first noted in 1207, at Venice – was the inescapable companion of the voluntary loan, and (it hardly needs saying) both of these became increasingly familiar to the citizens; there is a certain monotony about the fiscal development of all states. Specific forms of revenue, particularly indirect ones, were assigned to secure the repayment of loans. In time, loans were used more and more to finance the city-states, the public debt was consolidated and shares in it were dealt in a commercial property, but such later developments fall outside the period of this book.

Since the military obligation of citizens and *contadini* implied a very considerable administrative commitment it requires some explanation at this point, though the actual conduct of warfare will be discussed in chapter 5. All the communes compelled their nobles and other prosperous citizens to maintain a suitable horse for cavalry service. This requirement went back to the early period of the communes' development: by 1162, if not earlier, three hundred Pisan *milites* had to swear that they would provide war-horses. Normally the obligation required a man to serve in person, but he might be permitted in some circumstances, such as ill-health, to furnish a substitute. There were also cases where the politically unreliable were forbidden to serve in person, as happened with the Bolognese Ghibellines in the late thirteenth century. Joint inheritance might cause the obligation to fall on a number of co-heirs, particularly at a time when there had been no recent review of cavalry service; those owing it would then have to provide a cavalryman between them. This must considerably have complicated the task of organising the militia, for nearly two-thirds of the Florentine horses recorded in the *Libro di Montaperti* (1260) were owed jointly by *consortes*. Since cavalry service fell on all who could afford to perform it, there was a large class of men who owed it although not nobles in the sense of having been dubbed knights; they were known as 'knights for the commune' (*milites pro commune*). To single men out for this expensive honour must have been an invidious task; it may normally have been possible to make a distinction based on men's way of life but some line had to be drawn. Arezzo at one time found it convenient to base it on an *estimo* assessment of 500 L and Parma put it at 600 L. The size of the cavalry force (*militia*) of course varied greatly; in the larger thirteenth-century cities it often approached or even surpassed 1,000 men, rising at Bologna to 1,600 in 1298. Naturally these were not all called on to serve at the same time; Florence summoned from one to five of its six regions (*sesti*) according to circumstances. The man who provided the war-horse received payment for its upkeep (forty florins a year in thirteenth-century Florence) and was compensated if it was injured or killed when in the service of the commune. In addition he received pay when on active service.

The infantry obligation fell on the remaining adult male population, this usually being defined as all between the ages of four-teen and seventy, though more humane limits (such as eighteen to sixty) are also known. The organisation of this force was also regional. Its men received some pay when on service, and local commanders a small 'retainer' throughout the year.

Officials were required not only to impose the cavalry obligation (*ad equos imponendos*), but to inspect, review and value the horses and to investigate claims to compensation for death or injury. They also had to levy fines in cases (which were frequent) of absence and desertion. When the city's own forces were supplemented by mercenaries further officials had to negotiate terms with them and to secure their observance.

The podestà of Modena, as previously mentioned was required to bring four judges as part of his *familia*. Naturally the local 'consuls of justice' had found themselves unable to cope with the growing amount of judicial work in the commune. Sometimes this institution continued to exist alongside the external judge – thus Verona in 1201 had sixteen judicial consuls (of whom six were qualified lawyers) as well as two judges from outside the city – but in the end the professional benches ousted the indigenous product. The number of judges increased and they were further reinforced when the podestà (and later the Captain of the Popolo and other officials) lost many of their general executive functions and became primarily judicial officers. Certain cities also developed specialised courts, according to the nature of their business, to hear commercial and maritime cases.

The podestà of Volterra had to take an oath that he would judge 'according to the form of the Volterran constitution or, where the constitution is silent, according to Roman law[19]'. However, the normal doctrine, at least by the thirteenth century, was that judges should go by the commune's own statutes in the first place, then – failing these – by customary law, and as a final resort, in the absence of relevant *consuetudines*, by Roman law. The city-republic legislators liked to think of themselves as renewing and extending the law-giving achievements of the Romans, but in practice the influence of Lombard and other Germanic (i.e. 'barbarian') law was considerable, both in the municipal statutes and in the ways of the courts. It is to be seen, for example, in the use of local juries to give information concerning 'men of ill fame' and in some other aspects of the enquiries employed in criminal procedure, in a tendency to treat contumacy as a confession of guilt and in the ubiquitous employment of *bannum* (implying the loss of legal and political rights). Even the judicial duel is to be met, though its use became rare during the thirteenth century.

Church and state

By far the greatest juridical problem facing the communes was that of their relationship with the ecclesiastical power. The rivalry of Church and State is of course a major historical theme throughout western Europe from the eleventh century, when the Church, under papal leadership, first stated and pressed its claim to separateness and independence. The same drama which involved the Emperor Henry IV and Gregory VII, Henry II of England and Thomas Becket, Philip Augustus and Innocent III, was played out with no less spirit on the myriad stages of communal Italy.

Since the commune was in some respects the legatee of episcopal authority in the cities the relations of the two powers were from the beginning inevitably difficult, involving a lot of juridical precedents and boundary problems. As the commune's reach extended into the countryside, where the bishop always held considerable lands and seignorial rights, clashes were bound to become more serious and frequent – particularly since as often as not the consuls were themselves the bishop's own vassals.

The situation of the communes *vis-à-vis* the Church was much the same as that of the contemporary monarchies and the *casus belli* were similar. One ground for dispute was episcopal and monastic lordship in the *contado* and the commune's claim to exact military service and taxation from the bishop's or abbot's men. Particularly sensitive was the status of newly acquired rights and some communes legislated to prevent more land and men from passing into ecclesiastical hands. A city might also attempt to assert its control by ordering a monastic house to acquire property within the walls, as a pledge; this was the origin of a bitter quarrel in the twelfth century between Lodi and the papacy. The whole question of the rival jurisdiction of ecclesiastical lawcourts and those of the commune was supremely fruitful in disputes. The principal points at issue were jurisdiction in suits involving clerics as well as laymen and such controversial matters as usury, which might concern important secular interests as well as ecclesiastical law. There was less often ground for argument in cases involving

indisputable clerics or such undeniably ecclesiastical matters as testamentary or marital law, yet a rich crop of controversial circumstances survived around the dubious claimant to clerical privilege or the question of appeals from the spiritual to the secular courts, not to mention the bishop's seignorial jurisdiction.

No less important was the perpetually contested territory of ecclesiastical fiscal exemption. In city after city the clergy claimed to be exempt from direct taxation, the commune was reluctant to renounce a share in the wealth of its greatest property owners, and the papacy rushed to the defence of its own. The Church's achievement in generally securing exemption from direct taxation in normal circumstances was of course the commune's main motive for attempting to prevent more property from passing to the clergy. Nor was lay fiscality the sole point at issue, for the communal authorities quite often became involved in opposition to the tithe, or church taxation. Heresy could also lead to Church-State quarrels, for example when the eccesiastical authorities accused the secular power of failing to act against heretics, or when an indignant populace assaulted inquisitors, as occurred at Parma in 1279. Appointments to high ecclesiastical office, one of the principal occasions of dispute between monarchs and popes, perhaps played a less significant part in the communes, but this was merely because the latter possessed a weaker claim to have a say in such appointments. Their interest, however, was no less – the power of the secular clergy in the community is illustrated by the way in which city legislation treated them as 'magnates' – and in fact communes very frequently succeeded in securing the appointment of acceptable local candidates.

In view of this vast contentious territory it is not surprising that most of the communes were in a state of semi-permanent judicial war with their own clerical authorities. Bologna, for example, was placed under an interdict and its officials excommunicated three times between 1215 and 1232, as happened at Forli between 1257

Plate 3.4 Building work. Detail from Ambrogio Lorenzetti's fresco portraying the effects of good government in a city (Palazzo Pubblico, Siena, c. 1338–9). Building labourers are at work on the construction of a tower. The use of scaffolding is well illustrated here: the holes used for scaffolding can still be seen in surviving medieval towers. The balcony of a house is depicted in the centre. In a niche in the tower to the right of this a pot contains a plant.

and 1288, and at Parma at least four times between 1220 and 1293. Moreover, these were not brief clashes but usually wars which continued for years at a time and were ended only by negotiated truces that often proved quite ephemeral because the papacy would not ratify their terms or because a new controversy had arisen.

A dispute at Fano between 1218 and 1222 will serve to illustrate the nature of these hostilities. The quarrel originated over damage done by the commune to the lands of a neighbouring diocese (Fossombrone) and was exacerbated by a subsequent attempt to tax the clergy of Fano. The podestà forbade any communication with the bishop and his entourage, who had to subsist for three weeks on a diet of vegetables. After the podestà had refused to accept ecclesiastical arbitration, the bishop placed the town under an interdict and excommunicated the podestà and his leading supporters, a sentence which was then confirmed by a papal legate. The podestà and his men retorted by breaking into the cathedral sacristy and the bishop's palace. The bishop and seven canons fled to the high altar of the cathedral, but had to surrender after enduring three days without food. The pope (Honorius III) threatened to deprive Fano of its diocese and forbade all trade with the place, quite ineffectively. Negotiations over compensation to the injured parties were immensely drawn out and when Fano finally consented to offer hostages and pledges for payment more than five years had passed since the original clash. All this had occurred in the March of Ancona, within the lands of the Church. The events at Fano exemplify well the weapons available to the two sides. To ecclesiastical interdict and excommunication (sometimes the clergy withdrew from a city for years on end) the commune could retort with physical violence and measures depriving the clergy of civic or seignorial rights. It could also forbid attendance at services, decreeing a lock-out in answer to the Church's own form of strike, the interdict.

Yet it would be misleading to portray the officials of the commune as perpetually at strife with their own clergy. For one thing, it was very common in the twelfth century and not much less so in the thirteenth for the bishop to be a representative of one of the city's prominent families. At Piacenza during a period of 180 years, from the end of the twelfth century to the late fourteenth, twelve out of fifteen successive bishops of the city were from leading Piacenza dynasties, and of the three exceptions one alone came into residence. At Modena the situation was similar.

For some two-thirds of the period 1195–1290 the bishops were Modenese nobles, men thoroughly involved in civic affairs, as may be seen from the fact that in 1247 and again in 1264 a bishop went into exile with his family's party. And if peace between bishops and commune was sometimes the ephemeral result of revivalist enthusiasm (witness the short life of the 'pacifications' arranged at Bologna and Parma in 1233 by the friars John of Vicenza and Gerard Boccadabati), there was yet a very considerable community of interest between the two powers. In 1258 the commune of Arezzo promised to help its bishop (who confessed that he had found the 'spiritual arm' useless) to regain his lordship at Cortona. In return the bishop was to pay the commune 2,000 L and to give it land at Cortona for a fortress, also a quarter share of his seignorial rights there. This may have been an alliance at the expense of the Cortonese but it shows how harmony between city and bishop remained a practical possibility.

The pre-suppositions of government

A contemporary, asked to describe the government of his republic, would have discussed all that has been mentioned above: officials, councils, judges, financial and military institutions. To see his world clearly from the enforced vantage-point of our own we must take into account what he would have omitted because he would have taken it for granted. One presupposition was constant intervention by the commune in every aspect of social and economic activity. This was connected with the confident belief that problems were soluble. Discussion in council could find solutions which could then be enforced by legislation. If experience showed that this was not the correct solution then another would have to be tested.

This optimistic outlook went with a codifying mentality such as may be seen in action in the Florentine decision to reorganise the city's statutes in 1293–4. Clauses in different codes dealt with identical matters, so that 'many are superfluous, some are obscure, some contradict each other and others resemble each other; ambiguities and differences arise daily . . . and daily cause increasing troubles and complaints'. These statutes (of the podestà, of the Captain of the Popolo, and of the Defender of the Laws) 'should be brought together in harmony (*ad consonantiam*) and superfluous ones removed, so that what remains is clear, comprehensible and more concise[20].

Any government worthy of the name must be able to control the price of bread, but the grain policy of the Italian communes (see below, chapter 4) implies an advanced degree of *étatisme* and bureaucratisation. The conditions of sale were naturally the commune's business. Prices (for example, of building materials) were often fixed and maximum rates of interest stipulated (at between twelve per cent and twenty per cent, in the thirteenth century). The commune might (as at Siena) claim a monopoly of the sale of flour, and at the same time legislate vigorously in the interest of the consumer against other monopolies, both generally and specifically. Such measures prohibited attempts by gilds to form cartels, to control the supply of goods or services or indulge in restrictive practices. Gilds were not normally supposed to fix prices or to exclude any qualified man from becoming a member. Most serious of all, gilds were quite forbidden in certain crafts concerned with building and food (such as milling and baking) and almost universally forbidden to the workers of the only craft employing an appreciable proletariat, the textile industry. While forbidding the gilds to fix prices, the commune normally accepted their wage maxima; its labour policy, in fact, fully reflects the attitude of the employer.

It was not at all uncommon for the commune itself to fix maximum wages for certain categories of worker, such as agricultural labourers, masons, carpenters and weavers. At the same time favoured industries might be fostered by grants of privileges to immigrants working in them; thus Padua at one stage gave new cloth-workers fiscal exemption for five years. A good deal of this (though not the last measure) might be seen as the business of the gilds, but in practice gild legislation concerning such matters was often preceded or reinforced by the commune's statutes. This is true even of the regulation of the details of craft conditions. At Modena the commune itself decreed that millers should always use lower millstones larger than upper ones, that every sack at the millers should bear the owner's name, that bakers should always have water and brushes ready in front of their ovens as a fire precaution. And Piacenza, with rare consideration for the traveller, forbade touting for business by innkeepers and their employees.

The voyager who found his journey most organised was of course the seafarer. Venice provides the best of all examples of a state-regulated commercial life. The Venetian travelling to the Levant on business was likely to go in a state-built galley, commanded by a captain chosen by the state, within a convoy organised by the state, and when he reached Alexandria or Acre he might well be ordered to join other Venetians in a joint, state-organised purchase of cotton or pepper. The advantage of the last system was that prices would be kept lower if Venetians were not competing against each other. The convoy system for longer voyages goes back at least to the twelfth century. By the thirteenth the routine arrangements allowed for two convoys of galleys a year to the eastern Mediterranean and by the beginning of the fourteenth there were also annual sailings to England and Flanders, to north Africa ('Barbary') and to Aigues-Mortes (near the mouth of the Rhône). The arsenal, the state shipbuilding yard, dates back to the early thirteenth century and the materials used there were usually purchased directly by the Venetian republic. In all this, Venice is only an extreme example of a general characteristic; the Genoese allowed no galley to go south of Portovenere without a certain minimum cargo and a force of at least twenty crossbowmen on board.

A great deal of legislation bears witness to a struggle to keep the streets and other public places in a hygienic and agreeable condition. The Sienese went so far (in the constitution of 1309) as to forbid the erection of any new dwelling for which planning permission had not been obtained from the *pretori*; the aim of this measure was 'to prevent those who build from trespassing on public streets or on any of the rights of the commune'. A few years later Cremona proclaimed that 'no man is to demolish his house except for the purpose of building a better one[21]'. At Parma a man might be deprived of his house on account of debt, but if this happened the building was not to be destroyed 'lest the city be disfigured by ruins'. Legislation also forbade the obstruction of the roadway by balconies, arcades, external stairways, overhanging trees and similar hazards. Pisan dyers could hang up cloth in the street, but not so low that a man on horseback might hit his head on it[22]. In 1286 the Brescian 'judge concerning the repair of roads, streets and bridges' ordered eighty-eight men to remove external staircases obstructing various public streets, and gave the population of the *contrada* of San Benedetto two weeks to remove their arcade[23]. It was forbidden to throw rubbish into the streets and most communes had ordinances for the regular cleaning-up of streets and squares. There were severe rules prohibiting the fouling of rivers by sewage and by the industrial waste of dyers, tanners and others. No doubt such regulations were often flouted, but the hygienic intentions and paternalistic attitude to which they testify are nonetheless notable. This attitude is also to be found in the strict curfew – only bakers, doctors and priests on duty and (more mysteriously) students, were exempt – tried out by Modena. Fines on curfew-breakers were also a quite significant source of revenue at Siena.

Sumptuary legislation, both economic and religious in intention, greatly increased from the fourteenth century onwards, but it is to be found earlier. The principal motive seems to have been the partially justified argument that if the rich ruined themselves by extravagance the city itself was poorer. In thirteenth-century Pisa, women were forbidden crowns or garlands of pearls; elsewhere the number of pearl buttons, the length of scarlet robes, and so on, was limited. By the following century the Florentines were hopefully trying to restrain gluttonous eating in taverns.

Possibly under sumptuary legislation – though here the motive was quite clearly puritanism and not economy – one should include a Sienese measure of 1248 'concerning hair, which men are wearing too long; it must be cut so that at least some of their neck is visible from the back[24]'. Such a law merely stresses what is everywhere observable, that nothing lay outside the scope of the commune's business. All financial aspects of family and marital life were also the subject of legislatory regulation, including entail, dowries, wardship, wills and intestacy. For example, Volterra would not permit a husband to make his wife a gift on marriage worth more than a quarter of her dowry. Also Parma dealt with the problem of the spendthrift by decreeing that 'fathers notorious for gambling and dissipating their property are to be compelled, if their relatives request it, to emancipate their children and give them a share', even if the children are minors. Such intervention was not confined to statute-making; the minutes of council meetings are full of discussions of action in these matters. In 1288, for example, the Council of the Popolo at Bologna was occupied in giving permission to a lady named Fiordalisia to sell a house which was part of her dowry and in declaring invalid any contract made with one Nicholas de Catellanis 'who had become a prodigal, dissipating all his property and his mother's in taverns and gambling-houses . . . so that unless action is taken soon neither his wife or children will have anything to eat[25]'. In this instance the commune was not merely protecting the relatives but even protecting the man against himself, thereby giving its answer to the dilemma which was to perplex John Stuart Mill.

A number of communes made agreements with doctors who came on to the city's pay-roll as a sort of 'medical officer of health'. Thus in 1214 Hugh of Lucca reached terms with Bologna whereby he accepted citizenship and agreed to buy a house and live there for at least six months each year (and up to eight if requested to by the podestà) in return for an annual salary of 600 L. He could accept as payment from men of the *contado* twenty soldi or hay from the rich, firewood from the *mediastrini*, nothing from the poor. He was to serve in the army when called, no doubt as medical officer. It was hoped that one of his sons might succeed him and should this not eventualise he was to pay Bologna 200 L on resigning his office.

The previous year five teachers of law in Bologna had been ordered to take an oath of loyalty to the city. They had to swear that they would do their best to expand the *studium* (university), that they would not teach elsewhere nor assist pupils to study elsewhere. Bologna was the city whose prosperity and prestige were most dependent on a famous university and it naturally feared the loss of ground to rivals[26]. Meanwhile other cities wished to found or preserve their own, less famous, schools, and it was thought worth while to use alluring bait when angling in educational waters. Exemption from military service for both teachers and pupils was a commonplace and the Modenese went so far as to offer citizenship to anyone studying in their city and to subsidise a student bookshop by paying an annual salary to a dealer in legal texts. By the thirteenth century many towns had set up municipal schools in which Latin was taught and more advanced courses offered for future notaries and lawyers: the teachers were paid a salary by the commune. Naturally the civic authorities had a say in the education provided. Arezzo, for example, laid down very full ordinances in 1255 for its eight teachers of law, and Parma stipulated sixty (later fifty) as the maximum size for a class taken by an assistant master.

Nevertheless, education at the school level remained mainly in the hands of ecclesiastical bodies and of private individuals teaching for their own profit. The educational tone continued to be set by religious schools. Nowhere is this more evident than in the outlook of Dante, whose scholastic cast of mind is probably the product of a schooling provided by the Franciscans of Santa Croce and perhaps also the Dominicans of Santa Maria Novella. Meanwhile a great many of his contemporaries were picking up a vocational education in reading, writing and commercial arithmetic – learning to *scribere omnes litteras et rationes*, as the contracts said. Such a grounding no doubt led to a job as clerk with a business house or a notary. By the late thirteenth century, at least in the larger cities, the literacy rate was probably very high, though with poor data one hesitates to guess at it. Teachers were numerous – Bonvicino speaks of seventy elementary teachers at Milan – and so were pupils, though there is little evidence except Giovanni Villani's often-quoted figures for early fourteenth-century Florence[27]. He estimated that between 8,000 and 10,000 children were then receiving an elementary education in the city, while 1,000 to 1,200 attended the six schools giving a commercial grounding (in 'the abacus'), and between 550 and 600 had gone on to a training in Latin and logic in ecclesiastical schools. If these figures are roughly correct they suggest that something like half of Florence's male population had attended some type of school and this would confirm the impression of a wide diffusion of education.

Citizenship

The city-republic did so much to mould the outlook of its citizens in their upbringing and through the milieu provided by its political life and institutions that they could not but feel committed to its well-being. But before discussing their involvement in its affairs we must give some consideration to the nature of citizenship and how this was defined and obtained. It may seem strange that most city codes pay little attention to the matter and that there was not a large element in the population knocking angrily at the door for admission to the privileges of citizenship. The explanation seems to be, first, that eligibility for civic office v.as sometimes distinct from (and more important than) formal citizenship, and secondly that the conferment of citizenship was rather a recognition of duties already performed than promotion to an enhanced and privileged status. At Padua civic position was a qualification for citizenship, so clearly non-citizen residents (*habitatores*) could also hold office; on the other hand some towns granted a form of citizenship which carried no right to hold office. Other communes, such as Pisa, seem to have regarded eligibility for councils and office as identical with citizenship, using the terms synonymously and applying the same criteria for qualification. Movement from one city to reside permanently in another was relatively rare; of 2,816 inhabitants named in Orvieto's census of 1292, fifty-eight only had originally lived elsewhere and only nine of these came from outside Umbria. This contrasts with the mobility of the citizens of (for example) the Hanseatic towns and was both a symptom and a cause of strong civic patriotism. In consequence those who hankered after citizenship must have been for the most part residents recently moved in from the city's own *contado*; hence the emphasis on the requirement that the aspirant should be assessed for tax on city property. The lack of disputes about citizenship and civic eligibility suggests that men of standing who moved in from the *contado* and sought to play a role in communal politics were rarely denied the chance.

At Parma the General Council consisted of all 'old and true citizens who perform and undertake the burdens and services, both real (i.e., on property) and personal, of the commune[28]'. This was the pre-requisite for citizenship. It implied of course that the citizen was a householder. Parma would admit as a citizen any 'stranger' building a house worth 100 L – the house itself was a pledge to the commune 'that he would undertake and perform its duties (*onera*)' – so long as he was 'a true friend to Parma, not a usurer or murderer and not exiled or banned for any crime'. Any citizen not in possession of such a house was to buy one. The Pisans[29] also insisted on the rendering of taxes, loans and 'other services' based on an assessment within the city itself and residence there for at least nine months of the year; the summer months (July to September) might be spent in the district provided that the citizen did not himself do agricultural work. Pisa also demanded a birth qualification (the citizen or his father had to be born within the city or *contado*) and a period of residence, originally twenty-five or twenty years, though later this was reduced to ten and even three (1319). The last of these measures made citizenship obligatory for those otherwise qualified whose tax assessment was over 50 L and voluntary for those below this level. The demand for a quite lengthy period of residence was normal, though the period varied greatly from city to city; it might be five, ten, fifteen or twenty years or even as many as forty.

The oath taken by the new citizen insisted on his loyalty to the commune; he was to obey its statutes and officers, to attend meetings and give counsel (not revealing secret discussions), to perform military service and make his house or tower (*torre*) available when required for military purposes, to pay his taxes, and so on. If he were a noble from the *contado* his oath would include a clause about a period of compulsory annual residence within the city. This admission of a new citizen might be an occasion of some solemnity, as when the consuls of Viterbo conferred citizenship on the lords of Soriano in Piazza San Silvestro on 10 September 1258 'investing them with staffs, which they held in their hands, and saying: "Now you are citizens of Viterbo, admitted to all the usual benefits of Viterbese citizens"[30].

The attitude of communes to citizenship varied considerably with the time. In the 1280s Modena sold citizenship to a number of men at 100 L each because it was pressed by urgent debts to mercenaries. In times of depopulation after outbreaks of plague some towns offered tax exemptions and citizenship to any new resident (see above p. 22). The Pisans' action (mentioned above) in radically shortening the period of residential qualification also suggests a buyer's market in citizenship.

To what extent were the citizens drawn into a direct, personally-felt involvement in the commune's well-being through participation in the conduct of its affairs? The size of the greater councils, running to a thousand members or even more, and the survival of the general assembly, at least in the smaller communes, show that a high proportion of the citizens acted as councillors. No doubt many by temperament were passive attenders rather than orators, but the minutes often reveal an impressive number of active participants. At Genoa in 1292 a council, which appears to have had about 600 members, met to discuss the very urgent and controversial question of the commune's policy *vis-à-vis* France and the Sicilian war: the sessions lasted for seven days and during them no less than 105 councillors made speeches[31]. The proportion of men holding some form of office was very high, as the account given above of fiscal, military and other arrangements has shown. The early 'oath of the consuls' at Pisa (1162) mentions specifically ninety-one official posts in the commune, beside others of which the number of holders is not given[32]. The ninety-one include measurers, assayers of currency, watchmen, valuers for the tax estimate, overseers of streets and drainage and of the city walls, chamberlains and inspectors of financial accounts. The Sienese volume recording communal expenditure during the first six months of 1257 mentions some 860 offices held by Sienese in the city[33]. These were concerned with every aspect of the city's life. They include 191 *mensuratores*, 171 night watchmen, 114 supervisors of tolls and customs, 103 syndics of the regions (*contrade*) and ninety officials for tax assessment. Besides these there was a miscellaneous host: moneyers, supervisors of weights and measures and of grain and salt sales, custodians of fountains, gaolers, hangmen, officials for streets and houses, supervisors and masons for the upkeep of the cathedral, trumpeters, as well as six 'good men' to oversee taverns and prevent swearing and six others to keep out wild donkeys, swine and lepers, and to prevent people from spinning wool in the street. The suggested total of 860 omits all military officials and though there may have been some overlap through men holding more than one part-time position, it nevertheless reveals a high proportion of civic participation in a city of which the adult male population was probably not much above five thousand. The examples from Pisa and Siena do not exhaust the varieties of civic employment that were available. Bassano in the later thirteenth century had fifty-six overseers of communal lands and the payroll of Modena in 1327 included no fewer than fifty-one notaries employed to record the various aspects of the commune's administration. Like the great majority of the officials mentioned above, these notaries would generally only devote part of their time to the service of the commune and only receive part of their income from it. The part-time civic employment of the citizen is of course the essence of the city-republic. The body of full-time bureaucrats constantly tended to grow through the increasing scale and complexity of communal affairs and through bureaucracy's own natural propagation ('Parkinson's Law'). Pistoia had no full-time officials in 1100, fourteen in 1200 and eighty-two in 1300[34]. The amount of paperwork, especially in financial administration. was enormous; for example every payment, however small, made by or to the commune of Siena was recorded in three copies. But the expansion of bureaucracy did not have the effect of diminishing the number of 'amateur' officials, at least not before the middle of the fourteenth century.

A Pavian writer quoted above mentioned that in his city everyone knew where everyone else lived because they met each other daily in the open: the institution of the evening concourse (*passeggio*) is of course still a familiar one in Italian towns. He might have added that a very high proportion of his fellow-citizens would also be well known to each other through having served together on councils or in office. Turning briefly to

Periclean Athens, we note that an informed guess (by Gustave Glotz) has it that one-third of Athenian citizens held office in any given year. Such calculations are hazardous and moreover the figures given above are not strictly comparable because the numbers of those possessing formal citizenship in the Italian republics is unknown and a good many of the minor 'officials' listed, such as watchmen, were probably not citizens. But it is evident that the Italian participation in government and administration was of the same order as the Athenian.

4 Town and country

The contado

The assertion of the city's authority within what became its subject-territory played a primary role in developing the commune's institutions and personality.

There has, however, been misunderstanding of the motives involved in the city's expansion into the county or *contado* (=Latin *comitatus*) by historians who have seen the early commune as mainly representative of mercantile interests. In fact it was a political entity seeking power and dominion in its own vicinity in the same way as any other lord. There are close parallels between this process in Italy and the expansion of contemporary feudal lordships in France and elsewhere by the patient acquisition of new lands and rights. In the case of the republics there was an existing frontier at which expansion could aim: the diocesan boundary. Already by the early twelfth century the idea was current (though there was no precise legal justification of this doctrine) that every city possessed a claim to the diocese of its bishop as its subject territory, its *contado*. The connection with the bishop was expressed and strengthened by the bishop's own role in the early phase of the commune's expansion. The earliest 'submissions' of feudatories and villages to the larger towns were often made jointly to the bishop and consuls, or even to the bishop alone. Such an arrangement was characteristic of a period when the commune had yet to gather full confidence in its juridical status. In the major Tuscan communes (Pisa, Florence, Siena, Lucca) it was only around the middle of the twelfth century that the archbishop or bishop ceased to be the city's main representative at the submissions. He was soon to disappear from them altogether, but at first the link between diocese and *contado* was close. Thus on the occasion of Lodi joining the Lombard League in 1167 the other members promised it aid in exerting authority over its diocese 'as other cities do over men within their dioceses'. Three years later than this Milan claimed Seprio, in face of the opposition of Como, with 'all the rights that every city of Lombardy has in its *contado*'.

There is nothing puzzling about the motives underlying this expansion. The purpose of the communes was to extend the area within which they could levy taxation and troops, recruit paid armies, and demand the importation into the city of food, particularly grain. As the struggle for juridical and fiscal rights developed it was bound to affect every commune, for even a town which had been slow to expand had to seek to defend its own vicinity against the aggression of its more enterprising neighbours.

An agreement reached in 1198 between Arezzo and the men of Castiglione Aretino will illustrate the many thousands of transactions whereby the communes extended their authority into the *contado*[1]. By the terms of this deed the 'subject' people agreed to take an oath promising Arezzo aid in peace and war, with infantry and cavalry (*ostem et cavalcatam*), and with counsel (*parlamentum*). Each May they would pay Arezzo a hearth-tax of two soldi for each hearth (with the exception of certain specified categories) in their town and district: if, however, the Emperor or an imperial podestà levied the hearth-tax, Arezzo would not also demand it in the same year. Castiglione Aretino was also to make an immediate payment of 500 L. Another clause concerned tolls, from which the Aretines were to be exempt at Castiglione and the Castiglionesi at Arezzo 'like the other men of our *contado* who are our citizens'. Minor adjustments made in 1214 to these terms substituted an annual payment of 50 L for the tax assessed

Plate 4.1   The countryside. Ambrogio Lorenzetti's fresco portraying the effects of good government in the countryside (Palazzo Pubblico, Siena, *c.* 1338–9). This is a highly original work, the earliest European landscape on a broad scale. The figure of 'Security' (holding a gallows) dominates the scene and the theme most emphasized is the safety of the roads and fields; peasants can harvest, till their vineyards and bring their livestock to the market, merchants can carry their wares and the wealthy can go hawking.

by hearths and promised Castiglione compensation for losses suffered when fighting on behalf of Arezzo.

A much fuller agreement defining the terms of subjection to Pisa of the town of Scarlino (1276) will serve to emphasise the military and economic advantages of overlordship[2]. Scarlino's military obligation was very clearly set out as follows. If a *generalis exercitus* was proclaimed for a campaign 'this side' (north) of the river Cecina, Scarlino owed six horsemen and fifty infantry for the duration of the campaign; if the call-up was not 'general' she might send fewer than fifty men but they were to be 'adequate and well armed'. In the case of fighting beyond the Cecina they were to owe service for one month 'at their own expense' (i.e. Scarlino was to pay the men); if their troops were required longer Pisa would have to pay them. Scarlino was to permit its men to take their grain to Pisa, but there was no compulsory levy. Apart from this there were the normal signs of submission: Scarlino was to have a podestà and a notary who should both be 'Pisan citizens and permanent residents of Pisa'; it was to offer 25lb. of wax for candles in the cathedral each year at the feast of the Assumption; offences committed at Scarlino either by or against Pisans were to be tried in the Pisan court.

Scarlino was exceptional in not owing the hearth-tax, for this was a conventional obligation in the *contado*, as was the provision of grain and the general judicial subjection implied by promises to prevent crime, to expel outlaws, and to receive any garrison sent by the dominant city. Normally superior and appellate jurisdiction also passed to the city's court. Sometimes a clause might mention the duty of protecting merchants, particularly at night. The older view that the *contado* was subdued 'to make the roads safer for merchants' was based on misapprehensions about the nature of the commune and its population, but these clauses show that it contains a grain of truth. Certainly an itinerant merchant's life was a dangerous one. When the podestà of Orvieto was murdered in 1199 the victim was not at once identified because the monks who saw his corpse by the roadside on their way to the mill merely took it for 'some merchant who had been killed by robbers'[3]. And in the fourteenth century Paolo da Certaldo thought it wise to advise travellers, on account of danger from robbers, that they should look as poor as possible and should never mention where they were going, 'in fact, if you are going to Siena, say that you are going to Lucca'[4]. In practice the clauses in these 'submissions' which were most important to traders were probably concessions concerning tolls; such as the promise made by the Tuscan marquises Ugolino and Uguccione in the general assembly of Arezzo in 1201 that they would renounce all rights to payments of tolls by Aretine merchants[5].

The view that the twelfth century saw the military conquest of the *contado* by civic militias, a triumph of burgher soldiery over feudal castles, is also an over-simplification, if not a misunderstanding. While many campaigns were indeed fought by the communes at this time and castle sieges were the normal form of warfare against feudatories, the essential facts are that submissions were very often the effect of threats rather than of force and that subjection could only be secured by permanent intimidation and not by an isolated victory. Moreover the so-called 'submissions' frequently represented something that came close to being a treaty of alliance.

The considerable part played by purchase in expanding the communes' jurisdiction also shows that this story was not solely a military one. Some cities bought up feudal rights; for instance, Brescia in the later twelfth century acquired two-thirds of the Counts of Lomello's lordship at Buzzolano, including rights of hospitality and a whole complex of attached seignorial dues. Verona did the same in 1193 when she virtually doubled her subject territory by purchasing Garda and the surrounding region from the emperor Henry VI. Cremona's terms made in 1118 with certain nobles of the neighbouring town of Soncino show the characteristic element of alliance common to many of these feudal 'submissions'. The knights swore an oath of fealty to the people of Cremona 'as a vassal to his lord' and promised to make a token annual payment of five soldi on St. Emeric's Day. But the agreement concerning military assistance was a mutual one; the men of Cremona took an oath in front of their cathedral to render aid to Soncino when requested[6].

For terms involving a greater degree of submission one may quote a chronicler's account of Pisa's dealings with Count Aldobrandino in 1161 and 1163[7]. In the former year 'the vassals of Count Aldobrandino Novello captured Pisan ships laden with grain and other goods' and humiliated the Pisans by making two of their citizens carry a cross through the city. When the Pisan consuls started to organise a punitive campaign the Count was frightened, and on his mother's advice he went to Pisa with the bishops of Soana and Massa to deny his responsibility for these episodes. 'He took an oath in his own defence in the public parliament of Pisa. And in the same parliament the Count swore homage and fealty to Villanus the archbishop of Pisa. He swore to protect the men of Pisa, both those who had been shipwrecked and others, them and their property, by sea and land, throughout his district. So the consuls made peace with him and gave him large gifts and special honour. They invested him honourably with a flag in this parliament, as standard-bearer of the Pisans, after which he left for his own lands.' Two years later the Count 'renewed his oath of fealty to the entire people of Pisa' and promised 'that he would cause all his men aged between fifteen and seventy, throughout the cities, *castra* (fortified towns and villages) and "places" of his district, to swear an oath to preserve the people of Pisa and to obey all the orders and bans of the Pisan consuls'. Then a consul and two other Pisans 'rode with the Count throughout the Count's lands and received oaths to the honour of the city of Pisa'. Such a degree of overlordship, if it could be maintained (and in this case as in many others it could not), constituted true suzerainty. In these circumstances feuda- tories often swore oaths to reside in the city. The commune itself might offer them a residence, as did for example Piacenza to Marquis Malaspina in 1194, when the Marquis for his part agreed that two of his castles should be destroyed and not rebuilt, and that he should 'not keep in our lands any man or men making war against Piacenza[8]'.

In this early phase of expansion the rural gains of the communes consisted largely in the indirect acquisition of feudal or seignorial rights. When a lord took a vassalic oath of fealty to a commune, there was no direct consequence for his own tenants. Only in the thirteenth century did it become customary for the commune to buy out the lord by purchase of his fief, thus making the peasantry – unless they had secured recognition for their own rural community – direct subjects of the commune. In 1256 the commune of Arezzo bought from the Pazzi two places in the Casentino, Capraria and Pontenano, 'with their jurisdictions and courts and districts', including rents, taxes, dues and all services formerly owed there, with the homages and burdens, church patronage, 'and the villeins and rustics[9]'. In this instance the commune had become the successor to the Pazzi in their lordship.

The terms agreed by the cities with lesser communes, as with feudatories, varied from quasi-alliance to full submission. An instance of the former is provided by Bologna's agreement with Nonantola (1131)[10] whereby the men of the town and abbey of

Nonantola promised to render all taxes to Bologna and to give the city military assistance, taking an oath 'to aid the people and Church of Bologna from henceforth in perpetuity'. The terms included an alliance, directed against Modena, with which city Nonantola promised to make no separate peace; also the men of Bologna took an oath relating to military assistance to be given to Nonantola. The submission to Bologna promised a few years later (1144) by the small localities of Cellola and Savignano was much fuller. The former of these agreed 'to hold the new castle to the honour of Bologna and to be under the jurisdiction of Bologna', paying a tax of four denarii per household to the city each August, while the latter owed infantry and cavalry service and promised 'to give the castle and court of Savignano to the people of Bologna . . . and to be true and faithful to that people'.

The advantages to be derived from the submission of a sizeable community are evident from the terms reached by Rimini with Urbino in 1202. The citizens of Urbino then promised Rimini half the proceeds of direct taxation and also military service by fifty cavalry and 100 archers for a week (or longer at Rimini's expense) twice a year. Urbino was to pay 400 L and its podestà to take an oath to obey 'all the orders' of Rimini's officials[11]. This was another subjection which did not last. Inevitably some towns were constantly changing masters. Bassano during the thirteenth century submitted to Vicenza, then to Padua, then to Vicenza again and finally once more to Padua. The rate at which successful cities enlarged their frontiers naturally varied enormously.

As the process of winning overlordship in the *contado* became general some agreement arose as to the status of the population of the subject region. By 1269, when the men of the *ville* of Marzana confirmed their subjection to Arezzo[12], there could be no question of their being regarded as *cives*, as the men of Castiglione had been loosely styled in 1198 (see page 70). They were 'true *comitatini* of the city of Arezzo . . . within the jurisdiction and *comitatus* of Arezzo', wherein the city possessed '*merum et mixtum imperium et omnem iurisdictionem et speciem iurisdictionis*'. They had to obey the order of Arezzo's officials 'and to render, pay and recognise *datia* and *collectas* (direct taxes) and all services . . . to be answerable in all civil and criminal cases before the judges of Arezzo . . . always to accept the rector or podestà given or sent them by the commune of Arezzo: and to obey all the bans, edicts, statutes, ordinances, decisions and decrees of that commune' – and all this *in perpetuum*. In the event these arrangements came to be qualified, though not totally superseded, in the late fourteenth century, when Arezzo in turn fell to the domination of Florence.

Administration in the contado

As the communes extended their authority beyond the walls, receiving 'submissions' from feudatories, *castra* and villages, they were faced by the need to set up new institutions. The administration of rural areas called for the appointment of special officials and it was normal to divide such regions into *capitanie* (as at Pisa) or *pleberia* (as at Florence and Orvieto). Orvieto's *pleberia*, in a *contado* of which the area was some 750 square miles, numbered thirty-one in 1278 but were later reduced to twenty. These were administered by viscounts holding office for six months; the office was farmed out, normally to an Orvietan, though an occasions the *pleberium* purchased the right to appoint its own viscount.

In subject communes, *castra* and *ville*, the dominant city normally exerted its overlordship through appointing a podestà or rector: these were men from the city, acting for the normal yearly or half-yearly period. The *podesteria* of a subject commune – for example, of Arezzo or Pistoia, when Florence gained lordship over these very considerable places – might be a well-paid post. A Florentine mentioned by the fourteenth-century chronicler Velluti 'held other offices of the commune and *podesterie* and castellanships and he lived on the proceeds of these, having no craft or trade[13]'. Such offices, which were also seen, as they had been in classical times, as *honores* and *dignitates*, were much

Plate 4.2   Florence, portrayed in a Florentine manuscript of *c.* 1340 (the 'Biadaiolo Fiorentino', Florence, Biblioteca Laurenziana, MS Tempi 3). The work is a detailed treatment of Florence's grain supply in the first half of the 14th century. The scene is an episode of the famine of 1329. The author relates that after bread riots at the 'proud, perverse and mad' city of Siena, the poor were driven out and then fed through the 'benevolence towards the poor of the noble city of Florence'. The rioting and subsequent executions are authentic, the official expulsion of the poor probably not.

sought after. Even lesser posts provided experience for the young and ambitious, and they were numerous: Padua, for instance, appointed twenty-seven podestà within its not particularly extensive *contado* (1276). The Sienese permitted the communes of their *contado* to select their own rectors, as long as they chose a Sienese subject. This arrangement was probably not altogether exceptional, but the suzerain city must always have retained a power of veto.

Apart from appointing the podestà, the city usually reserved to its court higher jurisdiction and sometimes (as an alternative to farming out) kept a share of the profits of local courts. Lower jurisdiction normally remained entirely the affair of the subject institution, though in 1272 the Milanese decreed that no community within ten miles of the city could hold any court. Subject communes had also to submit their statutes for inspection. Within these limits the subject towns were self-administered and the main call of the *contado* on the commune's energies must have been the work of enforcing taxation and military service.

The military obligation of the *contado* was primarily an infantry one, though some nobles and dependent communes owed a fixed number of cavalrymen. It was normal to divide the *contado* into areas for the purpose of organising its infantry force. Commonly each region (*quartiere, sesto,* etc.) of the city had attached to it for military contexts a region of the *contado*. At Siena, however, for a *contado* of perhaps 2,500 square miles, there were special 'vicariates'. In the thirteenth century these numbered three, the forces of each being commanded by a 'knight' from the *familia* of the podestà. After reorganisation in 1310 there were nine vicariates, captained thenceforth by Sienese citizens, who had to be *popolani*. The number of men called from a particular zone might be determined by its tax assessment. At times very large numbers of *contadini* were summoned, mainly for pioneer and engineering duties. Siena had 3,000 *contado* infantry assembled in 1292 and possibly 7,000 in 1318, while Florence had no fewer than 12,000 of them under arms when threatened by Henry VII in 1312.

The most significant of the commune's administrative measures relating specially to the *contado* were those concerning food and agriculture. Each commune normally laid down a prescribed amount of grain which had to be delivered by the different areas of the *contado*. This *impositio blave* was levied on all grain-producing territory, in proportion to the usual yield of the community in question (sometimes the amount was based on the number of plough-teams). This could constitute a form of taxation, the grain not being paid for; or in other cases (as at Parma) the *contadini* might be compelled to take all their surplus grain to the city for sale, retaining only enough for seed and for feeding themselves and their horses. Occasionally substitution of a money payment came to be permitted, but normally fear of famine was such that grain was considered the more desirable alternative. The Sienese automatically granted safe-conduct for five days to any outlaws who came to the city bringing grain for sale. Naturally the obligation could be extended from subjects to dependent allies. Venice used its power in this way to secure its corn supply; so did Bologna to insist on grain from the towns of Romagna such as Imola and Faenza. The obvious complement to compulsory importation was a ban on exportation and this measure seems to have been universal. In practice it was not enforced in years of plenty (at one period Siena even encouraged the export of grain from part of its *contado* in order to stimulate production), but it stood on the statute-book in case of need. Furthermore many communes made purchases of grain, as a matter of routine, for storage in municipal granaries. Such a system existed at Florence as early as 1139 and Florence remained, even after its territorial gains in the mid-thirteenth century, particularly dependent on importation for its grain; a later calculation was that in an average year the city could only draw from its own *contado* sufficient grain to feed its inhabitants for five months in the year. However, such was the strength of the commune's authority that famines were felt more severely in the subject towns and even in the countryside than in the dominant city.

The communes also passed strong measures, common to all medieval states, against various malpractices in the purchase of food by middlemen. Many cities required a considerable bureaucracy (*ufficio del biado, grascerii*, etc.) merely to deal with the import of cereals. Although legislation concerning other food was less voluminous, it was common for towns to encourage imports of all foodstuffs and timber. Sometimes they forbade the import into the *contado* of wine, in order to protect their own growers. The viticulturalist naturally encountered despotism as well as benevolence and it was normal for towns to lay down a compulsory date for the vintage, the statutes at Modena ordering that this should not be before September. The same city prescribed a minimum proportion of land in the plain which was to be planted with vines and, in common with other communes, encouraged the growing of flax and various fruits. Volterra ordered all men living in certain hilly areas to plant at least four fruit trees each year, whereas Pisa required all *contadini* to plant six a year, as well as insisting on cabbage-patches and beans. Parma decreed that all sharecroppers plough at least four times before sowing and specifically forbade the export of almost all foodstuffs, including cheese, poultry, eggs and vegetables.

Immigration from the contado

The danger of shortage of agricultural labour and thus of food was of course the paramount consideration with the authorities; hence the laws promulgated in many places forbidding those engaged in agriculture to move into the city. In the early period this attitude was reinforced by the predominance in the commune of men who were themselves lords in the countryside; there is no real paradox in the Milanese statute of 1170 requiring peasants to remain on the land and to 'show reverence' (*reverentiam exhibere*) to their lord. Nevertheless there were times, particularly after visitations of plague, when communes attempted to reinforce their economic and military strength by encouraging immigration from the *contado* and other territories. 'A hundred men from the *contado* are to come and live at Siena[14]', the Sienese once decreed, and similar statutes can be found elsewhere; the essential mobility of population, as has been noted above, was assumed.

Normally the magnetism of the city – as in more recent times – was such that immigration could be expected to proceed steadily in the absence of official intervention. The spectacular growth in the size of many cities in the twelfth and thirteenth centuries was probably more attributable to immigration from the countryside than to a 'natural' increase in the town-dwelling population. Urban death-rates were so high (to judge from the following centuries, the earliest for which these can be calculated) that only rural immigration can explain a rapid rise in urban population. It seems certain that mortality from plague tended to be higher in the cities where, rather later, the only remedy against the pestilence was thought to be 'pills made of three ingredients called *cito, longe* and *tarde,* namely run swiftly, go far and return tardily[15]'. It has been suggested (on the inadequate basis of a single set of tax returns) that at Pistoia in the early fifteenth century life expectation was higher in the city than in the countryside[16]. The probability is that any centre whose population achieved five figures was more unhealthy than the country.

Studies of immigrants have shown that a high proportion of those who moved into the cities were men of some standing, owning land and small businesses, and semi-professional men, such as notaries. Normally they did not 'sell up' or part with their rural and village concerns, but retained their possessions in the countryside when they added to them a new town house. The runaway serf, that stock figure in the conventional picture of the medieval town, is curiously hard to find in the Italian records, though it is difficult to believe that the heavy work of the textile and other industries can have been carried on without help of this kind. Moreover there were primarily agrarian areas, such as the March of Ancona, in which a great many peasants moved to the towns without ceasing to be peasants. They were attracted thither by the strength that the commune afforded them in their dealings with their lord, as well as by the greater security of the town in time of war. Whatever the explanation, this movement was a very considerable one; in the years 1211–17 alone the population of Iesi increased in this way by at least 1,000. Many of the peasants must have walked extremely long distances to work on their land, as peasants in southern Italy still do to this day.

Tenurial change in the countryside

To assess the influence on rural developments of the rise of the city-republics is particularly difficult, since the most striking of these developments are already observable before the cities acquired much political strength and they have parallels in other parts of western Europe where the towns did not achieve independence. The manor and other agrarian seignorial institutions had begun to decline in Italy before the rise of the communes and were to decline in the late middle ages over most of western and central Europe, even in areas of backward urban development.

Yet there is clearly a direct connection, in an economic and social sense, between the developing greatness of the communes and contemporary agrarian changes. Naturally the impact varied greatly, according to the strength of the cities and to the resistant powers of different rural milieux. In the early sixteenth century

Machiavelli was to name not merely southern Italy and Latium but also Romagna and Lombardy as areas still subject to lords who 'command castles and have subjects who obey them[17]'. Everywhere the higher land proved particularly tenacious of older social arrangements. The Maremma uplands of the Sienese contado were still largely under seignorial domination in the fourteenth century; the holdings of the Pannocchieschi there were assessed at around 100,000 L in 1317–18, and only the Salimbeni, with castles and lands in the neighbouring Valdorcia, could rival them. Even the Florentines, always determined to press forward against their feudal neighbours, made slow headway in the upper Apennines. They founded five new towns as bastions against seignorial influence in the mountains, yet after this, in 1329 a charter lists 25 castles belonging to the Della Faggiuola and twenty years later the Ubaldini were still deriving considerable revenues from tolls on the grain trade in the higher Apennines.

One force, slowly strengthening, which wrought change in the rural areas was the tendency to produce for the market, particularly for constantly increasing urban markets. The major developments affecting tenure were the substitution of labour-services and money rents by forms of share-cropping (*mezzadria*) and the passage of much of the land to families which had made their money in the city and continued to reside there. Share-cropping took many forms, but the essence of the arrangement was that the lessor provided the land and buildings and at least part of the agricultural equipment, the tenant retaining half (whence *mezzadro* and *mezzadria*) or some other fixed proportion of the produce. By the early fourteenth century *mezzadria* had become the most common form of tenure in Tuscany and was gaining ground there as elsewhere: figures for the Sienese *contado* in 1317–18 show that over half the land belonging to Sienese townsmen was held by *mezzadria* and in many areas the proportion was above 85 per cent[18].

Where there was not a change to share-cropping there was often one from money rents to rents in kind, another symptom of production for an urban market. Owners preferred rent in food for which a better price might be secured as hungry towns spread, rather than a sum of money whose real value diminished. Whatever the change, the cultivators found themselves in a new position. Once most had combined the cultivation of a very small area of their own with labour on the lord's domain. They had been 'owners', though normally extremely poor owners. But as men from the towns bought up land and put together, when possible, compact *poderi* or farms, the tenants, now share-croppers, had lost the standing of ownership.

The process of large-scale land purchase by the city-dwellers is sometimes called 'the return to the land'. This is a misleading expression, for many of the purchasers were adding to rural property already held for a long period before they had moved into the city: rather than returning to, they were remaining on, the land. Figures from early fourteenth-century Siena, so far the only ones available, show that about two-thirds of the city's taxed population owned some rural property. The wealthier the men, the higher the proportion of their landed property that was rural. Thus those whose total property was valued at over 5,000 L had over 85 per cent of the value of their holdings in rural property, and no man in this category was without land in the country. Those whose property was valued at below 200 L had just under 40 per cent of their total holdings in rural land. In the higher ranges almost all had land both in the city and outside, but among the poorer this became less and less common, so that a mere 5 per cent of those in the lowest category had both urban and rural property. Among such as these there was naturally little difference between the average urban (77.2 L) and the average rural (77.8 L) holding, but in the wealthiest category (total valuation 5,000 L and above) the average rural valuation was ten times that of the average urban holding.

The nearer to the city, the higher the proportion of land held by city-dwellers – not unnaturally, since the owners must have included peasants and near-peasants residing within the walls. Close to Siena (i.e. within 3 or 4 miles) some three-quarters or four-fifths of the land was owned by city residents. Every Italian city had its horticultural suburbs (as was of course the case with cities elsewhere) and vineyards were usually conspicuous in that zone. The Bolognese Pietro dei Crescenzi (died 1321) mentioned in his treatise on agriculture 18 different types of grape grown for wine in his home region. Large vineyards existed close to Bologna's walls and much special legislation protected them, regulated their culture and even made provision for the construction of new roads 'so that men who possess vineyards and other property may come to and fro, both with carts and without them'. To be able to offer the produce of one's own vineyard was clearly a social, if not an economic, necessity. Nor were the advantages merely social and gastronomic. At Cremona a high proportion of the vineyards close to the walls belonged to the cathedral chapter[19]. The canons let out these very desirable plots at absurdly low rents to middlemen who drew a substantial profit from their allotments. Evidently these clerics, who came from the city's major families, saw the vineyards as a means of doing a helpful turn to their political allies and clients rather than as a source of income.

Everywhere the poorer soil and the less easily accessible terrain must have been much less affected by the city's influence, but the invaluable Sienese fiscal records show that in the 1320s property was changing hands freely, in most cases from *contadino* to *cittadino* ownership. Leading citizen families, such as the Salimbeni and Tolomei, acquired extensive lordships in the *contado* and tended to favour tenure by *mezzadria*. Generalisations about the cities' 'domination' of the countryside may be wide of the mark, since the policy of the communes was based on the realisation that authority there was shared between the city itself, its own citizens (particularly the wealthier and more powerful among them) and ecclesiastical and lay lords who survived from an earlier age.

The liberation of the serfs

The policy of the communes *vis-à-vis* the inhabitants of the countryside shows most clearly in their legislation concerning the unfree population, 'tied to the land' and subject to a lord. In this respect the cities intervened to direct and hasten the general process of change which was affecting seignorial institutions. Legislative action took various forms. The terms of a Bolognese judicial 'award' (*lodo*) of 1256 included the provision that lords were to sell their serfs to the commune, the price to be paid being fixed at 10 L for adults, 8 L for children. The following year the commune took the more general step of condemning the principle of servitude and decreeing the liberation of all serfs in the Bolognese diocese. Not surprisingly, it was found necessary to repeat this measure. Some thirty years later similar but less comprehensive action was taken by the Florentines. In 1289 a petition from the area of the Mugello argued that the forthcoming sale of the cathedral chapter's lands to the Ubaldini would weaken the authority of the commune in that region. This was followed by an order of the priors that no person could sell his men (*fideles, colonos perpetuos*, etc.), nor could any person or institution acquire them, except the commune of Florence. During the next year the commune duly purchased the chapter's rights in the Mugello.

Both these episodes – the Florentine one more clearly – illustrate the principal motive of the cities, which was the extension of their own authority, with all the fiscal and military advantages that this implied, at the expense of the older seignorial tie. This motive, after all, was not merely a feature of policy in the *contado*; within the city itself, vassalage was rightly seen as a contradiction to the commune's own claims. Another factor was the desire of the townsmen, many of whom found a wife in the *contado*, to avoid the danger that their children would be of servile status. But humanitarianism played a very small role in this 'liberation' and cities tended to protect the lord's rights against fugitive serfs in cases when the lord was himself a citizen of the commune.

What were the consequences of the serfs' liberation? Recent writers emphasize that it put them at the mercy of a new type of landowner, often a city man, producing for sale to the market. These men exploited the rustics – so it is implied – as their predecessors had not, and the peasants, juridically elevated, became economically depressed. This verdict cannot at present be accepted with any confidence. Certainly juridical liberty could not help a peasant if he was economically weak; it was his economic situation that mattered to him and legal status on its own could signify little to a family sunk in poverty. Yet it is just because this is the case that the history of the peasantry is in need of an infinitely greater supply of information than that at present available. Generalisation based on the traits and motives of the 'new' landowning class takes too little account of all the unknowns, not only those concerning general wealth – a lower proportion of wealth derived from the land did not necessarily imply a lower *per capita* income – but also individual or family wealth. These must have continued to depend on soil, harvests, health, family size and so on. Obviously judgements about the advantages or otherwise of 'liberation' are also dependent on judgements about the well-being of the serfs under the regime of the lords. There is the further difficulty that peasants, like treason, can never prosper, since if they prosper they cease eventually to be peasants. With so many unknowns in this equation it is certainly not yet possible to say whether the decline of lordship and the manor was in general a development disadvantageous to the peasantry.

The feudal nobility

It is no easier to generalise about the fortunes of the older landed families of the *contado*. In mountain fastnesses and in the more remote interstices of the Italian political map older feudal ways of living and thinking continued. The tradition of military command and the survival of the retinue of armed *fideles* helped some families to remain prosperous as *condottieri*. Those who rose to greatness in this way were quite exceptional; more normally military command was a convenient sideline, a supplement to inadequate revenues from agriculture and other seignorial sources.

Some descendants of feudal stock lost their identity entirely and became merged in the city population, but more commonly the old families recalled the past tenaciously and sought to retain something of their former position. The greatest families of the Florentine *contado*, the Guidi and Ubaldini counts, fell back greatly by the fourteenth century. Yet almost all the communes were compelled to compromise in some degree with the potentates of the surrounding countryside, and indeed there were many cities which in the course of time fell under their domination (see below, pages 158–65).

To talk of entire families either as throwing in their lot with the commune or as remaining rooted in the countryside is quite unjustifiable. It was natural that of the descendants of a single feudal dynasty some should come to opt for the city wholeheartedly, some should cling to the soil, while many more both retained rural territories and took on new property, interests and responsibilities in the city. The numerous branches of the Berardenghi in southern Tuscany provide instances of these variations[20]. The Berardenghi lords of Orgiale were represented by three branches at the beginning of the thirteenth century, two of which seem to have remained predominantly interested in their rural estates to the east of Siena. A third line, that of the seven sons of Ugo di Ruggeri, lord of Montaperti, became much more closely involved in Sienese affairs. Five at least of Ugo's seven sons moved into Siena, joining forces to build a residential fortress, with tower, known as the *castellare degli Ugurgieri*. They also had vineyards in the Sienese suburbs and other land in the immediate vicinity of the city. These five sons of Ugo are all recorded in positions of communal responsibility, as consuls, councillors, electors, militia officials, ambassadors and diplomatic arbitrators, chamberlains and so on. Who better 'to inspect the fortresses which are to be defended' than Ciampolo di Ugo, and who to serve (1236) as ambassador to the imperial court? Such people as he and his brothers were essential recruits for the commune's military and diplomatic business.

With these preoccupations of Ciampolo di Ugo of Orgiale one has returned to the fundamental interpenetration and interdependence of town and country, of burgher and feudatory. A later Florentine, Giovanni Morelli, has been described as 'engaged in trade, engaged in agriculture, engaged in politics and office . . . a man of business in them all'[21]. This formula is of general application. Paolo da Certaldo thought a man should keep in his house two years supply, or at least eighteen months', of grain and oil[22]. The notion of the governing and politically-conscious elements in the commune as quintessential 'burghers' in their attitudes and ways of life is incorrect and so is the idea that their regime saw the victory of the city over the countryside, followed by exploitation and over-taxation. The land was – or came to be – for the most part in the hands of the *cittadini*, but it is doubtful whether this fact in itself affected the welfare of those who tilled the soil. The changes in the tenure and status of the peasantry have a connection with the growth of the town, in Italy as elsewhere, but the essence of these developments is mutual interdependence.

5 External relations

Civic patriotism viewed internally in a previous chapter, cannot be explained solely in terms of government and administration. A man will only become fully aware of his allegiance to his own state if he knows of other states to which he has no allegiance, and his loyalty will be sharpened all the more if it becomes engaged in opposition to other states. The Italian city-republics were supremely capable of eliciting such loyalty, since a man had every chance to know neighbouring cities and the important differences in geographical site, in architecture, in economic life, in political constitutions and traditions between other cities and his own. Traditions of enmity for rival cities were in fact an invariable ingredient in fully developed civic patriotism.

Relations between the cities not only created civic spirit but also developed the muscles of the commune through institutions formed to conduct war and diplomacy and to exert authority in the subject territory. So much was this the case that the commune of 1200 may be considered essentially the product of such relations. In the first place 'external relations' inevitably amounted to the city's dealings with its neighbours. This was the process mentioned by the mid-twelfth-century German chronicler, Bishop Otto, who relates that

practically the entire land is divided among the cities . . . and scarcely any noble or great man can be found in all the surrounding territory who does not acknowledge the authority of his city[1].

During the period when many of the communes were engaged in asserting their authority in the *contado* (the twelfth century in particular) it was common for most of their energies to be absorbed by this undertaking. When claiming lordship in its immediate hinterland a commune was unlikely to try conclusions with a neighbouring city which was concentrating on a similar task. Hence friendly or neutral relations between neighbouring republics are very common – though by no means universal – during this phase. There was at least a certain potential community of interest, as appears from the agreements reached by Perugia and Arezzo in 1198 and 1216 defining their respective spheres of interest[2]. But such understandings were the ephemeral products of circumstance; Città di Castello, for example, designated by the agreement of 1216 for equal partition between the two cities, was by 1230 committed to a Perugian alliance against Arezzo.

Once neighbouring cities had become effective neighbouring powers, the struggle for better frontiers and more territory was launched and a conflict of economic and strategic interests made 'neighbour' a synonym of 'enemy'. This state of affairs is evident from a very early period in the maritime cities, whose interests clashed sooner and more directly. Pisa's vulnerability is illustrated by the predations of Count Aldobrandino (see pages 73–4) and before the end of the twelfth century this city had become involved in wars against Genoa, thenceforth its perpetual rival, and Lucca. Genoa, too, dependent for its existence on grain imported from Provence and the Maremma (the coastal zone between Pisa and Rome), had from early on to protect the galleys engaged in this vital trade. In some other regions the process of 'absorbing' the *contado* had already proceeded far in the twelfth century and set neighbour against neighbour. Bologna's war with Modena early in that century has already been mentioned, but Milan and Pavia were enemies in the century before. 'The dissension arose', explains a chronicler, under the year 1059, 'because both cities were populous and ranked above the other cities of the kingdom [of Italy]. Milan was truly the leader, as all knew. They were neighbours and so each was ashamed to yield to the other. And so they mutually inflicted on each other killings, looting, fire and robbery[3]'. The effect was to make the political map of northern and central Italy resemble a chessboard, seen at its clearest in Tuscany, where Pisa was early ranged against its eastern neighbour Lucca in a struggle for the commercially important Via Francigena, thus making Lucca an ally of Genoa. To the east Lucca's enemy was Florence, itself the enemy also of Pistoia (to its north-west) and of two southern neighbours, Siena and (less implacably) Arezzo. In the face of Florence's emergence as the greatest Tuscan city, Siena could find little direct support from Arezzo, another neighbour-enemy. But as the Florentines advanced their power so they formed maritime ambitions and threatened Pisa more directly, thus ending the era of their co-operation against Lucca.

The role of the Empire and Papacy

Like all historical similes, this chess-board pattern is a misleading oversimplification. In part this is so because it ignores the exist-ence of a spasmodically powerful force, the Empire. Frederick I Barbarossa (1152–90) in particular pursued a policy of reasserting imperial authority south of the Alps which had a momentous impact on the communes. From the imperial viewpoint it was obviously unsatisfactory that the most economically advanced and wealthiest regions of the Empire ('a very garden of delights', as Frederick's chronicler said) should have been permitted to evade imperial control and taxation and above all that this should have come about through no process of juridical recognition but mainly by mere assertion on the part of the cities and tacit accept-ance on that of the emperor. There is no room here for a chron-ological account of imperialist action and its consequences. The essence of Barbarossa's original policy was to assert imperial judicial and fiscal rights, thereby ending or at least lessening considerably municipal self-government, particularly in the Lombard plain. After 1183, when this attempt had failed, Fred-erick (and later his son Henry VI) transferred the main weight of his pressure to Tuscany and central Italy, seeking a compromise with the cities of the north. Henry's son Frederick (1220–50), launching his venture from his south Italian kingdom instead of from Germany, renewed the ambitious attempt to rule all imperial Italy, that is, Tuscany as well as Emilia, Lombardy, Venetia, Liguria and Piedmont. Nor was Frederick II content to resign the centre of the peninsula to its lawful overlord the pope. Even in this century (1152–1250) of greatest imperial pressure, the result fell very far short of what was aimed at; in practice the Empire tended to play the role of a powerful third party involved in the contention of rival cities and coalitions. The part of the other superior power, the papacy, was not essentially different from this. Engaged in a continual contest for lordship over the cities of their own lands, the popes also at times intervened with some effect to strengthen and encourage anti-imperialist alliances in the north.

In the eyes of the citizens of the greater communes the Empire was less a suzerain than a formidable but desultory military force; Barbarossa undertook six expeditions into Italy between 1154 and 1184 but was never able to concentrate his strength there for more than three years on end. Cremona and Milan's other neighbours (Pavia, Como, Lodi and Novara) welcomed and supported Frederick's campaigns against Milan and it was these cities – threatened and at times oppressed by the Milanese – which played the chief part in the destruction of Milan in 1162. The Emperor's role as an ally shows in a whole series of privileges derogating from imperial authority. In Piedmont Frederick was able to win over Asti and Tortona in this way and even for a time Alessandria, the city founded by Genoa and the cities of the Lombard League as an anti-imperialist stronghold. In Lombardy, Pavia (1164) gained the right to choose its own consuls freely and to hear all lawsuits, and Cremona benefited by a stream of privileges issued in 1157, 1162 (two), 1164 and 1176. Later in 1176 the Emperor promised Cremona a garrison of 1,000 troops whenever the city requested it, besides which he would not make a separate peace with any of Cremona's enemies. Genoa and Pisa, valuable for their shipping as well as their situation on lines of communication, were other beneficiaries. The great privilege to Genoa of June 1162, which might better be termed an alliance, exempted the city from imperial taxation and recognised its right to self-government. Pisa received a similar diploma in the same year. There were times when the Emperor seemed to veer towards the tempting policy of backing one of these two cities against the other, though he never quite succumbed to it. But to both Genoese and Pisans Frederick I and Frederick II must have appeared primarily as potential allies whose terms required consideration. There were others who saw them in a similar light. The great feudal lord of the Veneto, Ezzelino da Romano, was a member of the anti-imperialist league until 1232, but changed sides in that year – later recapturing Verona and taking it over with him – merely because he had concluded that Frederick II would make a more satisfactory ally than the anti-imperialists.

If imperial authority were to be asserted successfully, it would entail fiscal and administrative pressure unacceptable to the unprivileged communes – and if all were privileged there would be virtually no authority. In particular, rule by imperial podestà could mean, as it did at Piacenza in 1162–4, heavy taxation, confiscations, forced labour and the taking of hostages as a pledge for 'good conduct'. Situations like this lie behind the anti-imperial rebellions of the 1160s and help to explain why Frederick failed to keep the friendship even of Milan's enemy Cremona. In 1164 a military alliance was formed between Verona, Vicenza, Padua and Treviso. Three years later this coalition was strengthened by the adherence of another league comprising Brescia, Bergamo, Mantua and Cremona, once the Emperor's closest Lombard ally. Other cities, including Milan, Ferrara and the main communes of Emilia (Parma, Modena and Bologna) joined at the same time. This 'Lombard League', of which later versions were formed in 1185 and 1195, was not a supra-communal authority but rather a form of alliance concerned primarily with the organisation of military and diplomatic co-operation. It held 'parliaments', assigned to its members areas of military responsibility and settled the precise contributions of each to field armies (*tallia militum*) and garrisons. To the communes the *societas* or League was, like the Empire, an institution to be judged by its utility rather than by any theoretical implications; only an immediate imperialist threat could keep it in being. Though the League acquired a seal and a banner and achieved some success in promoting economic co-operation between its members, its vitality faded with the diminution of its raison-d'être, the fear of imperial control.

The Lombard League's military successes forced the Emperor to modify his aims in northern Italy. After the Treaty of Constance (1183) Frederick resigned himself to a policy of compromise with the Lombard cities and the terms of an agreement reached with Milan in 1185 read in many respects like a settlement between equivalent powers. Mutual engagements were made, the Emperor promising that 'we shall maintain the city of Milan and aid . . . the Milanese to maintain all their possessions and rights' and that 'we shall make no alliance with any city, place or person of Lombardy, the March (of Treviso) or Romagna except with the consent of the Milanese'[4]. The effect of the military struggle was naturally to sharpen the citizens' awareness of their constitutional singularity. Something of this enters into the reported speeches of the city representatives at Ferrara in 1177, of which we may accept the purport if not the exact words. These orators spoke of imperial 'persecution', of the Emperor's oppression of 'Italy and the freedom of the Church'. The aim of the cities was 'never to relinquish that liberty which we inherited from our fathers, grandfathers and great-grandfathers': 'we would rather meet a glorious death with liberty, than live a wretched life in servitude'[5].

In the realm of action the League had set a convenient model for the organisation of city alliances. This was followed in the Tuscan League after Henry vi's death (1197), in the second great anti-imperialist Lombard League of 1226, and later in a whole series of military alliances, many of them fostered by the papacy. A characteristic occasion was the 'parliament' of the 'cities of Lombardy and the March of Treviso devoted to the Church' held at Brescia in March 1252: here plans were drawn up for the campaigning season and a division of expenses arranged, each member being responsible for the payment of a proportion (*tallia*) of a total force of 600 cavalry. After the intervention in the peninsula of Charles, Count of Anjou (1265) and his conquest of the kingdom of Sicily (1266), the 'Guelf' military alliance of the Angevin power with its supporting cities was maintained by a series of such agreements. The Angevin monarchy to some extent inherited the polarising role of the Empire, for after Frederick ii's death (1250) imperial power became a yet more desultory influence in Italy: the continuation of a pro-imperialist tradition (Ghibellinism) will be discussed in chapter 6. Meanwhile imperial and (to a much smaller extent) papal intervention had in the later twelfth century had the effect both of crystallising the chess-board pattern of northern Italy and of forwarding the development of the diplomatic and military institutions of the republics.

The conduct of diplomacy

The diplomacy of the Italian communes has been little investigated. This is strange, since the conduct of diplomatic negotiations by republics presents special difficulties and, for historians, special interest. The nature of these difficulties is well illustrated by an embarrassed reply made in 1308 by the Florentine Signoria (the seven leading officials of the commune) to the Duke of Calabria, heir to the king of Naples; they feared, they said, that they could not permit the Duke's ambassadors to address the General Council of the city, as he wished, before

Figure 4
Affiliations to the
three Lombard Leagues

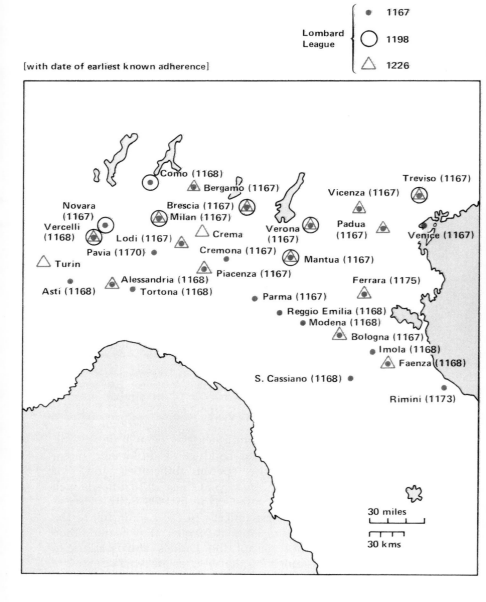

speaking to the Signoria. Such an arrangement would be unsuitable because the Florentines were not in agreement on policy and because the councillors included 'common, uninformed men of the lowest class *(vilissimi et improvidi et vulgares)*[6'].

The cities' conciliar institutions and the need to gain consent from large bodies must have hindered the preservation of secrecy and the achievement of quick decisions concerning diplomatic policy. The actual conduct of diplomatic business, on the other hand, did not vary greatly from the forms followed by contemporary monarchies. Ambassadors, who were always travelling representatives of the commune (resident embassies of the modern type do not make their appearance till the fifteenth century) received, at least from a quite early date, 'letters of credence' and written instructions. The obligation of furnishing a written report at the end of the embassy seems to have become common by the thirteenth century: Venice, the pioneer and leader in all matters of diplomacy, legislated in 1268 to make such a report compulsory. Can any other single piece of legislation have conferred so great a benefit on historians?

It was not uncommon for the podestà to serve as an ambassador on important occasions, but the most usual form of embassy comprised a small number (often two or four) of citizens. The rates of remuneration for expenses for ambassadors were precisely fixed. Parma (in the mid thirteenth century) paid according to the number of horses used; within the district the daily rate was four soldi per horse, outside that but within Lombardy five soldi, further afield six soldi, and the maximum number of horses authorised was two in the district and three beyond. The pay for accompanying notaries was also fixed. These rates could at times involve a city in considerable expenditure; Cremona, for instance, spent over 500 L on ambassadorial expenses in six months in 1234[7]. But men with businesses to supervise were not as a rule anxious to be chosen for embassies and normally communes fixed by legislation the frequency with which a man could be required to serve. At Perugia a man could refuse to serve more than once a year, but missions of particular importance – secret ones and embassies to the pope, the emperor or the city of Rome – could be imposed in addition to this. Here as elsewhere men refusing to go on embassies were liable to fines. Qualified citizens who were not reluctant to travel might act as ambassadors many times in a year. A Perugian, Maffeo 'Cinturalie', in the course of the year 1260 travelled as ambassador to

Assisi in January, to Siena and Lucca in March, to Fabriano in July, to Città di Castello in August, Orvieto in September and to Assisi once more in October[8].

As the Perugian clause about 'important' missions implies, it was necessary and difficult to find men whose appearance, manner and entourage would impress. This was particularly the case in dealing with emperors. Barbarossa's chronicler Rahewin records admiringly of the Milanese that their envoys were 'men of learning, and very good speakers' (though he thought some other ambassadors 'men of much eloquence but little wisdom'). The Pisans too were proud of having despatched 'three wise men' to the Emperor, 'who were honourably received and whom he later sent back to us with great honour'. No doubt these citizens were conscious of making a début in 'the world's debate', somewhat nervous newcomers to the courts of princes. They may have feared the attitude to be found in Frederick II, who once amused his courtiers by doing an imitation of the Cremonese ambassadors; one of these (according to the chronicler Salimbene) used to begin with a long-winded speech in praise of the other, saying what a noble man he was, and how clever and rich and powerful, and mutual panegyrics in this style had to be gone through before they would proceed with their business. No doubt Frederick II was a peculiarly difficult person to deal with; a Genoese chronicler has a melancholy account of an embassy from his city which travelled round with the Emperor's court in 1220 trying to get Genoa's privileges confirmed and constantly being fobbed off with excuses and postponements[9].

Embassies were a feature of the commune's existence in which the noble families were called on to play a disproportionate part. Ambassadors, the author of the *Oculus Pastoralis* advises, should normally be 'the greatest and most eloquent citizens'. Chroniclers refer constantly to 'great and solemn' embassies of 'the greatest and wisest citizens[10]' and naturally this meant frequent calls on the families of aristocratic descent. When the Popolo limited the magnates' share in office-holding (see pages 136–43) the proportion allotted to them in embassies tended to be greater than that given them for internal positions; thus at Piacenza after 1222 they received a two-thirds share of embassies but only half of other offices. 'Let the reply be made by an old knight [i.e., one of old descent] who is thoroughly familiar with the matter and knows about the precedents (*qui bene sciat totum et res antiquas*)', the Florentines decided on one occasion[11]. But was not their feeling really that nothing could replace the well-bred polish and 'style' of the aristocrat?

Military organisation

The military obligation in the communes has been described above (on pages 53–4). But the armies which assaulted castles in the *contado*, ravaged the territories of neighbouring cities, garrisoned fortresses and (on rare occasions) clashed in open conflict, very often comprised mercenaries as well as civic troops. From an early period many of the communes recruited strangers to serve for pay; Fiesole had recourse to them, for example, in 1124 when struggling to preserve her independence against her close neighbour Florence. By the thirteenth century such mercenary forces were often of appreciable size: in 1216 Rimini paid off a mixed force of some 300 cavalry and infantry raised by the Counts of Montefeltro to fight for the commune. A single feudal magnate might suffice as military entrepreneur for a small city but not for a wealthy one. In 1224–7 Genoa collected considerable mercenary forces through the services of the Count of Savoy, the Marquises Malaspini, the Counts of Lavagna and of Ventimiglia and a number of other feudatories; many of the details are lacking, but the contract (*condotta*) of Count Thomas of Savoy in 1225 committed him to send 200 cavalry for two months at a rate of 16 L per man per month. Although feudal nobles were the principal agents of recruitment, the mercenary cavalry in Genoese pay in 1227, which numbered over 500, included 'many knights and squires from Lucca and its district and a good many others from both Tuscany and Lombardy[12]'. Already the cities were willing to go further afield. In 1229–31 the Sienese, involved in a bitter struggle with Florence, employed hundreds of mercenaries, mainly Umbrians and men from Lombardy and the surrounding regions (Emilia and Liguria) but also some French and Germans. When the Sienese urgently needed crossbowmen in the summer of 1231 they sent recruiting officials to Umbria, Lombardy and Liguria, and raised no fewer than 700 at Genoa and in the region of Spoleto. A financial effort on this scale could not be sustained; for the next quarter of a century Siena spent little on mercenaries.

The development of mercenary armies was thus a spasmodic

affair, but around the middle of the thirteenth century they were accepted as a regular feature of Italian life. The authorities of a papal province, the March of Ancona, began in 1255 to abandon demands for military service, substituting for this a fiscal due earmarked for the payment of mercenaries. At this time the Milanese had 1,000 cavalry mercenaries on their books 'from various parts of Italy', which they found so costly that they had to call in a Bolognese to advise them on new ways of 'extorting money' for the commune[13]. When Frederick II's bastard Manfred made his impressive attempt to reassert Hohenstaufen power throughout central and northern Italy (1258–66), he did so with a force of many hundreds of German cavalrymen which was maintained by the money of the Ghibelline communes.

Whether these Germans or their conquerors and supersessors, the Frenchmen of Charles of Anjou, are to be regarded as turning the scale in favour of sizeable mercenary bands (as opposed to mere mercenary recruitment) is a matter of definition. The 1260s saw new developments in the organisation of armies, in that alliances used the *tallia* system (see page 93) to keep bodies of mercenary troops permanently in employment and, at a lower level, the bands of which these troops were composed acquired increasing cohesion. In the years following Charles of Anjou's conquest of the Regno (1266), the position of Angevin power in central and northern Italy in many ways represented a restoration of that enjoyed by the Hohenstaufen. One manifestation of the strength of the Angevins and their allies, the Guelfs, was 'the *tallia* of cavalry of the Tuscan *tallia* alliance', primarily a force of Provençal and French cavalry (but including Catalans, Spaniards and even Lombards and Germans). This usually numbered some 1,500 horsemen in the 1280s, but at times rose to a strength of 2,500 cavalry and an infantry component of no less than 20,000.

When the Sienese had sought mercenaries in 1229–31 they had to send out men to distant regions to enlist individuals or small groups. It was far easier for the communes if they could find a middleman able to provide a body of soldiers already accustomed to his leadership. The normal term for such a body was a 'constabulary' (*conestabileria*), its leader being the 'constable'. The word is found in the Sienese records in 1267 and was soon to become a very common one: the usual size of a constabulary was then fifty horsemen, though twenty-five and one hundred were also common. As the recruitment of such bands became the norm, cities began to legislate to regulate the employment of mercenary companies and a sort of customary law came to apply to the contracts of employment (*condotte*). 'Let us recruit mercenaries on the usual terms' (*ad pacta solita*) was a common decision: the *pacta* related to such matters as rates of pay, horsing, armour and weapons, compensation for horses wounded or killed, capture in battle and so on.

The very big role of mercenary cavalry, both Italian and foreign, is noticeable throughout northern and north-central Italy from the 1260s onwards. A war fought in 1275–7 between Milan (then under the domination of the Della Torre family) and the exiles from that city was conducted largely by German troops on one side and Castilians on the other. Nor was it only leagues and the largest cities with made use of mercenary bands. When the Perugians attacked the neighbouring town of Foligno in 1282 they had in their pay six constabularies comprising 380 cavalrymen. But, like other communes, Perugia was using such men to strengthen its own civic forces, not to replace them. The typical army now taking the field on behalf of a commune was a mixed force. The increased importance of crossbowmen, both on foot and horsed, certainly hastened the dominance of professionalism. Genoa went to war in 1248 with 400 Genoese cavalrymen and the same number of mercenary horse recruited at Piacenza, in addition to 600 of her own crossbowmen and big Genoese garrisons in her fortresses: she also had no fewer than thirty-two galleys on a war footing. *Mutatis mutandis*, the Florentine forces arrayed against Pistoia half a century later (1302) comprised the same sort of combination; the 500 cavalry were all Florentines, whereas 1,000 of the 6,750 foot were mercenaries[14]. The civic militia and infantry 'host' lived on into the fourteenth century, reinforced but not superseded. The nostalgic moralists who groaned at the decadence of their own times and saw their contemporaries as lacking in public spirit and interested only in making money are quite misleading. The approximate numbers of Florentine cavalrymen engaged in the four great battles of 1260 to 1325 are as follows:

1260 (Montaperti)	1,400
1289 (Campaldino)	600
1315 (Montecatini)	300 (or more)
1325 (Altopascio)	500

There was thus a sharp initial decline in the period when mercenary bands first became a regular feature of the scene, but no

FORMA DEL CARROCCIO DE' BOLOGNESI.

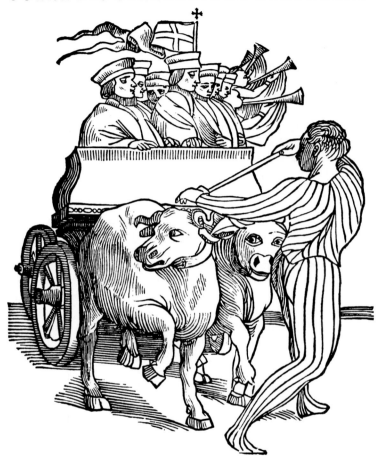

Plate 5.1   The Bolognese carroccio in a woodcut of *c.* 1605
(from C. Ghirardacci, *Historia di Bologna*). This late reconstruction
portrays the use of the carroccio in a civic ceremony rather than
its military role. As a symbol of patriotism it was both useful as
a rallying-point in battle and on occasions of peaceful
ceremony, for example when officials swore oaths on taking up
office or when important visitors were received.

continuous decline thereafter. The numbers of the civic cavalry and infantry forces remained considerable.

Patriotism

It has been suggested above that fully-grown civic patriotism was the product of enmity and warfare between cities. This patriotism did not merely expand by 'natural' growth in these circumstances, but was consciously nurtured. An instance of this process is the communes' use of the *carroccio*, a special waggon to bear the standard in battle. The earliest known appearance of the *carroccio* was in 1039 at Milan, where Archbishop Heribert had constructed 'a high wooden pole like the mast of a ship which was fixed to a strong waggon; at the top was a gilded apple and from this descended two ribbons of dazzlingly white cloth, and in the centre a holy cross was painted with our Saviour portrayed, his arms extended'. The use of a standard as a rallying-point for infantry was not new and waggons played a ceremonial role before under the Merovingian kings, but the archbishop's combination of the standard with the waggon may have been an innovation: it was to become (in Italy at least) a regular feature of warfare. By the later twelfth century a number of cities had adopted the use of the *carroccio*, sometimes giving it a special name (Parma's *carroccio* was called 'Blancardus', Cremona's 'Bertha') and always appointing a body-guard to accompany it into battle. This force was an élite body, primarily of infantry; in the thirteenth century it numbered 1,500 at Bologna, at Florence 152, reinforced by forty-eight horsemen. The Milanese did not retain the *carroccio* without making modifications. In the later twelfth century St Ambrose, the city's patron saint, was portrayed where Archbishop Heribert had preferred a crucifix. A century later, now draped in scarlet cloth and drawn by three pairs of fine oxen decked in white cloth marked with red crosses, it incorporated 'a tree with a wonderfully gilded cross at the top'; from this fluttered a white banner with a red cross. Pavia's *carroccio* had a wooden 'tabernacle', a red tent and a long banner with a white cross on a red background; as well as having a pole with a gilt apple at the top, it was adorned with olive branches. It was customary to use this tabernacle for the celebration of Mass before battle. Religious symbolism was common to all the *carrocci*, as was the use of oxen to draw the waggon.

The loss of the *carroccio* in battle was a grievous disgrace. When Frederick II captured the Milanese *carroccio* at Cortenuova (1237), he sent it first to Cremona (with Milan's podestà Piero Tiepolo, son of the Venetian doge, tied to its supporting ropes) then on to Rome. Even more humiliating was the loss of the Florentine *carroccio* (which the victors apparently burned) to the Sienese at Montaperti (1260), but perhaps worst of all was the fate of the Paduan waggon, which Ezzelino da Romano left in the open so that it should rot away by degrees. For the *carroccio* was much more than a military symbol, being used as a focus of civic patriotism on all ceremonial occasions. Thus the Bolognese sent an embassy to greet the queen of the victorious Charles of Anjou (1267) accompanied by their *carroccio*. The solemn peace between Parma and Cremona (1281) was symbolised by an interchange of waggons. Oaths of submission from subject communes, oaths of fealty sworn to the Popolo by its members or by new podestà to the commune, and the great internal pacifications such as those achieved by the Dominican John of Vicenza in 1233, all these were occasions that called for the presence of the *carroccio*.

The portrayal of St Ambrose as an emblem of Milanese patriotism during the struggle against Barbarossa has already been mentioned. The feast day of a city's patron saint was always a special occasion, marked by religious processions and notably by the participation of representatives of subject places bearing wax candles for the cathedral. The weight of wax due was specified in the terms of submission; the 200 or more places subject to Siena owed a total of more than 30,000 lb. Siena's devotion to its patron, the Virgin, was particularly fervent, for the Sienese had marched bare-foot to her altar in the cathedral to offer her the keys of their city, and a few days later had been rewarded by the astounding victory of Montaperti. Foot-races for prizes (the *palio*) also took place on the patron saint's day, at least at Florence and Siena. Celebrations also took less respectable forms, as one would expect, and Pistoia had to recruit ten extra watchmen during the festival of St James to try to check 'unlawful converse between men and women' in the cathedral[15].

One of the clearest of witnesses to the growth of city patriotism is the appearance of a new literary genre, the work describing and praising the writer's own commune. One of the first examples of this – certainly the first that can be clearly linked with the communal movement – is a poem about Bergamo, the *Liber Pergaminus*, written by one Moses de Brolo in the early twelfth century. Moses describes the city's strong walls, its gates, its piazzas, its excellent water supply, and he emphasises the virtues of its citizens. They are peaceful folk, justly governed, respecting the law and living in dignity, charity and concord. The young receive a Spartan education and Bergamo is formidably strong in war.

Later writers in the same tradition tend to combine Moses' approbation of the qualities of their fellow-citizens with a more statistical assessment of their achievements. A prose description of Asti, written in the late thirteenth century, assures us that the city is 'adorned with wise, noble, rich and powerful citizens', with 'a wise, good and wealthy *populus*, which guards the goods and honour of the commune' and with 'most beautiful ladies, who wear gold and silver ornaments and costly clothing; their gold and silver garlands are filled with pearls and precious stones'. The author boasts of the value of the city's possessions in houses and land (which he estimates at 500,000 L), of the total fiscal assessment on mobile property (2,000,000 L) and of its cavalry force (160 or, according to another edition, 600). He remarks on the number of religious houses, on the excellence of Asti's grain and wine (the latter a sentiment with which many will agree), but he has a few complaints: some of the citizens are 'full of falsehood and wickedness', others seek office so that they can 'take the commune's property'. These criticisms are all the more interesting for being untypical of the normally laudatory descriptions provided by proud citizens. Opicino de Canistris writing of Pavia in about 1330 and Giovanni Villani presenting Florence at about the same date are more conventional. Opicino thinks his city 'the most noble of Italy, the flower of Liguria', having 'most healthy and subtle air', and possessing an army of 2–3,000 cavalry and over 15,000 infantry, able to fight on land or water. 'All the citizens are most affable and familiar' in their deal-ings with each other; they are sociable and polite, rising to their feet when anyone enters the room. Pavia's lawyers are learned and are proved lovers of justice, often chosen for office in other cities. Villani's confident account of 'the power of our commune' in 1336–8 is based on the belief that 'figures talk'. He overwhelms his reader with statistics, fiscal, bureaucratic, military, demo-graphic, educational, ecclesiastical, industrial, financial and commercial. He rejoices as he gives figures for the consumption of food and recounts how the Florentines have built such villas 'that most strangers coming to Florence, seeing all the costly houses and fine palaces all around the city for three miles on every side, thought that, as at Rome, these buildings were all part of the city'. The accuracy of Villani's statistics is still the subject of learned controversy, but the important point is that they are not *prima facie* incredible. He too has his misgivings, about heavy taxation and the sinfulness of 'insane' expenditure on building, but the main impression that he leaves is of Florentine self-esteem.

For a modern reader the most enjoyable of these city pane-gyrics is probably Bonvicino da Riva's prose description of Milan, the *De Magnalibus Urbis Mediolani*, which was completed by 1288. Bonvicino, a schoolmaster, wrote in order that 'all lovers of this city should glorify God' on account of her greatness, that 'strangers to Milan should know her nobility and dignity and so should revere, honour, love and defend them above all mortal things' and that 'my fellow citizens should consider from what a *patria* they derive their origin and should never degenerate from that nobility'. Liberty being natural to Milan, he fears no external tyrant, though he passes over the existence of a native lord. All Lombardy is fertile and well-populated, but Milan is like a rose within it, outstanding for its fertility, fortitude and good faith. Bonvicino devotes Book 1 of his work to the praise of Milan's site; it is not too hot or cold, the water supply is excellent, food is plentiful and the population numerous and long-lived. The second Book is 'praise of Milan for its dwellings'. The city has 12,500 houses, but these are not overcrowded. The streets of Milan are wide and its palaces beautiful, 'the houses packed in, not scattered but continuous, stately and adorned in a stately manner'. The *contado* includes fifty towns and 150 villages (*ville*); 'if a man travelled the entire earth he could find no such paradise of delights'. Book 3 praises the inhabitants. These are friendly, affable and honest; Bonvicino thinks he has demonstrated their natural goodness. 'In regard to population, it seems to me to outshine all the other cities in the world.' Its population he puts (almost certainly exaggerating) at 200,000 for the city, 500,000 for the *contado*. He gives statistics about clerics, professional men, some crafts and provisions; he knows 'from the books of the commune', for example, that Milan has 300 bakeries. Book 4, on Milan's 'fertility and abundance', is also statistical and very informative about the supply and consumption of food; about seventy oxen are slaughtered in the city daily, and so on. 'It is an excellent life for anyone who has enough money', there is

Figure 5
A large city-commune:
medieval Milan

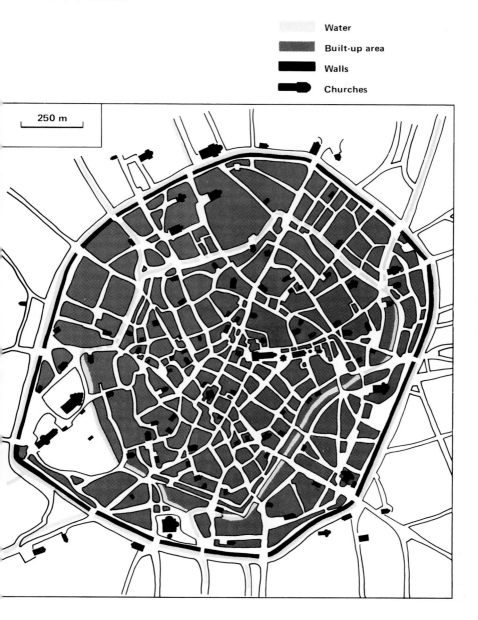

work for all and the Milanese ladies have the dignified bearing of kings' daughters. There are cities in Italy, he feels sure, whose total human population consumes less food than do the dogs of Milan! Book 5 is on Milanese fortitude. The city has won many victories, even against emperors, and 'from what I have read and heard' has never been defeated except when outnumbered. The city has a great arms industry (100 smiths work at the production of armour) and Bonvicino goes on to describe the *carroccio*. Book 6 praises the Milanese for their fidelity, particularly to the Church. Book 7 is on Milanese liberty; 'the divine goodness' has always prevented its occupation by external tyrants.

The final Book praises the 'dignity' of Milan. The city 'has no equal in the world; indeed it is like a world in itself'. If internally united it could easily conquer all Lombardy. The six things in which Milan specially excels other cities are plentifulness of water and of good monks, the size of its law school, its special liturgical offices, the dignity of its archbishopric and its faithfulness to the Church. It lacks only two things, 'civil concord' and a port. Bonvicino, however, seems worried about some unnamed threat to 'the wonderful splendour of the world, the city replete with manifold graces, the venerable city, consecrated by the holy blood of many martyrs'.

Bonvicino's eulogy of his own city is not more illustrative of civic pride than are the *obiter dicta* of the chroniclers. The Florentine Dino Compagni (I, 1), writing about 1310, having told his readers of Florence's good air, well-behaved citizens and beautiful women, goes on to say:

the buildings too are most beautiful and are filled with necessary crafts, more than those of any other Italian city are. So that many people come from distant countries to visit Florence, not through necessity but on account of its crafts and the city's beauty and adornments.

One may also instance Martin da Canale, author of the thirteenth-century *Cronique des Veniciens*, written in French. Martin writes of his city (and who can blame him?) as 'the noble city called Venice, the most beautiful and delightful in the world'. Piazza San Marco is 'the most beautiful square in the whole world, and on the east side is the most beautiful church in the world, the church of the lord Saint Mark . . . and if anyone wants to know the truth concerning this beautiful church, let him go and see it'[16].

The maritime cities perhaps outshine all the others in the

fervour of their patriotism, just as they did in the ferocity of their mutual hatreds. No chronicler gives a more direct impression of this spirit than Caffaro, the twelfth-century Genoese: 'Caffaro who wrote this book daily offers a triple prayer for the present and future consuls, that God may ever grant them to rule the people of Genoa in peace and concord and to increase in good works'. This too is the outlook of Jacopo Doria, who as one of Caffaro's successors kept the official record of Genoa's achievements between 1280 and 1293. He wrote, he said, 'so that every Genoese by reading this may learn more about the excellent deeds of the commune and his own predecessors; and that through their example and the acceptable rewards which they deservedly gained, he may be the more eagerly inspired to work for and maintain the honour and advantage of the commune[17]'. Here again is the very vocabulary of patriotism.

Civic spirit and the visual arts

To these proud citizens, their city's outward aspect was an important element in its prestige. It was in this spirit that the Sienese decided to have a public meadow within the city because

among those matters to which the men who undertake the city's government should turn their attention its beauty is the most important. One of the chief beauties of a pleasant city is the possession of a meadow or open place for the delight and joy of both citizens and strangers, and the cities and some towns of Tuscany, as well as some other honourable cities, are honourably supplied with such meadows and open places[18].

The element of pride in the city's appearance, and above all of a competitive determination to outshine their neighbours, was particularly strong among the Sienese, though the trait is to be found everywhere. The immensely ambitious cathedral which the Sienese began in the fourteenth century was a retort to the cathedral begun by the Florentines in 1296. Their Palazzo Pubblico, which was being built at the same time, was another attempt to show that Siena could build more impressively than its northern neighbour. The Sienese councillors decided, when discussing this building, that

it is a matter of honour for each city that its rulers and officials should occupy beautiful and honourable buildings, both for the sake of the commune itself and because strangers often go to visit them on business.

This is a matter of great importance for the prestige (*secundum qualitatem ipsius*) of the city[19].

A particular subject of pride to the Sienese – and rightly so, every visitor to the city will surely agree – was their Piazza, the *Campo*. Hopeful plans were formed as early as the thirteenth century for keeping the appearance of this piazza uniform by insisting that all the houses giving on to it should have the same type of window. And in 1346 the chronicler Agnolo di Tura proudly recorded 'on 30 December they finished paving the *campo* of Siena in stone, and it is considered the most beautiful square, with the most beautiful and abundant fountain and the most handsome and noble houses and workshops around it of any square in Italy[20]'. Even a city that lacked this almost pathological urge to compete could feel the same pride in its piazza. At Parma the authorities were not permitted to use the piazza for carrying out punishments which involved the spilling of blood. This was a measure directed 'towards the beauty of the piazza and of the things sold there', and in general it seems to have been felt that the piazza was a place of dignity, deserving special protection; a number of activities were forbidden there, including spinning, suckling children and eating figs.

Naturally the appearance of the commune's own palace was a matter of particular pride, as the Sienese observed in the passage quoted above. Siena started on its *palazzo* late. Till the second half of the thirteenth century its meetings were held in churches or a small hall and its officials lodged in rented houses; these were the normal arrangements before the construction of purpose-built *palazzi*. Discussions about a *palazzo* began in 1281, but the matter proceeded very slowly, as was normal for the communes' building projects: Volterra's imposing palace was helped on by a regulation compelling the authorities to spend at least 25 L a year on its construction till it was complete! The

Plate 5.2 The Palazzo Comunale, Piacenza. The development of the Lombard municipal palace culminated in this fine building, begun in 1280 but never completed. A great deal of clearing work was necessary (two churches and a castle were destroyed) to make room for the *palazzo* and its surrounding piazza. The form of the battlements denotes Ghibelline allegiance. Within a few years of the construction of the *palazzo* Piacenza was under the domination of Alberto Scotti, *anzianus perpetuus*.

Sienese chose their site in 1288, a plan was agreed on by 1297 and the building partially finished in 1310, though the tower was not completed till 1344. This tower had to be particularly imposing so that it rose above the cathedral. The curious site of the Sienese *palazzo*, on low ground where huge foundations were required, was dictated by the wish to choose neutral territory between the three hills on which the city lies. The result was a triumph, and indeed Siena had benefited from postponing for so long the erection of a palace. When the remarkable edifice was complete it eclipsed the fame of the palaces of most communes which had been built earlier, though perhaps not that of the Florentine *Palazzo Vecchio*. The greater Lombard cities had, for the most part, built palaces in the twelfth century and then extended them in the thirteenth. In some cities the site of the Roman forum survived as the piazza and provided an obvious setting for the palace. Continuity of this sort may be seen at Todi and at Assisi, where the classical Temple of Minerva was put to use as an annexe of the commune's palace. Since the Popolo could not allow its architectural achievement to be overshadowed by that of the commune, money and care were also lavished on *palazzi del Popolo*, such as those of Florence (the Bargello), Orvieto and Todi.

Second only to the palace were the walls, another great source of pride; Giovanni Villani devotes two chapters to the Florentine walls which were being constructed in the 1320s[21]. Most communes had officials entrusted with the upkeep of the walls; Pisa's *capitanei murorum* figure in the 1162 statutes. A good deal of legislation was devoted to the walls and in particular to the attempt – always destined to frustration – to keep them entirely clear of private and public buildings. Compulsory work by the population played a big part in the construction and maintenance of walls; in some cities each region had the obligation of providing labour for its own section of the walls and its gateway. Often the walls were a very expensive item in the commune's budget; Florence's second medieval circle, mentioned above, cost about 6,000 l a year in the first years of the fourteenth century and in 1324 nearly 20,000 l was spent on it in five months, which represented roughly a quarter of the commune's total expenditure.

Besides the palace and walls there was a third item of architecture which was both essential and aesthetically important; this was the water supply, in particular the fountains. No subject played a larger part in the deliberations of some communes;

reading the minutes of their meetings one is confronted by page after page of discussion of hydraulic engineering and architecture. Nor is this surprising, since many of the towns were situated on hilltop sites where water supply set specially difficult problems. Siena was one city which worried perpetually about shortage of water, another was Orvieto, which constructed an extremely ambitious aqueduct and later sank a well some two hundred feet deep. Great pride was taken in the elaborately adorned fountains from which the precious water eventually flowed. Siena's Fonte Branda is immortalised by a reference in Dante's *Inferno*, but perhaps the finest of all the fountains is Perugia's, on which much of the sculptural work was probably done by Nicola Pisano. The very complicated scheme of this fountain, involving fifty reliefs and twenty-four sculptural figures, had an encyclopedic general theme; as well as the Labours of the Months and the Liberal Arts, Roman and Perugian political and ecclesiastical history are represented. Figures stand for Perugia itself, Lake Trasimene and Chiusi (a prized Perugian possession), and there are portraits of the podestà and the *Capitano del Popolo* for the year (1278) in which the work was done.

Rivalry between cities naturally extended to ecclesiastical as well as secular architecture; it was inevitable that the grandeur and beauty of its cathedral and the number and size of its parochial and mendicant churches should be regarded as an index of a city's greatness. The construction of new cathedrals at Florence and Orvieto, both of which were begun in the last decade of the thirteenth centuy, certainly influenced Siena's decision (1337) that the size of its own cathedral was inadequate and its strange experiments in enlarging this building. The ideal was still that on the solemn occasions of the year – Christmas, Easter, Whitsun and the day of the patron saint – the entire population could find room in the cathedral. The largest cities probably failed to achieve this, but the Florentine Duomo has room for 30,000 and could probably have taken the entire adult population of the city after the mid-fourteenth-century decline.

While the citizens urged on church-building and justified expenditure on it in terms of beauty and *decorum*, they also showed their willingness to meet the cost by special taxation; at one stage over eight per cent of Florence's revenue was going towards the construction of the cathedral. When the laity had played a considerable part in initiating and paying for a new cathedral or church they were often able to secure some control

over the architectural work and the future upkeep of the building through an original type of institution, the *Opera* (works). The evolution of the *Opera* did not signify a general transfer to the laity of control over ecclesiastical buildings; many ecclesiastical bodies managed to keep control over their own church fabric, but even in cases where laymen had not taken the initiative in building they were often able to gain some influence by fostering the existence of the *Opera* as a separate entity. Nor was the commune committed to support of the cathedral only. An effective letter from the Franciscans of Siena in 1286 asked for financial assistance from the city authorities, pointing out that 'if the cardinals and bishops and other priests or ambassadors from other Tuscan cities came and saw the unfinished façade (of San Francesco), this would by no means add to the honour of the city[22]'.

The great mendicant churches ranked only after the cathedrals in size and hence in their involvement in civic pride. In 1309 the Sienese asked their Dominicans to remove a wall which partially hid the grandiose church of San Domenico and thus detracted from the dominant architectural feature of the western part of the city. For the same reason it was normal for cities to try to keep the areas around the cathedral and major churches clear of houses. The authorities were in fact dedicated town-planners, as may be seen at Pisa, where it is still possible to admire the careful layout of the central precinct containing the cathedral, the baptistery and the Camposanto.

The outward appearance of the city was treated as a unity and men were employed to foster it as a whole. In the thirteenth century Bologna retained a series of architects whose task was to supervise all public buildings and works; between 1245 and 1267 one of these, Alberto, was concerned with the cathedral and baptistery, the tower of the *palazzo* and its bell, the walls, streets and water supply. Such versatility continued to be expected. In 1310 Orvieto welcomed the Sienese Lorenzo Maitani as *universalis*

Plate 5.3 The Palazzo dei Priori, Volterra. The *palazzo* was begun in 1208 and finished in the 1250s, perhaps the first purpose-built municipal palace in Tuscany to be completed. It is certainly the oldest Tuscan *palazzo* to have survived and was an important influence on the great Florentine *palazzi* of the Capitano del Popolo (now the Bargello, begun *c.* 1255) and the Signoria (the 'Palazzo Vecchio', begun in 1299).

Plate 5.4   The Piazza del Comune, Assisi (from the fresco cycle in the upper church of S.Francesco, Assisi, by 'the Master of the St Francis Legend', painted *c*.1300). A simpleton lays down his cloak for St Francis. The painting shows the Piazza del Comune, with the palace of the Capitano del Popolo (left, with tower) and the Roman temple of Minerva. The *piazza* occupies the site of the Roman forum and the temple was used in the medieval period as an annexe of the palace.

caputmagister. He was granted Orvietan citizenship and fifteen years' exemption from taxation, on becoming overseer of civic buildings and bridges as well as *capomaestro* of the cathedral. Over the next twenty years he was occupied in supervising all the work carried out on the cathedral façade. Probably – though the evidence is far from conclusive – he was the sculptor responsible for the finest parts of the superb marble reliefs which decorate the lower part of that façade. He also busied himself with work on the commune's palace and the *Palazzo del Popolo*, on the walls and gates, fountains and bridges.

To combine headship of the cathedral work with employment as chief architect and engineer of the city seems to have become conventional. At Siena at the same period Lando di Pietro worked on the defences, constructed military 'engines', made the machinery for chimes of bells, undertook work on the cathedral, the *palazzi*, fountains, streets and bridges, apart from being a goldsmith and a painter of crucifixes. Probably Arnolfo di Cambio undertook a similar diversity of tasks when he was *capomaestro* of Florence's cathedral in 1300 (Vasari attributes to him work on the walls and the Palazzo Vecchio as well as various churches), and it was to the same post that Giotto was appointed in 1334, to superintend the cathedral, walls and other fortifications, 'and the other building work of the commune pertaining to his offices as master'. Most people today think of Giotto as a painter, but he was also the architect of the Florentine campanile and probably of fortifications, bridges and churches.

The gild system was an intrinsic part of the arrangements under which men we now consider as 'artists' were treated as craftsmen. Painters were expected to turn their hands to all sorts of useful work. The statutes of the Venetian gild of painters, which date from 1271, envisage the production by its members of 'escutcheons, shields, chests, caskets, patens, tableware, dining tables and altarpieces[23]', and this list omits much of the work they must have undertaken such as decorating walls and designing banners. Painters no doubt usually planned and constructed their commune's *carroccio*. At Siena they painted the elaborate and often beautiful covers in which the accounts of the *Biccherna* were bound. They were also employed to paint the pictures of hanged criminals and political exiles with which many of the cities decorated their palaces. To be depicted thus was to have fallen into particular infamy, but painters were also required to portray protective saints and the heroes and great deeds of the commune. The Florentines, for example, had pictures of the victory of Campaldino in the Bargello. Among many portraits which commemorate successful podestà and captains one may mention Simone Martini's striking portrayal in the Sienese Palazzo Pubblico of Guidoriccio da Fogliano (*c.* 1330), near two fortified places in the *contado*, presumably the scenes of recent military success; below this painting is one (revealed only in 1979–80) of figures standing outside another town[24].

A great deal of visual propaganda, in fact, was entrusted to artists and this form of publicity was taken very seriously. The Milanese decorated one of the city gates with reliefs depicting the misdeeds of Barbarossa. A complaint voiced against Pope Boniface VIII at his posthumous 'trial' was that he had alienated papal territory to the city of Orvieto in return for that commune celebrating him with two statues. The truth was that, although the statues certainly existed, the pope's reward had been land and not immortality in stone; but the interesting thing about this accusation is the reminder that men longed for the portrait which went with true fame.

Naturally the commune was only one of many patrons of the visual arts. Ecclesiastical bodies and gilds also spent enormous sums on architecture, sculpture and paintings, families and individuals subsidised altarpieces and church monuments and had their homes decorated. Yet it is important that a great deal of art was 'official' art, and this may help to explain the comparatively slow development of changes in taste during this period. The main significance of the commune's direct role as organiser and patron of art lies in the emergence of a new form of secular building, the palaces of the communes and Popoli.

6 Internal divisions

The foregoing discussion of the government of the Italian republics and of their external relations has perhaps given an impression of unity within the commune. Such an impression would be very misleading indeed. 'War and hatred have so multiplied among the Italians', says the Florentine Brunetto Latini (*Li Livres dou Tresor*, book III pt. 2), writing in about 1284, 'that in every town there is division and enmity between the two parties of citizens'. Even in the eleventh century Milanese chroniclers had remarked of their fellow citizens that 'when they lack external adversaries they turn their hatred against each other'. This well-founded observation was to become a commonplace for other cities too. Florence was built under the signs of Aries and Mars, says Malispini: 'our ancestors were always fighting battles and wars and when they had no other opponent they fought among themselves[1]'.

Internal division was deep and completely ubiquitous; it is the very fabric of the internal history of the communes. The 'two parties' of which Latini wrote were the Guelf and Ghibelline factions. Later we will try to define these two diplomatic systems and the corresponding division within many communes. But it will be better to begin by considering the more far-reaching horizontal fracture of social division. 'The cause of all the ills that arise in cities', according to Machiavelli (*Istorie fiorentine*, III, 1), 'is the serious and natural enmity which exists between nobles and *popolari*, caused by the desire of the former to command and of the latter not to have to obey them.' Machiavelli's succinct formula introduces admirably the question of social factions, but does not fully define their nature. In practice two connected but distinct issues were at stake. In the first place, the powerful men in the cities inevitably manifested their social strength through lawlessness and violence; equally inevitably, the leading part in attempting to restrain them and to fortify the defences of law and order was played by those elements which ranked a little below the nobles or 'magnates' and might hope in combination to check their superiors. Secondly, the same popular elements felt themselves deprived of an adequate share in the political life of the commune and organised themselves as a pressure-group to insist on securing more political power.

Nobles and magnates

To explain the separateness of the 'magnates' within the commune and the hatred felt by many against them it is necessary to return once more to the strength of the landowning, knightly element in the early commune. Insistence on this point is required because it may entail unlearning what nineteenth-century historians saw as the very nature of the city-republics. For them – and the idea at its most characteristic is enshrined in the *Communist Manifesto* – the medieval citizen is the 'burgher', trading and not landowning, thinking not of his sword (except when challenged *in extremis* by the forces of feudalism) but of his profits; his milieu is the warehouse and the craftsman's shop, not the castle or the countryside, his horses are for carrying wares, not for hunting or fighting. But this quintessential burgher, to be found perhaps at Ghent or Lübeck or London (or perhaps not even there?), is not identifiable in the Italian cities, where, to a large extent, political independence was founded and the tone of politics was set by landowners. Furthermore these landed knights were often themselves involved in commerce and industry and even prominent citizens who were not themselves of 'feudal' descent derived much of their outlook from those who were. The ethos of the knight permeated the citizen population.

To understand Machiavelli's remark about the nobles and their 'desire to command' it is necessary to know something about the way of life of these nobles and their organisation within the commune. In many cities they possessed their own corporation, a *societas militum* capable of acting independently, so that, for example, Cremona could make an alliance in 1200 with the *societas militum* of Brescia and the following year the commune of Brescia with the knights of Cremona. As late as 1286 the Pisan *commune militum* had its own four captains, and at Chieri, a comparatively small place, two separate organisations, one of *milites*, the other of *populus*, continued to exist alongside each other, each with its own consuls, podestà and fiscal system. It was probably this survival of a formal social dichotomy that Frederick II was seeking to end when he issued an edict 'for the dissolution of *societates*' within the communes.

But the behaviour of the nobility is as important as their organisation. Again the modern reader must use his historical imagination to think away the polite compromises and innuendos of modern society and to summon up a world in which strength and pride ('the proud man's contumely') expressed themselves directly and brutally. He must think of men like the sixteenth-century nobles at Belluno who used to shout 'Take your hat off, dastard!' and to show their scorn for the multitude by writing on the walls *meccanici et plebei*. Their houses and clothing to some extent set the wealthy apart, as did their rural estates on which they and their families would spend the hot months of the year. Pisan legislation made allowance for citizens who lived for three months (from July to September inclusive) in the *distretto*, but Giovanni Villani remarks that Florentines who were 'rich, noble and well-off' spent as much as four months a year in the country 'and some more'. When Oberto Spinola attempted a *coup d'etat* at Genoa in the early days of October (1265) he ordered his supporters to close the gates to keep rival nobles away from the city 'because he knew that all the Genoese nobles were living out at their villas at that time, as was their habit[2]'.

The existence of a characteristic aristocratic way of life does not imply an absolutely clear-cut, unmistakable social division. A witness in a lawsuit at Arezzo in 1238 knew a man was a noble because he had often seen him at exercise with his horses and weapons, like a nobleman (*ludere cum armis, more nobilium, cum equis*), yet 'equestrian' and 'noble' were certainly not synonyms. The class of non-nobles who were sufficiently well-to-do to be compelled to perform cavalry service on behalf of the city (*milites pro commune*) has already been mentioned. When nobility began to imply certain automatic constitutional handicaps, a new ambiguous class came into being, which was paradoxically privileged by being declared 'popular' although in fact of noble descent. And, as with all such categories, there was bound to be a difficult and controversial borderline. The family of Salimbene, the Parmesan chronicler (b. 1221) was indisputably 'popular', yet his father's first wife had been of noble descent and his own brother married into a family claiming kinship with Countess Matilda of Tuscany. When legal lines were drawn it was found very difficult to define a 'magnate'. Clearly lineage and dubbing as a knight were clues, but not the only touchstones. By the *popolo*, said the bishop of Cremona in 1210, when attempting to settle internal disputes, 'I understand the *popolo* excluding those great families which are members of the *popolo* but are counted among the knights'. The ordinances of the Popolo of Pistoia (1284) defined the powerful (*potentiores*) thus: 'knights or sons of a knight and other members of families in which there is a knight or has been one in the past . . . A knight is a man who is, or has been, held to be a knight by public repute[3]'. The family is defined for this purpose as 'those bearing the same coat of arms'. The Florentines, in the same context, instead of 'the past' wrote 'the last twenty years' and they too had recourse for their criteria to the vague and unsatisfactory notion of 'common repute' in defining '*potentes*, nobles or magnates'.

It will be observed that the law envisaged the noble as a member of a family group rather than as a mere individual. Sometimes a single noble dynasty might so predominate in the political life of a town as to prevent the evolution of even a nominally oligarchical situation. This would usually lead to the supersession of republican institutions by a formal tyranny (*Signoria*: see chapter 7). In some other towns a small number of families achieved a shared constitutional domination. This was the case at Belluno and Feltre in the Veneto where four and three families respectively gained, by agreement, complete shared control of the commune's offices. A document of 1267 records that 'by the ancient law and approved and recognised custom of Belluno, one quarter of the honours, offices and dignities belonging to the families and kindred of Belluno have long

Plate 6.1   Medieval towers, Pavia. View from Via L. Porta. A great Lombard city and the capital of the *regnum italicum*, Pavia owed its importance to its site on the river Ticino, at the highest navigable point, whence there were trading links by land with the river Po. In the later 12th century (when the population may have numbered 15,000) there were said to be a hundred towers at Pavia. A fresco of 1522 shows that a great many still survived at that date, but few now remain.

pertained to the Nossadani'. The Nossadani, like the other three great houses of Belluno, the Bernardoni, Tassinoni and Castiglioni, had a list bearing the names of their members and those of families allied to them. This last relationship is illustrated by a lawsuit of 1272 in which a family sought to establish its membership of the Bernardoni kindred; witnesses were asked whether the Borzani and the Bernardoni 'stood together through life and death against their enemies, as relatives and friends[4]'.

A formal alliance such as the above was known as a 'consortium' (*consorzeria*). Its nature is perhaps best illustrated by the oath sworn by the members of a *consorzeria* founded at Bologna in 1196:

We swear to help each other without fraud and in good faith . . . with our tower and common house and swear that none of us will act against the others directly or through a third party. If this tower should become necessary to any of the jurors for his own purposes . . . the others are to make the tower and house available to him and to help and not oppose him. Matters concerning the construction of the tower are to be settled by the decision of two men chosen from the jurors and they are to decide in good faith what is in the best interest of the kin who swear this oath. The jurors are to make their sons (if any) swear a similar oath before reaching the age of fifteen, either within a month of being requested or within whatever limit the rectors may set. If any disagreement should arise among the jurors the then rectors are to call together the disagreeing parties within thirty days to try to reach agreement; the latter are to accept the rectors' decision. No purchase in connection with the tower is to be made by an individual; everyone is to be consulted concerning such a purchase and whoever wishes to take part in it is to have a share, whereas the shares of those who have not taken part are to belong to those who have[5].

The oath goes on to name two families with which the jurors may not contract marriage, friendship or any sworn agreement except by consent of the rectors. Nine captains of 'the work on the tower' are named; the rectors are to be chosen from among these. The *consorzeria* is renewable at the end of five years.

The statutes of another *consorzeria* set up a century and a half later by a group of Florentines show how this versatile institution could cover any form of alliance for mutual support. These Florentines had no common tower, but they did possess a treasurer and three arbiters. They were to enter no quarrel except with the approval of their arbiters and any of them becoming involved in a dispute was not to make peace except in accordance with terms approved by the arbiters:

'*Item*, if it should so happen that one of us receives any outrage or offence at the hands of anyone, then each of us is bound to help, defend and revenge him with his own property and person, treating the quarrel as though it involved himself . . .'

'*Item*, if any of us should have any lawsuit in the court against any powerful person . . . then all the rest must accompany and aid and advise him like true relatives and brothers and consorts, if he who has the suit requests this . . .'

'*Item*, if one or more of us should be condemned for any cause arising from our interests or actions performed at the command or by the decision of our arbiters, then all are to pay the fine jointly, the size of their contribution being according to their tax estimate . . .'

This was a pact of mutual social aid and support. Its jurors do not seeem to have been nobles and may not have been related to each other, but their agreement illustrates the sort of assistance that 'consorts' normally promised each other, in litigation and financial matters, as well as in the wars and perpetual violent quarrels of communal life. It was usual for *consorzerie* to provide for the settlement of disputes among their own members. Their own officials, as may be seen from both the documents quoted above, possessed jurisdictional authority, but the commune might also intervene in their affairs, as at Pisa where a statute decreed that a 'consort' could be compelled to pay for any damage done to a tower as the result of his own action; until he did so, he lost the right to use the tower. Some *consorzerie* even assumed the power of making political decisions on behalf of their members; the statutes of the Corbolani of Lucca (1287–8) provide that

if there is trouble at Lucca, then the consul of the 'house' if he is at Lucca (or otherwise the chamberlain) is at once to call together as many of the 'house' as he can, without fraud. They are to meet at whatever place the consul chooses and to discuss among themselves what action should be taken, whether they should serve the commune of Lucca or one of their allies or should go to whatever place is settled amongst them. They must observe whatever is decided, on pain of paying a fine to be fixed by the consul (up to 100 soldi), if such a fine is agreed on.

The political and social aspects of the *consorzeria* are indivisible. In some ways, for instance in clauses forbidding marriages within the consortium and in arrangements for the maintenance of a chapel by consorts, the *consorzeria* would be recognisable to anthropologists as a kinship group.

Primarily, however, it was an instrument for mutual assistance among nobles. One of its forms was a settlement between

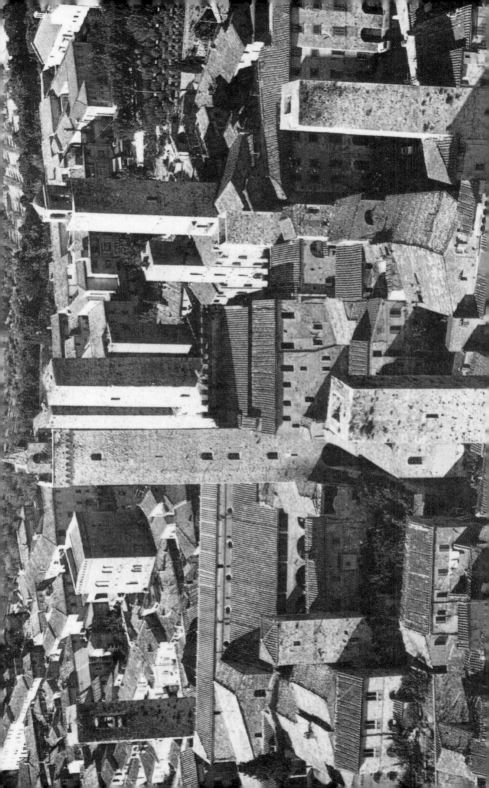

brothers for co-ownership, to prevent the fragmentation of an inheritance, an arrangement analogous with the shared obligation of cavalry service mentioned above. Its most common function was to provide for the erection and maintenance of a tower, and Bologna, which still preserves spectacular medieval towers, conveniently illustrates the typical clauses of such a contract. In 1177 eight members of the Carbonesi family (already, we may presume, consorts) came to terms with Marchesello de Vetralla over the construction and use of a tower, to be built above Marchesello's dovecot tower. He was to pay 30 L towards the cost of the first twenty *punti*, which height was to be attained by the next Martinmass. The Carbonesi could build higher if they wished, but would get no more financial help. If their building damaged Marchesello's dovecot they were to pay compensation for this, the amount to be settled by arbitration if necessary. The tower, which would have a door on to the piazza, might be designed to face whatever direction 'may be necessary for doing harm to their enemy or enemies'; it could be used against anyone except Marchesello or his family. If either party wished to sell, the other was to have the first offer 'at a just price'; moreover Marchesello could alienate his share to nobody but the Carbonesi and their share could apparently not be alienated, though they could divide it differently among themselves. The Carbonesi share could not descend through a female line and neither party could contract a marriage which might harm the interests of the other. The agreement was to be renewed after ten years.

The Carbonesi's insistence that their tower was both for defence and 'for doing harm to their enemy or enemies' leads on to the question of the role of the towers in the life of the city nobles. As early as the 1160s the Jewish traveller Benjamin of Tudela had been impressed by this picturesque feature of the cities. At Genoa, he says, 'each householder has a tower to his house and at times of strife they fight each other from the tops

Plate 6.2 San Gimignano, view of medieval towers. San Gimignano was a small commune, lying along a ridge on the main route from France to Rome (Via Francigena). Some twenty towers still survive close to the town's main street; prominent near the centre of this photograph are the towers of the Palazzo Comunale and the Palazzo del Podestà. The most impressive views of San Gimignano are to be had from distant points in the Val d'Elsa, from which the great towers dominate the skyline.

of the towers', while Pisa 'is a very great city, with about 10,000 turreted houses for battle at times of strife[6]'. Benjamin's statistics are not of course to be accepted literally; clearly they mean 'a very large number'. Some of the towers that he saw were already then very old. The earliest recorded attempt to fix a maximum height for the towers of Pisa and to control fighting from them dates from about 1100, and before the time of Benjamin's visit the consuls' oath included a clause promising that they would permit no towers above a certain height and would levy a fine of 10 L on any man attacking the tower of another. The maximum height permitted was that of the towers of Stefano and Lamberto and of Guinizone's on the other (south) side of the Arno. The earliest surviving Genoese consular oaths also date from before Benjamin of Tudela's time and contain similar clauses about a maximum height for towers and fighting from them. Legislation of this sort was characteristic of almost all the communes.

But this vertical quasi-military domestic architecture demands rather more explanation. It represents the existence in the city of a form of watch-tower which was also very common in the countryside. Moreover, the institution which made the tower a necessity was itself familiar in rural areas: this was the blood feud or vendetta, a tradition both of violence in settling (and prolonging) private disputes and of unwillingness to settle such matters in the courts. Essentially the purpose of the tower was defensive; its owner's home was his castle, to which he could retreat if under attack and where he might hope to conduct a prolonged defence. It became conventional for those who could afford it to inhabit a 'house-tower'. Many did so no doubt because they had inherited one from ancestors and this was the accepted form of residential architecture, rather than because an aristocratic way of life dictated an unending series of vendettas for all. It has been suggested that the high cost of land within the cities encouraged vertical building: there is probably some truth in this, but most cities normally had unused building space and in the main the towers should be seen as the product of fear, fashion and a taste for display, rather than of economic necessity. Some towers were set very close to each other, as may still be seen, for example, at San Gimignano and Bologna. In these circumstances fighting from tower to tower, as described by Benjamin of Tudela, may have taken place and some advantage could be derived from building higher than one's neighbour, but normally ostentation must have been the main motive for building very high.

Certainly the usual form of fighting involving towers was an assault launched from without, from ground level, against a defence within. This is the sort of warfare described by the Genoese chronicler under the year 1194:

The Volta and their party constructed a new and very powerful weapon. They directed a wooden spingard against Oberto Grimaldi's tower and Oberto Spinola's new tower. With this, in the sight of all, they managed to make a hole in the new tower of Bulbunoso, which is at the crossroads of St Syrus. In this way they destroyed most of the tower and caused it to collapse. Then the men of the [?archbishop's] court came and set up a 'machine' in the orchard of St Syrus with which they propelled many stones against the houses and towers of Oberto Grimaldi and the Spinola family. They later erected other machines and the other side also constructed many machines and shot many stones at the houses and towers of the court party.

A century later the fighting between Blacks and Whites at Pistoia was similar in essentials, in that men attacked towers from the ground, rather than 'fighting each other from the tops of towers'.

The Blacks had fortified the tower of ser Iacopo's sons and from there they did much harm to messer Ranieri's sons. And the Whites had fortified messer de Lazzari's house . . . That house did much harm to the Blacks with crossbow fire and stones, so that they could not fight from the street. When the Blacks saw that they were being opposed by servants [*fanti*] inside the house, Vanne Fucci and some of his companions went up to it, attacked it frontally with crossbow fire and then won it by setting fire to one side of the house and entering it by the other side. Those who were inside began to run away and they pursued them, wounding and killing and plundering the house . . . Then everyone returned to his own dwelling; the honours of that day belonged to the Blacks[7].

The tower was a family's refuge and stronghold, to which it could retire in disturbed times. Giovanni Villani relates[8] that when there was trouble in Florence in 1303 'many towers and fortresses were fortified in the old way (*al modo antico*), so that things could be thrown, and arrows fired, from them'. Once again it seems that the role of the tower was defensive. The destruction of their towers, because this deprived powerful men of the means of self-defence, was the supreme social penalty, carried out, for example, at Genoa in 1161 against some 'rebels' and again in 1187 against certain nobles and others who had been responsible for the murder of a consul, and often later against heretics and defeated Ghibellines and Guelfs. At Genoa the threat

Plate 6.3   Fighting from towers, from a manuscript of the
Genoese Annals (Paris, Bibliothèque Nationale, Ms. lat. 10136,
f.IIIv). Fighting is taking place at the base of the towers, while
some men (including an archer) are engaged in combat from the
towers. The object projecting horizontally from the lefthand tower
may be a battering-ram. For the events illustrated, see p. 127

Plate 6.4   Destruction of a tower by the Genoese authorities, 1190. This illustration from a manuscript of the Genoese annals shows the podestà of Genoa, Manegoldus de Tetocio of Brescia, supervising the complete destrution of the residential tower (*domus in castro*) of Fulco de Castello. This was ordered by a general meeting (*parlamentum maximum*) because three members of the de Castello family had murdered a consul, Lanfranc Piper. The guilty men had already escaped to Piacenza. (Paris, Bibliothèque Nationale, Ms. lat. 10136, f. 109v).

to destroy towers exceeding the permitted height was carried out in 1196 and the Pisan authorities were sufficiently in earnest to assign a use for the debris of towers destroyed on the orders of the commune; it was to be employed as ballast for cargo vessels.

The noble or magnate who defended his tower was unlikely to be dependent merely on his own relatives; he would have a *familia* in the wider sense, a household, including men like the *fanti* who helped the Whites at Pistoia in 1295. It was these retinues which made the powerful so formidable and helped them to defy the law. The Genoese annals once again illustrate this, when the chronicler explains that in 1237 'great contention and discord' broke out over the election of a podestà, 'so that all the magnates of Genoa kept serjeants with them and nearly all of them went about armed and fortified their towers'. After some fighting around a tower, in which there were several casualties, a truce was arranged and the archbishop pronounced an arbitration as the result of which the podestà originally named was accepted. But the troubles of 1237 were quite normal, and two years later the chronicler notes a rumour 'that some nobles and powerful citizens of Genoa wanted to bring men and serjeants into the city to reinforce their strength'. These 'men and serjeants' are of course the military retinues to be found at this date throughout feudal Europe. They figure in the Pisan statutes of 1286 as 'followers living in their houses with them' (*masnaderii morantes cum eis in domo*) of whom the magnates were to furnish a list; any Pisan 'keeping a serjeant or follower' was to pay a certain sum as a pledge for their good conduct[9]. Clients and vassals, though probably not the lower ranks of household retainers, could be included in the *consorzerie*.

Naturally the authorities of the communes recognised retinues and the institution of vassalage, together with the fortified towers and the blood feud, as the great rival and challenge to their control. The attempt of the Popolo to erect a legislative barrier which would deprive the magnates of the advantages of their social power will be discussed later, but something may usefully be said now about laws directed against vassalage, in order to illustrate the nature of this phenomenon and the menace that it presented to communal law and order. A great many communes ordered bluntly in their codes that 'no man is to become the vassal of any other or swear fealty to him' and the penalty was often severe, so severe that one may doubt its observance. At Perugia not only were both the juror and the recipient of an oath of vassalage to be decapitated, but so was any notary who recorded such a transaction. Modena, more reasonably, forbade notaries to draw up deeds of vassalage or serfdom for *potentes* and their familiars, but did not threaten the death penalty. The outward sign of vassalage was the wearing of the lord's livery or arms. Pisa prohibited members of the Popolo from bearing noble coats of arms, though it is significant that an exception had to be made for *popolani* of the *contado* who had been used to carrying such insignia for a period of at least ten years. Other statutes – which in themselves recognise the futility of forbidding all vassalage – made the lord responsible for the deeds of his serjeants and followers. A characteristic clause from the Spoletan 'Breve Populi' of 1296 ordains that 'whoever commits an offence against another through any "assassin" or through his servant or a vassal is to be punished, both he and the man committing the offence[10]'. Such measures were often associated with orders that magnates should provide the podestà with full lists of their household serjeants.

The Popolo

Set up against the commune's overmighty subjects, the noble and the non-noble but powerful 'magnates', were their self-appointed counterweights and adversaries, the *populares* (Italian *popolani*). Like the nobles, these men constituted a corporation within the republic, a *societas populi*. The only status which automatically excluded a man from the Popolo was membership of the *societas militum*, but in practice leadership tended to be exercised by prominent and well-to-do gildsmen. A Milanese chronicler saw that city's Popolo as composed of 'those who live by buying and selling and not by manual labour, such as merchants and men halfway between wealth and poverty'[11]. The really humble had no great part to play in the Popolo; it was hoped that they would answer its call to arms, yet they were suspect as being potentially both servants of the magnates and opponents of the gild masters. In 1277 the popular organisation of Padua forbade the presence at the election of officials of all 'sailors, gardeners, agricultural labourers, landless men and herdsmen' and various other categories, including all men assessed for taxation at less than 100 L[12]; presumably the danger was that the powerful might use them to intimidate the electors. Distinctions between richer and poorer *popolani* were commonly made, the former being accused of overawing the latter and of paying an insufficient share of taxation. Even the officials of the Popolo would refer to its own 'better and more powerful' members (*de melioribus et potentioribus ipsius populi*)[13]. In its aspirations and leadership the Popolo was essentially the organ of the wealthier craftsmen and of educated professional elements such as the notaries.

The description 'pressure group' is inescapable for the Popolo, though it hardly explains a complicated and varied social institution. It has already been suggested that the Popolo was concerned with two different but related aims, the general one of seeking to counterbalance the social weight of the powerful and lawless and the more specific one of achieving for the *popolani* a considerable constitutional role in the commune. In both of these it gained a good deal of success. Its constitutional ambitions and victories have parallels outside Italy, for example in the communes of Flanders and Germany, where the gild elements in the later middle ages usually contrived to sap the monopoly of an early established oligarchy of merchants and craftsmen. But it may be better to introduce the Popolo by way of a brief discussion of its more general social objective.

The Popolo regarded as an enemy any special alliance or party among the powerful to exert political pressure within the commune – partly, of course, because such an alliance was a rival to itself. No citizen of Spoleto or its district, so the Popolo of that city decreed, could contract or swear any 'conventicle, plot (*coniuratio*) or conspiracy' except by consent of the podestà, Captain or councillors. Every member of Bergamo's Popolo took an oath that

I shall do the best that is in my power to see that the council of the *credencia* and all the offices and honours of the commune of Bergamo should be chosen in the interest of the community [*communiter*] and not by reason of any party or parties.

Furthermore

if any party or alliance in the city of Bergamo or any gathering takes up arms or begins to fight and if they intend to act against the honour and good estate of the podestà, rector or rectors of the commune of Bergamo or against the commune or this corporation (the Popolo) or any member of it, I shall not take up arms with them or join them, nor give them assistance or advice. Instead I shall hasten to the palace or wherever the rector, podestà or rectors may be. I shall defend and aid and maintain

Plate 6.5 The Capitano del Popolo of Pisa swears an oath on assuming office (Pisa, Archivio di Stato, Breve del Popolo et delle Compagnie del Comune, Com. A.N.6, fol. 6). The Capitano places his right hand on the Scriptures as he promises to 'defend and maintain' the Popolo and the city itself and its *distretto*.

the rector, podestà or rectors and the commune in every way of which I am capable, to the advantage of whoever is then in office as the podestà, rector or rectors[14].

The constitutional organisation and development of the Popolo are intricate (and have been the subject of controversy among historians) on account of its twofold nature. Two distinct aspects, one regional and military, the other corporative (that is, connected with the craft gilds) merged in a single *societas*, which continued to bear the signs of this dual origin. The more common form of evolution, it seems, was one where the original main basis of the Popolo was the *vicinia* or region; at an early stage (in the early thirteenth century in most larger cities) the Popolo was a primarily military phenomenon, a *societas* uniting the bodies of regional infantry whose task was to check the power of the magnates in times of crisis. Moreover each *vicinia* was an organisation within which families could find allies in times of faction and discord. The craft-gilds (*arti*) might already have some connection with the Popolo but this was likely to be a subordinate one. There were exceptional cities where there was no connection between gild and Popolo and others where the organisation of the Popolo was from its origin connected with the gilds. Often there was a stage – which must have involved much administrative confusion – in which the *popolano* had military and political duties both *qua* inhabitant of a certain region of the city and *qua* member of a gild. Membership of these two bodies approximately coincided, the only gildsmen who tended to be treated as magnates being merchants and judges. The gild element in the Popolo usually came to the fore as it became a more sophisticated and a less purely military body. Certainly the most common form of evolution was in this direction, with the gilds increasingly asserting themselves as the organising force within the Popolo; in many of the larger cities they predominated over the regional element by the mid thirteenth century, though arrangements varied greatly.

In its fully evolved form the Popolo retained a military organisation. The body of 'popular' infantry which was in perpetual readiness for employment against the magnates numbered 1,000 in many cities, though naturally not all could raise a force of this size, while in some it was 2,000 or yet more numerous. Normally the Popolo had its own Captain. This was an office modelled in many ways on the podestà; its holder was recruited from another city and his period of appointment was usually six months or a year. Presumably the office originally came into being because the *popolani* felt that the leadership of an individual would further their cause more effectively than joint leadership by committee, and this decision was often hastened by ambitious men (in the first place sometimes renegade local nobles) who offered such leadership. No doubt also there was conscious imitation of the commune's constitution.

The first recorded Captain of the Popolo, it seems, was at Parma in 1244. The institution is to be found at Piacenza and Florence in 1250, in most of the Tuscan and neighbouring cities (probably imitating Florence) within the next few years, and in the large majority of communes by the 1270s. As with the *podesteria*, the degree of active leadership exercised by the *Capitano del Popolo* varied greatly from city to city and even from tenure to tenure. The post became one which was held by members of the same body of judicially-trained knights as acted as podestà and it was common for them to play both parts at different times, acting now as podestà and now as *Capitano del Popolo* according to the vacancies that arose and offers that were received. Like the *podesteria*, the captaincy of the Popolo tended to decline into an essentially judicial post in the course of the fourteenth century.

The Popolo also had its own local officials, most commonly known as 'elders' (*anziani*), though other titles such as 'priors' existed. Such men had usually led the Popolo, at least in the more precocious towns, before it had its captain, though the contrary order of development, captain preceding *anziani*, was not altogether exceptional. In normal circumstances the *anziani* were probably the effective leaders of the Popolo, not surprisingly, since local *popolani* might be expected to have its interests more at heart than external nobles. The method of electing the *anziani* usually reflected the dual nature of the Popolo, some of them being chosen by the gilds, others by the various regional divisions (*rioni*); at Parma for instance there were sixteen, of whom eight were gild representatives, while each of the city's quarters appointed two others. Commonly the *anziani* held office for a brief period of from two to six months, during which time they resided in a special *palazzo*. In many communes the local *anziani* tended to supersede a captain in the leadership of the Popolo. At Florence the six priors to some extent effaced the captain after 1282 and a similar process seems to have taken place around the same time at Siena, Perugia and Orvieto. Thus in some cities the Popolo's institutional evolution was the reverse of the commune's, which had earlier shifted from a joint regime of local men (the consuls) to a single external official (the podestà). The Popolo's repetition of the commune's institutions extended also its conciliar structure: it often had a greater and an inner council.

There are few cities in which the story of the rise of the Popolo goes beyond the early years of the thirteenth century. The eleventh-century social disputes at Milan were essentially quarrels between different categories of feudal tenant. A chronicler of Piacenza[15] attributes the first noble-Popolo troubles in that city to the year 1090. Their origin he ascribes to a fight between a noble and a *popolano*, in which the latter was being defeated, so that other *popolani* had to come to his aid. This led to a general battle in which men were killed on either side and to a decision by the nobles to leave the city and blockade it, making it impossible to hold the market there. This story may be apocryphal or its date incorrect, but it gives a credible and interesting idea of the form taken by noble-Popolo disputes. Evidence from a number of cities suggests that commonly the substantial point at issue concerned taxation. In the period when the consulate itself was often shared on agreed terms between nobles and non-nobles, it was apparently normal also to fix what proportion of the commune's revenue should be provided by each of these two elements. Inevitably this arrangement led to bitter quarrels. When such disputes culminated in civil war this in turn often involved other cities, for each party looked to its counterpart in neighbouring cities for support, as, for example, the Brescian *milites* did to the nobles of Cremona in 1202–8.

The 'popular' party makes a sporadic constitutional appearance in the early years of the thirteenth century – the *populares* of Vicenza, for example, chose their own podestà in 1206, though the city seems as yet to have had no regularly organised Popolo – but its first substantial and lasting gains were only made in the century's third decade. At Piacenza the Popolo chose its own podestà in 1220 and three years later a settlement was achieved whereby nobles and *popolani* jointly chose one mutually acceptable podestà by a complicated process of indirect election. Meanwhile, in 1222, they had reached terms which allotted to the Popolo half the offices in the commune (*honores et officii*) and one-third of the members of diplomatic missions. In the same year the Popolo of Vicenza won the right to one-third of all offices there. Such arrangements, which became common, were usually arrived at through the arbitration of some third party, such as the podestà of another city. At Modena the first popular gains were achieved in 1229 when a fixed proportion of popular representation in the council was secured, though there was no firmly organised *societas populi* till twenty years after this. At many other cities similar victories were won but did not last; quite often, indeed, the Popolo was forced into dissolution.

From about the middle of the century – the period of the early *Capitani del Popolo* – the Popolo was normally on a firmer basis. At this time a new and more radical Popolo was formed at Piacenza and it is worth recounting this development in some detail to instance the Popolo in action[16].

The movement began in 1250 as the result of a grain shortage. A protest meeting gathered in a church and those present took an oath of mutual support as well as despatching a deputation to the podestà to complain about the export of Piacentine grain to Parma. The podestà's response was to arrest the main organiser of the meeting on the grounds that it was 'to the harm and detriment of the city'. The General Council backed the podestà and decided that 'not more than three people should meet together in the city and the podestà should have full permission and power to enquire into the actions of the said Antolino, and if he found him deserving of death then he should be certainly killed'. The more timorous of those who had been at the assembly now attended gild meetings at which they explained their own innocence in the matter. But other members of the Popolo rang the bells, gathered together in arms and frightened the podestà into releasing the ring-leader, Antolino. This was the chance for Antolino to harangue the people in arms, 'provoking them and inducing them to do what he wanted and reminding them of the many ills suffered by the Popolo of Piacenza over the last fifteen years, how many men had been condemned to death and driven from place to place', and so on. The re-formed Popolo now elected twelve consuls, explained to the council of the commune that Antolino's actions 'had not been against the podestà but on behalf of the Popolo', and determined to gather its own council and to issue statutes. The council assembled in the church of San Pietro, found insufficient room there, and adjourned to San Sisto. It was decided to elect a *rector populi*, but at once 'a great division arose in the Popolo; some wanted one, some another, and there was a great deal of noise. Then Tado de' Tadi said: "Why don't you have Uberto de Iniquitate, because he has suffered much harm and damage on your account?" So he was elected, by voice.' A considerable party of 'traitors to the people' disapproved this choice because they thought Uberto too favourable to the imperialists. These people tried to get out of the church to raise a force against Uberto but failed to because the church doors had been closed by those who had attempted unsuccessfully to get in.

There followed an orderly election of consuls from the gilds and these, together with the regional consuls, unanimously elected Uberto as podestà and rector of the Popolo for one year. Soon after this, Uberto's supporters were to be heard saying that one year's office meant 'little good and little harm' and he was chosen as *potestas populi* for five years, his son to succeed in the event of his death. Already many opponents of the new regime, not all of them nobles, had gone into exile, and controversy rose over whether they should be readmitted. One of Uberto's opponents over this question was the original popular leader, Antolino, who now himself suffered exile in turn. 'And so', says the chronicler, 'parties arose within the Popolo'. After de Iniquitate had disputed control with the commune's podestà, a Genoese, the nobles persuaded this man, Nata de' Grimaldi, to become 'podestà of the nobles in exile'. Fighting, alternating with abortive attempts at pacification, continued for another two years and only in December 1252 did the nobles of Piacenza return to their city.

The events of 1250–2 at Piacenza reveal a great deal about the nature of the Popolo. Firstly they serve as a reminder that this was not just an 'institution', but a generalisation covering the activities of energetic and ambitious men spurred to action by grievances such as arose in a year of bad harvest. They also show how, as might be expected, the Popolo could seek its ends by a display of unity and force and then, having apparently gained them, become divided over personalities and questions of policy.

Piacenza, like most of the communes mentioned so far in connection with the Popolo, was a large city and its institutional development was precocious. A smaller centre, Matelica in the March of Ancona, shows no trace of 'popular' gains before 1237, when the nobles lost certain fiscal privileges including exemption from direct taxation. Further fiscal gains were made by the *populares* in 1278, but not till near the end of the century did a Popolo emerge, with a captain, and at the same period the leading gild officials gained control in the commune. The formation of an infantry force of 1,000 *popolani*, found in so many larger towns in the thirteenth century, is not recorded at Matelica till 1340.

Whenever it happened, and whatever means of pressure were used by the Popolo, there was likely to come a time when the supreme authority of the commune itself would be challenged by the pretensions of this state within the state. The rivalry is expressed clearly enough in the title of a statute of the Pistoian Popolo: 'Statutes of the Popolo are to prevail over statutes of the commune'[17]. 'If there are any clauses in the constitution of the commune of Pistoia', this explains, 'which are harmful or contrary to any clause of the constitution of the Popolo of Pistoia, then the clauses of the constitution of the Popolo are to be valid and binding and are to be observed and acted upon, and not those clauses in the commune's constitution which are contrary to them.' At Pistoia the podestà might open official letters only in the presence of the *anziani* and the letters had to be read out to them. A straightforward clash of authority occurred at Siena in 1257, when the podestà acted without consulting the Capitano del Popolo and in the subsequent controversy each of these officials invited the other to visit him but declined to make the visit himself lest he derogated from the dignity of the body which he represented. This Sienese dispute originated over the political, fiscal and judicial clauses of an abortive agreement between commune and Popolo reached in 1256. The Popolo proceeded to claim a half-share of the membership of inner councils, the main council, the electors to the *podesteria* and the 'amenders' of laws, as well as one of the three functionaries of the accounting-office (*Biccherna*): by 1262 most of this had been gained. Pressure and compromise somehow prevented constant confrontations between communal and popular authority, in a situation which anyone accustomed to clear-cut modern notions of sovereignty must see as a paradox and nightmare.

When one moves on to consider the legislation promulgated by the Popolo it is impossible to maintain firmly the distinction suggested above between the Popolo's general social objectives and more specific constitutional ones. The declared aim of the popular code of Bologna (1282) was 'that rapacious wolves and meek lambs should be able to walk with equal steps'; the lambs of course were the *popolani*, the wolves the nobles. Such a code was intended to neutralise the situation described in one of its clauses: 'many men of the popolo of the city, *contado* and district of Bologna are daily troubled and disturbed in their property and the fruits of their property by the magnates'. The legislative measures against the strength of the magnates include those (mentioned above) directed against vassalage and retinues, as well as laws forbidding seignorial justice and fiscality and 'private' prisons. Other related measures attempted to remove *popolani* from the threatened control of the powerful, by forbidding them to accompany magnates in the streets, to go to their houses or to take news to them, to seek their suppor'. in any judicial matter. Normally the officials of the commune were also forbidden to associate with magnates. In the same general category belong the many laws regulating the height of towers and seeking to prevent the nobles from feuding.

Apart from this the magnates were placed under precise constitutional and juridical disadvantages, which confirmed or augmented the institutional victories of the Popolo. They were naturally excluded from all the institutions of the Popolo itself, including the gilds, and their share in the now more circumscribed offices of the commune itself was limited. Total exclusion from all political office was rare, particularly as nobles were needed as ambassadors and military advisers; more commonly the magnates were allowed a fixed degree of participation in certain councils and offices. In judicial matters a sort of 'double standard' was proclaimed, to the disadvantage of the magnates. Crimes committed against *popolani* by magnates were not to be punished by the normal penalty for the offence; this was to be doubled, trebled or quadrupled. At Parma, for example, 'the oath of any member of the Popolo is to be full proof against any magnate or powerful man' and if any magnate was accused of wounding or attacking a *popolano* the authorities must act even if there was nothing against the accused man but 'rumour and reputation' (*si sola vox et fama fuerit contra talem magnatem*). The word of a magnate was *ipso facto* of less juridical worth than that of a *popolano*. 'In any accusation concerning damages', it was decreed at Modena,[18] 'the oath of a powerful man (*potens*) is not to be believed, nor is that of their sons or squires.' Proof against a magnate was to be easier and the proceedings such that a verdict could be obtained more quickly. At Bologna the word of the offended party was to be accepted concerning his attacker; if he said the man was a magnate, *potens*, knight or noble, then he was automatically to be regarded as such.

Ultimately this sort of penal system depended for its effectiveness on officials, backed by armed force, whose task it was to supervise its operation. At Florence in 1281, and at Bologna in 1288, lists of magnates were drawn up compelling those named to make a payment (of at least 1,000 L at Bologna and 2,000 L at Florence) as a pledge for their future good conduct. The Bolognese list included about forty families (ninety-two individuals), a rather later Florentine list about 150, of whom seventy-two resided mainly in the city. These were the men whose repression was the particular task of such officials as the 'Standardbearer of Justice' (*Gonfaloniere di Giustizia*), appointed at Florence in 1293 by the 'Ordinances of Justice' and imitated in a number of other cities. In the event of a magnate killing a *popolano*, the *Gonfaloniere* had the responsibility of seeing that the magnate's house was at once destroyed by the Popolo's infantry, his property confiscated and he himself automatically sentenced to death.

The family solidarity of the nobles was turned against them; if the guilty man could not be traced, his next of kin was liable to the same punishment. The ferocious Popolo of Parma, which decreed a fine of 10 L for any of its members 'not recommending it as a good thing that vengeance should be done on magnates offending *popolani'*, had a special body of one hundred *antiqui cives populares* 'to take vengeance against magnates who offend *popolani'*. This was additional to the normal thousand popular infantry force.

If the popular codes had been fully and constantly effective they would have made the life of a magnate a Kafkaesque nightmare. To what extent did the reality correspond to the law? The answer to this question must be a provisional one, largely because codes have survived better than judicial records and such records as exist have been little investigated. When it came to a straight armed struggle with the nobility, there is no doubt that the Popolo could be an effective force, as it showed at Genoa in 1288 when defending its own captains in their palace and foiling an attempt at an armed coup by the Grimaldi and other nobles. But was it able to convert its outlook into the routine of day-to-day business in the courts? One's impression is that the magnates received juster treatment than the codes directed against them would suggest. At Bologna the statutes laid down that 'the (sworn) accusation of the offended party is to be regarded as sufficient proof concerning both the wound and the person inflicting it', but in practice witnesses, often including medical witnesses, were required and the unsupported claim of a plaintiff that his aggressor was a magnate was insufficient. Magnates sometimes succeeded in establishing their innocence and occasionally *popolani* were found guilty of false accusations. On the other hand, magnates were often convicted, and quite often the guilt was tacitly confessed by failure to appear in court, but the sentence was not always as relentless as the codes suggested. In 1292 a Pistoian noble condemned for inflicting a facial knife wound on a *popolano* was fined 500 L. The following year another noble of the same city, having been arrested for beating a *popolano* about the head with a cudgel, got away with a fine of 300 L[19]. When a man was known to have money there was a strong temptation to let him off with a fine, particularly if the Popolo's funds were low – and good sense suggested the uselessness of inflicting fines so heavy that they were unlikely to be paid. Again and again fines levied on members of the Pazzi, Frescobaldi and other Flor-

Plate 6.6 The ending of a feud between families. Sienese painting of the mid-14th century (in the Museum of Fine Arts, Boston, Mass.) made for Arigo di Neri Arighetti. Presided over by an archangel, the former enemies exchange the kiss of peace having flung away their weapons and shields. Below the main panel, which depicts the mystical marriage of St Catherine of Alexandria to Christ, the predella also shows St Margaret and St Michael warring with demons. An attribution to Barna da Siena has not been generally accepted.

entine magnate families were eventually commuted for a much lower payment; it was not unusual for pardons to be sold for as little as fifteen per cent of the original figure.

Not only did magnates survive the measures of the 'meek lambs', they continued to prosper, to feud and to have successful public careers. The extent to which they were still required as ambassadors, military commanders and officials in the *contado* has already been emphasised. Of the Florentine families mentioned above, the Pazzi, as well as the Guidi, Ubaldini and Ubertini, continued to hold widespread and flourishing lordships in the regions around the city.

There is perhaps a sense in which the Popolo, like treason and peasants, could never prosper, or was doomed to achieve nothing better than partial success. Since a *popolano* who 'made good' was on the way to becoming a magnate, the Popolo was perpetually menaced by the loss of its leaders. If it was a product of social mobility – had the situation been static, the *popolani* might have been prepared to accept their inferior position – the Popolo was also its victim. In practice, of course, the process of recognition of magnatial status was liable to lag behind the attainment of wealth. As 'new classes' rose it was inevitable that not all their members should be absorbed rapidly into the nobility, nor even into the *de facto* associated categories, the magnates, *potentiores*, etc. Had the 'older' families followed a systematic policy of pressing office on the parvenus, they could have hindered, perhaps even prevented, the rise of the Popolo; but the supposition is in itself a slightly absurd one. New men rose to wealth and prominence with rapidity and sometimes in large numbers: clearly not all of them would find all they wanted in the way of civic office or social recognition. In any case there were bound to be men like Piacenza's Antolino Saviagata and Uberto de Iniquitate whose temperaments cast them for a popular role and others to whom opportunism recommended it; and there was necessarily always a stratum in society immediately below the magnates, with a role which was to claim for itself a greater share in the commune.

Other private city organisations

Since associations of nobles and *popolani* and the *consorzerie* all challenged its hold, it was natural that the commune should feel its authority threatened by these rival loyalties. Some communes hopefully outlawed all 'parties', whereas another, more realistically, confined itself to ordering that no citizen should take an oath or bind himself to membership of 'any corporation (*societas*) for mutual assistance except the companies of armed men and the gilds [whose oath is] made for the honour and advantage of the commune' of Bologna (1211)[20].

The Bolognese *compagnie delle armi*, which are mentioned in this law, provide a particularly interesting example of a powerful organisation within the commune. Since the twelfth century, or even earlier, Bologna had been divided into four *quartieri*, each of which was in turn divided into a number of *contrade*. The latter exercised minor police authority and each (there were seventy-two) corresponded to the area of a chapel. The Bolognese *quartiere* possessed its own military organisation, as was normal for the regions of the cities, having its own standard-bearers (for both cavalry and infantry), councillors and other officials. But by the early thirteenth century there was another structure of twenty (occasionally twenty-four) *societates armorum*. The latter differed greatly from each other in size, had no firm regional basis, and cut across class divisions. At one time one of them had as few as 130 members, another almost 600. Some insisted on all their members living within certain boundaries and recruited in one *quartiere* only, others had members in all four. Some, such as the *Lombardi* and *Toschi* (Tuscans) had names referring to the area of origin of men who were not native Bolognese, others had gild associations, yet others links with aristocratic *consorzerie*. Everything about them, most of all their topographical insouciance, suggests a voluntary origin. This impression is strengthened by their varying statutes and financial arrangements: the annual contribution ranged from two to twelve *bolognini*. These *compagnie* were for mutual protection, as is clear from the statutes of one, the *Spade* (Swords), of 1285:

> Our members should maintain and defend each other against all men, within the commune and outside it. If any of them should have a suit against any knight, *potens* or lawyer . . . in the court of the podestà, captain or any other judge, lay or clerical . . . the *ministrales* (officials) are to select one hundred of the best and wisest of our members and divide these up into units of twenty and sub-units of ten. These men are to stand by our member . . . in the court and out of it . . . all hundred of them if necessary[21].

This *compagnia*, in the judicial protection it hopes to offer its members, looks like a *consorzeria* or even like the Popolo. But even if it is recognisable as a distant relative of the Popolo, there is one very significant difference indeed: the *compagnie delle armi*, at least in their thirteenth-century heyday, comprised both nobles and non-nobles, members together of the same *compagnie*. All these organisations have in common a distrust of the commune's judicial machinery, in so far as it affected the unaided individual, and all attenuate the commune's authority.

These Bolognese *societates* have a peculiar interest, largely because the statutes reveal their voluntary origin, independent of action by the commune, but one could cite many other examples of loyalties lying within the commune and rivalling it. Among these the *consorzerie* were very strong, but so too were the regional organisations mentioned above, both the small *contrade* associated with the watch and similar duties and the larger regions, which (at least in some towns) possessed their own councils and officials. Feeling between regions was often of genuine hostility, even violent hostility, and has sometimes remained so up to very recent times. In some towns the inhabitants of the different *rioni* gathered in the main square to throw stones at each other, a violent sport in which there were many casualties; at Siena the *bactallia in campo Fori* between the three regions (*terzi*) is witnessed by documents as early as 1238. Stone-throwing of this sort was an organised sport in a number of towns, as were various other forms of fighting and wrestling. Obviously such occasions must have strengthened the local, regional loyalties within the city.

Yet another and very important competitor of the commune was the gild, which itself normally had direct representation in the Popolo. Indeed there were many cities in which the Popolo came to be nothing but the collective body of the gilds. The legislation of the gilds to a large extent controlled the economic and even social activities of their members, who must normally have comprised the majority of the adult male population. The gild could also express political views and even take political action. Thus in 1293 the gilds of Padua resolved to form 'a single body, society, brotherhood or league to maintain and conserve the city of Padua and its district in a peaceful state as a commune, free from the domination of any tyrant or any other single person'[22]. And the hold of gilds over their members could be extremely strict. The gild of notaries of this same city (Padua) not only forbade its members to express opinions in council meetings which did not represent the majority of the gild, but positively ordered that they must speak in the terms laid down by the gild council.

Guelfs and Ghibellines

The division mentioned at the start of this chapter between what Latini called 'the two parties' involves a difficult problem of historical nomenclature and interpretation. 'Who *were* the Guelfs and Ghibellines?' is a question which has been put to every teacher of medieval history: there is no simple answer. In a strange way, due perhaps in part to their picturesque names, the Guelfs and Ghibellines have assumed too much importance in the common historical imagination – and at the expense of social factions – so that even general histories of the period have been entitled *The Guelfs and the Ghibellines*. This is the outlook satirised by Max Beerbohm (in the short story *Savonarola Brown*) in the stage direction 'Enter Guelfs and Ghibellines fighting'. Yet although they may have usurped too much of the limelight, these great parties require explanation.

Such an explanation has to begin from the special position of the Empire as a political force involved in the Italian peninsula, yet essentially external to it. A crucial problem for each city (and hence for each citizen with an opinion on foreign relations) was the diplomatic attitude to be adopted towards imperial power; did a policy of friendship or one of hostility appear to present the greater advantages? In other words, the Empire had a polarising effect and as communes came to form pro- or anti-imperial traditions so two rival diplomatic systems tended to crystallise. This situation was already present in the period of Barbarossa and the rectors of the Lombard League took an oath to oppose their own anti-imperialists: 'if he is a citizen of my city I shall in good faith do my best to bring it about that any house he may have in the city should be destroyed and that he himself should be expelled from the city[23].

But the twelfth-century Lombard whose sympathies were pro-imperial was not a Ghibelline. The two words 'Ghibelline' and 'Guelf', though often used anachronistically by later writers, do not come into the vocabulary of Italian politics until the time of Frederick II (1220–50). The words themselves are derived from the German 'Welf', the family of Frederick's Saxon opponent Otto IV, and 'Waiblingen', a castle of the Hohenstaufen the name of which was used as a battle-cry. Hence they passed to partisans and opponents of Frederick II's power in Italy. There was a tendency to identify an 'imperial party' and a 'Church party' in some of the cities before these came to acquire the labels of 'Ghibelline' and 'Guelf'. The famous names for the two factions seem to be attested first in Florence around 1242 and the convenient usage spread very rapidly. In the critical years of the 1240s both Emperor and Pope (Innocent IV) referred to the rival Florentine parties as the 'Guelf' and 'Ghibelline' parties of Florence. Before the end of the decade the names were in familiar use in the neighbouring cities; Arezzo apparently had its own Guelfs and Ghibellines by 1249 and by 1251 certainly possessed a formal Ghibelline party (as did Pisa, Siena, Pistoia and Prato) with a captain and councillors. At the same time (1251–2) a network of Guelf and Ghibelline diplomatic alliances began to spread throughout Tuscany. Already the words had become a common-place; at San Gimignano legislation forbade 'the singing of any songs between Guelfs and Ghibils (*Ghibillos*)'.

The spread of these terms beyond Tuscany is of course a matter of terminology rather than of substance. The Genoese pro-imperialists had their own captain in 1241, the 'party of the Empire' a captain at Parma in 1247 and the existence of pro-imperialist and anti-imperialist parties is of far more importance than the names given to them. It is worth emphasising nonetheless that only around 1265, when the anti-Hohenstaufen cause was transformed by the passing of its leadership to the house of Anjou, did the terms 'Guelf' and 'Ghibelline' come to adhere firmly to the anti- and pro-imperialist factions throughout northern Italy. Men remembered that these terms had originated in Florence and had been used there to describe the friends and opponents of Frederick II's power. Salimbene, the Franciscan from Parma, was aware of it and in so far as his chaotically loquacious history has a principal theme, this is it. 'All these parties and schisms and divisions and maledictions', he says, 'in Tuscany as in Lombardy, in Romagna as in the March of Ancona, in the March of Treviso as in the whole of Italy, were caused by Frederick, formerly called emperor[24].'

Giovanni Villani, the fourteenth-century Florentine chronicler, also explains correctly the derivation of 'Guelf' and 'Ghibelline' from Florentine factions and their subsequent diffusion. He further attributes the alignment of the Florentine nobility into two hostile groups to a quarrel in 1215 between the Buondelmonti and the Donati, which he sees as the ultimate origin of the local Guelf-Ghibelline feud[25]. These events took place a century before Villani's time (and he was not quite right in thinking 'Guelfo' and 'Ghibellino' two castles in Germany), so that his unsupported version cannot be accepted. But this story does illustrate one very important point. In no city can the parties have originated as pure political entities divided by a difference of opinion on foreign policy. Local divisions within the nobility, dictated by envy, rivalry, family vendettas and sympathies, existed quite independently of the imperial question and usually long before this had been posed by Frederick II. Family and party allegiances and alliances within the cities served first of all to promote the polarisation of noble factions into two opposing systems. This was closely connected with the survival of strong kin loyalties and the tradition of the blood feud. When the question of the Empire arose the magnates, as the most politically-conscious and powerful of the townsmen, naturally tended to take sides, and so their divisions once again became polarised, this time by the external rival principles, imperialism and anti-imperialism. But the success with which the individual could express his view was in turn dependent on the prevalent policy and traditions of his own city. As was mentioned above, some communes such as Cremona, Pisa and Siena had strong pro-imperialist traditions, others such as Milan and Florence anti-imperialist ones. Each city had to take account of prevailing winds and thus at times to change its course, but a strongly-principled Florentine Ghibelline or Sienese Guelf knew that he was a paradox, that commonly the wind would be blowing fiercely into his face.

The defeat of the Hohenstaufen cause in 1265–8 marks the end of one phase in the history of the terms 'Guelf' and 'Ghibelline' and the beginning of another which lasts beyond the period with which this book is concerned. In the period *circa* 1270–1350 the significance of both terms is unstable and elusive, but Guelfism was primarily a system of alliances dedicated to the maintenance of the 1265–8 settlement, that is to say of the Angevin cause. Its principal representatives were normally the Angevin rulers of southern Italy (initially of insular Sicily also), the papacy and Florence with its associated powers in Tuscany and Emilia (often including Bologna), with less firm affiliations in north-western Italy. The papacy, which had done so much to promote anti-imperial alliances in Frederick I and Frederick II's time, supported the Guelfs with its spiritual weapons, in particular the interdict and excommunication. Possibly it conferred also a certain spiritual prestige, though of a rather worn and battered quality. The common bonds of the Guelfs consisted partly in the memory of shared experience (as a Modenese chronicler said, they remembered 'what the Italians had suffered from the fury of the Teuton[26]), partly in a common interest in the maintenance of the Angevin position. There was also a strong economic fabric to Guelfism. The Florentine bankers, the most prominent in Europe, financed the Angevin conquest and then took over entirely the financial organisation of the Neapolitan kingdom, levying its customs and guaranteeing its revenues. They were also bankers to the papacy. The economic dependence was mutual, for Florence drew much of its grain from the Regno, the papal lands of central Italy and the Romagna. Seen as a general phenomenon, then, Guelfism was an alliance involving the kingdom of Sicily and those other Italian powers dependent on its support.

Before turning to Guelfism as an 'internal', local phenomenon it would be well to attempt a general definition of Ghibellinism in the period after about 1270. In a sense this was the mirror-image of Guelfism: its common memories and prejudices, for examples, were anti-French (and specifically anti-Angevin) as those of the Guelfs were anti-German. 'The Pavians usually detest the French, Provencals and Picards', says a Ghibelline chronicler, 'for many reasons. One is that many Pavians were killed in the battle with King Conradin [Tagliacozzo, 1268], whom the Pavians greatly loved. Another is that they are great imperialists [*nimis sunt imperiales*] and keep faith with the heirs of the late Emperor the lord Frederick of happy memory[27].' The Angevins figure in Ghibelline writings as selfish supersessors of the Hohenstaufen, lacking any legitimate claim. The same chronicler reflected on the death of Manfred: 'now let the Church see whether French power is not one of those thorny sticks which wound the hand of whoever tries to use it'. The papacy, he believed, had introduced into Italy a new dynasty which would be its master – though in fact after 1282 the Sicilian war was to make the Angevins a much less dominant force *vis-à-vis* the popes. This Ghibelline remarks that when Piacenza – or rather its *intrinseci*, for the Ghibelline exiles remained defiant – accepted the lordship of King Charles (1271) 'most of them favoured this because they were the Scotti and the other merchants and gildsmen'. There is an aristocratic disdain in this viewpoint which could not be found in a Guelf's; the implication is that those who lived by trade needed peace, whereas a noble might prefer war. Although the old view which equated the Ghibellines with feudal aristocracy and the Guelfs with commerce is in general quite untenable, the imperial connection gave Ghibellinism a certain glamour denied to Guelfism. But after Conradin's death the Empire was so rarely a power to be reckoned with in the peninsula that Ghibellinism inevitably became an elusive and fugitive phenomenon, prospering only during the rare occurrence of favourable circumstances. The Piacentine chronicler quoted above produces an admirable (if biologically dubious) analogy to explain the nature of Ghibellinism:

Just as fishes' eggs may lie in the dry bed of a river and then, even after a hundred years, when a stream returns to the river-bed little fish may be procreated from those eggs; in the same way those cities, places and magnates who were formerly in the graces of his imperial majesty will freely return to the same once more whenever the strength of imperial excellence may reappear.

But the reappearances of effective imperial intervention after 1268 were rare, the only important ones being those of Henry VII (1308–13) and Lewis IV (1327–30).

Guelfism, when installed as the normally dominant cause, deteriorated more and more, its never very considerable doctrinal content dwindling as it became, at the local level, the party which stood for the maintenance of the status quo. It was also a property-owning party with a very big interest in the maintenance of arrangements which had sent hundreds of Ghibellines into exile and confiscated their property for the Guelf party and its leaders. Sinister manifestations of this aspect of faction and exile had probably always been a common and corrupting influence on the political life of the communes. At Milan, for example, a number of men were sentenced to exile and to the loss of their property for having supported Frederick II's ally Ezzelino da Romano. An inventory of this property was drawn up and a reward offered to anyone denouncing men who defrauded the commune by not declaring their holdings. The reward offered was so promising that in 1265 six men entered into a formal agreement to denounce one such individual, on his death, and to share the proceeds. Often the amounts involved were considerable. At Florence no fewer than 530 Guelfs suffered damage to their towers and houses during the brief interlude of Ghibelline rule (1260–6) and the total damage inflicted (according to the claimants) amounted to more than 132,000 L, a sum probably greater than the total revenue of the commune for one year. In fourteenth-century Florence, thanks to the political proscription of Ghibellinism, the Guelf party became the vehicle of a conservative oligarchy able, through its constitutional privileges, to outlaw any potential newcomers. Its principal weapon was its power to deny office to any man accused of Ghibellinism.

In the course of the fourteenth century this sordid form of Guelfism may have conferred some benefits on Ghibellinism, which had at least the glamour of a long-lost cause. The strength of its appeal to a historically-minded romantic in the time of Henry VII may be seen in Dante's imperialist letters and his *De Monarchia*. But Tuscan Ghibellinism was in practice the coalition of Florence's enemies, such as the feudatories and *condottieri* who continued the war against the Florentine-Angevin powers right through the long interval (1313–27) between Henry VII's expedition and that of Lewis IV. By then the true origins of the terms 'Guelf' and 'Ghibelline' in Frederick II's time were becoming mislaid. Andrea Dandolo the Venetian doge (b. 1306) recounts that 'there were once two brothers in Tuscany who were noblemen. One of them was called Gibellinus and he followed the Emperor, the other was called Guelphus and followed the Church, whence those of the imperialist party are called Ghibellines and those of the Church party Guelfs.' At least the memory of the Tuscan provenance of the names is preserved here. Around the middle of the fourteenth century the Lombard chronicler Pietro Azario attributed the troubles of 'the two discordant swords' to two contrary demons, 'one of whom was called Gibel and the other Gualef'[28]. Azario's bewilderment is not all surprising, for in his day the two terms had come to have a mainly local significance and meant quite different things in different contexts, so that, for example, a 'Guelf party' might be found organising a rebellion in papal territory. Even small towns like Chiusi (near Lake Trasimene) and Bertinoro (in Romagna) came to have their own Guelf and Ghibelline organisations – a chronicler relates that the Ghibellines of Bertinoro were exiled in 1295 – and in such places in particular the two labels described local factions whose connections with the increasingly unreal general issue were tenuous indeed.

Rolandino, the chronicler of the Trevisan March, remarks that at Verona feelings ran so high over the pretensions of Ezzelino da Romano that 'not only the knights but the *populares* and merchants also were divided into two parties'. These words carry the implication that normally only the magnates were deeply involved in the great external issue. Such people had a great deal at stake, as the enormous figure for the damages inflicted on the Florentine Guelfs makes clear. Meanwhile the majority of the population must often have remained cautiously uncommitted. Salimbene explains that general indifference was one reason why the party opposed to Frederick II recaptured Parma in 1247. 'The people in the city took no part in these matters; they would not fight either for the attackers or for the Emperor. The bankers and money-changers continued to sit at their tables and craftsmen went on with their work, all as though nothing was happening'[29].

Members of defeated parties faced the prospect of exile and the confiscation of their property or at least the loss of all political rights. Nobody of the imperial party may hold any office or be a member of any *balìa*, proclaims the late-thirteenth-century constitution of Parma, characteristically. The use of similar provisions by a well-entrenched oligarchy at Florence has already

Figure 6

A typical small commune: medieval Gubbio

Walls

Water

Built-up area

Churches

Open spaces

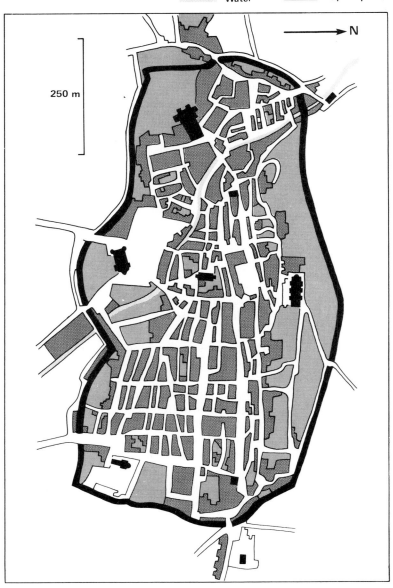

250 m

→ N

Figure 7
Guelf and Ghibelline
loyalties in Tuscany

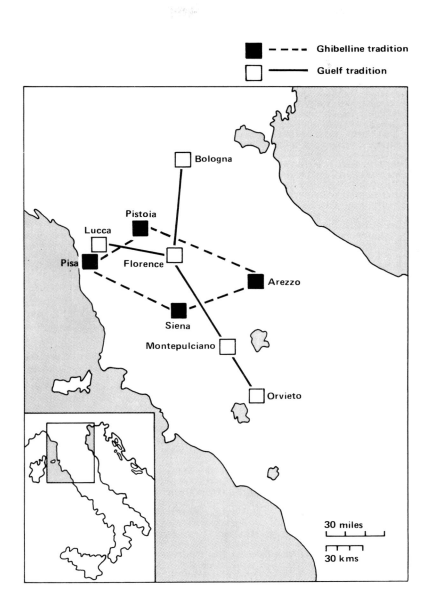

been mentioned. Other penalties were more ingenious. At Padua in 1279 a great many alleged pro-imperialists, though not rich, were promoted to knighthood so that they could be taxed more heavily. At Bologna Ghibellines owed cavalry service but might not perform it in person, so that they had to pay substitutes. Such penal legislation was naturally backed by other clauses 'making windows into men's minds'. Guelf cities, for example, forbade their citizens to criticise the Angevin dynasty or the papacy or the officials of either. One favourite vehicle of criticism was song and in 1269 a Perugian was sentenced to have his tongue cut off (since he could not pay a 100 L fine) 'for singing against King Charles' [of Anjou][30].

But the most ferocious penalty for defeat was exile, a fate peculiarly harsh for men formed by and devoted to their native city. Certainly exile was inflicted on magnates and their households rather than on other classes, but it was a regular and very important feature of the life of the communes (and it still awaits a satisfactory published study). Often it was the automatic punishment for 'political offences'. 'Any Ghibelline fighting or causing a disturbance with or against a Guelf is to be sent to forced residence 100 miles beyond the frontier of the district of Pistoia': thus the Pistoian statutes of 1284. Naturally, men often fled into exile of their own accord because they were frightened. A chronicler from Vicenza[31] tells us the sort of way in which this would happen. In 1262 some pro-imperialists had already left the city and others had been summoned by the podestà and tortured:

One day the podestà summoned ten men from each quarter of the city, from among the leading citizens (*de maioribus et potentioribus*): they were to be at the bishop's palace in the presence of the bishop and podestà, after dawn. At once some monks and other people went round the city telling all the members of the imperialist party who had been summoned: 'If you go to the bishop's palace, you're a dead man; you will all be taken prisoner and none of you will be released until the castle of Valdagno has been handed back to the commune.' Then nearly all the leaders of the imperialist party took flight.

They were then outlawed and their houses and property wrecked. Although exiles were most commonly defeated Guelfs or Ghibellines, social as well as political factions could be a cause of exile, as is illustrated by the story of how the entire noble population of Piacenza fled to the countryside and blockaded the popular regime within the city. The numbers involved might be considerable; when the Guelfs regained Florence in 1268 they drew up a list of Ghibellines which contains the names of 1,050 people, some 400 of whom had been sent into exile outside the district of the commune. No doubt there was a tendency for such bodies of exiles to decline over the years, as circumstances forced men to swallow their pride and accept terms on which they might be readmitted. Negotiations over such terms were a commonplace of city policy; they normally included the provision of guarantors and financial pledges for future 'good conduct'.

A party living in exile in no way lost its corporative nature as a party. It continued to reach agreements and to have its own funds, officials (podestà and captains) and councillors. It entered into alliances, just as a commune might. In 1247–8, for example, the podestà and corporation (*universitas*) of the Modenese exiles, 'both *milites* and *pedites* favouring the party of the Church' (note that the word 'Guelf' was not yet current in Emilia) contracted a series of military agreements concerning garrison duties with the commune of Bologna[32]. And when Charles of Anjou entered Italy in 1265 the (pro-Church) exiled party of Brescia came to terms with him as an ally. The years of Manfred's strength in Tuscany and north-western Italy (1258–66) were the great age of Guelf parties in exile. In June 1265 at Città della Pieve (near Lake Trasimene) the 'captains of the party and corporation of the Guelfs of the city and contado of Siena who are faithful to the Roman Church' forgathered to choose a representative with powers to make certain alliances and to receive instructions from the pope. In July of the same year the bishop of Arezzo was chosen as 'captain and rector of the said Guelf party', at a salary of 1,500 L for a year or until the Guelfs re-entered Siena, whichever was shorter. Not till May 1267 did the Sienese Guelfs succeed, under papal auspices, in negotiating terms which readmitted them to the city. Parties in exile were naturally prone – such is the optimism of all exiles – to make exaggerated promises to allies which they were later unable to keep; sometimes they were not above binding to a virtually perpetual alliance with another commune the city which had driven them out. But when it came to bargaining between the commune (*intrinseci*) and the exiles (*extrinseci*) of the same city concerning the latter's readmission, blank cheques could no longer be the order of the day. In these circumstances it was normal to agree on neutral arbiters to help to fix terms.

The men who remained in exile were those who found some economic *modus vivendi*, and since most exiles were of the magnate class almost the only possible answer was to fight for a living. Men who often had brought away little with them except a war-horse became the cadres of the paid cavalry forces. The pro-imperialists driven from Piacenza naturally tended to take service as mercenaries with Manfred (1258), who offered them 3 L each a month if they had a horse and twenty soldi as infantry. When this imperialist party regained Piacenza (1260) it proceeded to offer terms to another hundred exiled Ghibelline cavalrymen, from Milan. In the next decade or so northern Italy was a battle-ground for groups of Germans accompanied by Ghibelline exiled forces (*forestati*) on the one side and on the other Frenchmen, Provençaux, Picards and the Guelf *forestati*. After the great Ghibelline victory in Tuscany (Montaperti, 1260), many Tuscan Guelfs crossed the Apennines to Bologna, which became a centre of these disconsolate and often penniless characters. But in 1264 they in turn were recruited as mercenaries by the exiled Guelfs of Modena, succeeded in capturing first that city and then Reggio Emilia, and contrived to gather both necessary equipment and considerable loot. So well did they thrive that by 1266 the Tuscan Guelfs in exile composed a finely-mounted body of more than four hundred cavalry which contributed notably to Charles of Anjou's conquest in southern Italy. Thus, as might be expected, the interconnection of the Guelf and Ghibelline systems was military as well as diplomatic. If a definition of 'Ghibelline' and 'Guelf' is to be made, it should be in terms of a polarisation of local aristocratic factions by two external forces, one the Empire and the Italian heirs to its traditions (such as Manfred), the other the papal-Angevin connection.

The ideal of concord

After reading the foregoing pages one can easily imagine what quality constituted the ideal of the people whose lives have been under discussion. As hungry men dream of food and frozen men of warmth, so the men of the Italian republics dreamed of concord. The cry was for rule in the interest of the community and the menace to the community was the party. Under Ezzelino da Romano, says a critic, Padua 'was not ruled in the common interest but in that of a party' (*non regebatur communiter sed per partem*) and the measures he put forward were 'not based on justice but on party'. With this sort of situation he contrasted Venice, later to be the ideal of so many political thinkers: 'Oh happy commune of Venice, whose citizens look to the common interest in all their actions and regard its name with almost religious awe . . .'. And Moses de Brolo, in his agreeable if somewhat idealised description of Bergamo, thought his own city notable for the small number of its towers, its citizens' respect for the law and the prevailing concord:

> Fighting and disturbances are rare amongst them,
> Golden Peace ties the citizens with a firm knot.
> Both poor and rich live a peaceful existence.
> The place is no common one, for observance of the laws,
> For its dignity, its piety, the purity of its concord[33].

Moses, who incidentally wrote as an expatriate at Constantinople, was quite exceptional in thinking his own city harmonious. Guittone of Arezzo lamented in verse the disturbed state of his own city (*Ahi, dolze terra aretina*), which he attributed to pride (*soperbia saver si te tolle*). He also reminded the Florentines after their defeat at Montaperti: 'Oh wretched men, see where you are now, and consider well where you would be if you were ruled as a community' (*a una comunitate*)[34]. As Latini said, all should pull together on the same rope of peace and good deeds:

> . . . *tutti per comune*
> *Tirassero una fune*
> *Di pace e di ben fare.*

And in Lorenzetti's fresco of 'Good Government' in the Palazzo Pubblico at Siena the citizens are actually depicted holding the same cord, which runs through the hand of a figure representing Concord. In this fresco Pax and Concordia are among the chief figures, while the most prominent of all, the 'Ruler', seems to represent the 'lordship' or government of the commune.

Concord is naturally a topic also in Bonvicino's description of Milan (Chapters 5 and 8). The only possible circumstances, he thought, in which any king, tyrant or people might subjugate the city were if 'the citizens contrive to disembowel themselves by turning their own sword against themselves'. The two main things that the city lacked were a port and concord:

If only envy could cease, they could love one another and take thought in all good faith for their fatherland. Then I firmly believe that they could easily make all Lombardy submit to their domination.

The last reflection, with its reminder that men deplored civil strife because it enfeebled their contribution to external strife, seems a fitting one to conclude the chapter.

7 The failure of the republics

The existence of republican forms of government in the Italian city-states was intensely precarious. These institutions were so constantly under pressure or even in full crisis that there is little reason to be puzzled at their failure to survive in most of the cities. The factionalism discussed in Chapter 6 suffices on its own to explain why, in most cities, the regime of a single individual was able to secure acceptance before the end of the fourteenth century. Clearly the occasional survival of republicanism as an exception needs more explaining than do the triumphs of the *signori*. Republicanism in decline is seen as a puzzling historical problem only if the republic is regarded as the body politic in health, the 'tyranny' (*signoria*) as a pathological form. The general question of why republican forms did not last is very easily answerable in terms of their failure to provide stable regimes, but the descriptive question – *how* were they superseded? – remains an interesting one.

Feudal power

There is much insight in the remark that 'in the *Signoria* the two political principles which had so long fought one another in Italy, Municipalism and Feudalism, are joined together[1]'. 'Municipalism' as a principle is in this instance perhaps too philosophical an abstraction to satisfy the historian, because in every city-republic there had remained an important feudal element, in institutions and in ways of life and thought. Nevertheless,

Salzer's aphorism quoted above rightly emphasises that the essence of the *signoria* was the victory of landed power.

To look at the map of later medieval Italy as it has appeared to most historians is to see a landscape of powerful city-states, each dominant over an extensive region. But it is only necessary to blink one's eyes for this map to become one of wide feudal lordships, in the interstices of which the communes struggle to maintain a fugitive independence. Vassalage is well known to have persisted far into the modern period as a preponderant social relationship in central and southern Italy and in much of the Alpine and sub-Alpine north-west, but it has not always been noted that it also lasted, though to a lesser extent, in the rest of the peninsula. A view of north-eastern Italy that accords with the second rather than the first of these maps may be had from the chronicle of the March of Treviso by the thirteenth-century author Rolandino of Padua. Rolandino sees the history of this area in his time as, primarily, the history of four great families, the Marquises of Este and the other feudal dynasties of Da Romano, Camposanpiero and Da Camino. For him Veronese history is essentially a struggle between Estensi and Da Romano. The Sambonifacio and other families are involved as allies of the Estensi, that of Salinguerra (the Torelli) as an ally of the Da Romano, with the role of the commune itself almost that of a passive victim.

To read the account of a composite military campaign, even if the leading spirit in it was a city, is often to receive the same impression of the enduring strength of vassalage. The Guelf (primarily Florentine) force which took the field against Arezzo in 1288 included 250 cavalry raised by 'the Guelf Counts Guidi, Mainardo da Susinana, messer Iacopo da Fano, Filipuccio of Iesi, Marquis Malaspina, the Judge of Gallura, the Counts Alberti and other minor barons (*baroncelli*) of Tuscany', says Giovanni Villani[2]. Again we are in the world of retinues, of the *masnaderii* or followers discussed above, of men like the Pisan *comitatini* allowed to wear their lord's livery because they had done so for more than a decade.

One major town which consistently under the shadow of feudal lordship was Ferrara. This was an important centre of transit trade, on an arm of the Po, a party to early commercial treaties with Venice and Modena, and yet it failed to develop gild or 'popular' institutions of any political importance. Twelfth-century Ferrara seems to have been disputed between the

Torelli and the Adelardi. Then, from its first appearance (1195), the *podesteria* was dominated by the families of Salinguerra (Torelli) and of the Marquises of Este. After nearly twenty years of approximate alternation in this office the two *partes* reached an agreement in 1213 providing for joint decisions concerning the *podesteria* and the appointment of two arbiters to settle the matter in case of dispute. When Marquis Aldobrandino died young and the ambitions of the Estensi were checked also at Padua, Salinguerra achieved virtual control over Ferrara. This was certainly the situation by 1220 and he maintained his position till 1240, when he was ejected and replaced by the Estensi. A later chronicler attributes to Salinguerra a following of 800 horsemen, a large but not incredible figure. In the late thirteenth century, when the Estensi were lords of Ferrara *de iure*, the city's statutes reveal how the retinues which had once overawed the city had been absorbed into its constitution; it was now compulsory for the infantry to wear the Este badge, an eagle. Moreover, the characteristic legislation of the commune was stood on its head in the interests of feudalism: far from vassalage being forbidden, it had become illegal for any of the Marquis's retinue (*maxenata*) or vassals (*fideles*) to take oaths of fealty to any other person. The vassals had to reside in Ferrara and could not alienate their fiefs.

Ferrara's fate was not exceptional among the towns of the central Po valley. Its neighbour Mantua never escaped the domination of local dynasties, having Marquis Azzo of Este as its podestà in 1206–8, and remaining largely under the authority of that family, the Torelli and the Counts of Sambonifacio. In 1257 a later Marquis Azzo and a Count of Sambonifacio were chosen as captains of the Popolo 'in perpetuity', though both families were ousted in the 1270s by the *signoria* of the Bonaccolsi family. Verona, further to the north-east, also saw the Estensi and Sambonifacio podestà dominating from the very early thirteenth century: as already mentioned, this commune achieved little independence before falling after the mid-century to the more enduring lordship of the Scaligeri, a local family.

The Da Romano family, rival of the Marquises of Este in the March of Treviso, was in the thirteenth century the other immensely powerful feudal dynasty of north-eastern Italy. The main territorial base of the Da Romano, the land of their *homines de maxenata*, was situated around Bassano and the foothills of the Venetian Alps. Ezzelino III da Romano was brought into contact with Verona through his own and his sister's marriages into the

Sambonifacio family, and he began to build up his power in that city around 1226, though Verona only became the centre of his authority some ten years later. By then he was committed to an alliance with Frederick II, while the Estensi and Sambonifacio played the contrary, anti-imperialist, suit. To Verona Ezzelino added Vicenza and Padua (1237); though never formally declared lord of any of these cities, he nevertheless set up an effective supracommunal lordship which lasted well, surviving the death of Frederick (1250) and only crumbling in 1256–9.

The intensely disturbed years of Frederick's wars also saw the rise of a feudal lord as Ezzelino's neighbour to the west. This was Oberto Pallavicini, an experienced commander who had the support of a considerable body of German mercenaries; by origin a feudatory from the region of Parma, he secured recognition as imperial vicar first from Frederick and then from his son Conrad IV. Pallavicini's principal municipal victim was Cremona (1250), but he also gained Piacenza in 1253 as successor to the popular regime of Uberto de Iniquitate (see chapter 6) and by 1254 was 'perpetual' podestà at Pavia and Vercelli. He also attempted a coup at Parma, but was unsuccessful there. As *dominus perpetuus* at Piacenza he achieved the formal lordship which was denied to Ezzelino. The Pallavicini empire survived, in alliance with Ezzelino's, through the mid-1250s, lost some territory (including Piacenza) in 1257, but throve in alliance with Manfred in the next decade. Pallavicini kept control of Cremona till 1266 and even made an energetic though eventually unsuccessful attempt to gain the friendship of the Guelfs after the Angevin victory of 1266.

Further west still, the Marquis of Montferrat set up a comparable overlordship in Piedmont which may finally illustrate the type of state which replaced municipal independence in much of northern Italy around the middle of the thirteenth century. This was a powerful and historic dynasty, famous for its crusading achievement, with lands centred in southern Piedmont between the plain and Liguria. Since its foundation in the later twelfth century Alessandria had lain under the shadow of the Marquises; before 1200 one of them was styled the city's *dominus*, having had conferred on him by Henry VI half the imperial rights there. But the first extension of lordship over a number of communes was achieved in the three decades after 1260 by Marquis William. What he founded was a very extensive feudal overlordship rather than a tyranny. Beginning as captain and 'lord' at Alessandria,

Tortona and Acqui (1260), he added Ivrea in 1266. This city promised him *fidelitas et vassallagium*, with half its revenues; his status
gave him the right to name the podestà, to overrule any statutes
and to veto any treaty reached without his consent. These terms
suggest the type of loose suzerainty that the Marquis gained –
and in the main held, though very precariously – in the following
years. He lost Alessandria in 1262, regained it only in 1278 (as
captain for four years) with various other towns, including
Vercelli, which made him *Capitano di Guerra* for ten years. The
same year saw a redefinition of his status at Ivrea, where he was
to continue to appoint the podestà and to manage the commune's
finances, but not to meddle with its legislation nor commit it to
war. From 1278 he was captain for five years of a great League
extending from Turin and Genoa to Como, Mantua and even
Verona. He went on to accumulate lordships at Milan, Alessandria again (where he was granted *plenum arbitrium in perpetuum*),
Como and Vercelli (both of which made him captain for life) and
a number of smaller places. The north Piedmontese equivalent to
the Marquis of Montferrat, in a smaller way of business, was the
Marquis of Saluzzo, often a dominant factor at Turin. Piedmont
was to remain a strongly feudalised land.

The lordships of the Estensi, Ezzelino, Pallavicini and William
of Montferrat have been described merely as examples, though
they are significant ones through the number and importance of
the communes which they dominated. The widespread feudal
lordships which swallowed, or partly swallowed, the communes
within their dominion are in many ways reminiscent of great
lordships north of the Alps, of the duchy of Burgundy, the
earldom of Lancaster or the archbishopric of Cologne. But a
similar achievement on a smaller scale, of domination in a single
town secured by feudal power and soldiery, is at least equally
characteristic. The Visconti, lords of Milan from the later thir-

Plate 7.1   Ottone Visconti, archbishop of Milan, enters the city
in triumph, 1277. A scene from the frescoes in the Rocca
(Castello Borromeo), Angera. The Visconti emerged in the 13th
century as a politically powerful family of landed origins. After
defeating the rival family of Della Torre at Desio the
Archbishop became *de facto* signore of Milan. A period of
alternate Visconti and Della Torre control followed, after which
the Visconti assumed full authority, first as *domini generales*
(from 1330), then as Dukes (1395–1447).

teenth century, are described by the chronicler Galvano Flamma as *valde nobiles et antiqui*; 'they had vassals', he says, 'and they granted out fiefs to different families'. The Counts of Montefeltro also based their domination of Urbino on landed power; their ability to put 300 men into the field as early as 1216 has been mentioned above. Their feudal neighbours from the Tuscan-Romagnol Apennines gained control of the cities of the plain of Romagna, Rimini, Cesena, Forlì and Faenza. The Manfredi, normally predominant in the last of these places, neatly acknowledged the source of their strength with a quotation from Psalm 121 which preceded their statutes for the Val di Lamone: 'I have lifted up my eyes to the mountains from whence help shall come to me'[3]. Even where republicanism survived, it was often able to do so only after a struggle against the retinues of powerful feudatories. Genoese history provides many illustrations of this, such as the assault on the podestà and the Fieschi family in 1270, which was the work of the retinues of the Spinola, Doria, Volta and others. This coup led to the grant of a joint captaincy for five years to Oberto Spinola and Oberto Doria, but the intended *signoria* proved abortive. On the other hand, many communes never really escaped the shadow of the lord's castle. This was particularly true of small places, like Penna San Giovanni in the March of Ancona, which in 1248 formed a *comunantia* whose podestà was always to be the lord. Yet it could apply, as has been mentioned, to such significant towns as Ferrara and Alessandria.

No clear line can be drawn between the feudatory turned *signore* and the condottiere turned *signore*, since the origins of all the early condottieri were feudal. Nevertheless, there were some *signori* whose strength was based to a particularly notable degree on the mercenaries whom they led. One of these was Manfred Lancia, an imperialist commander in Frederick II's time, who in 1252 made use of his body of 1,000 mercenary cavalry to set up the first of what proved to be a series of short-lasting experiments in tyranny at Milan. The condottiere turned *signore* never became a common figure (a fact disguised by the fame of Francesco Sforza) but, in so far as he became a type, the pattern was set in Tuscany early in the fourteenth century. Here the prototypes were Uguccione della Faggiuola, lord of Pisa and Lucca (1314–6), and Castruccio Castracane whose lordship of Lucca lasted from 1320 to 1328.

It would be misleading to attribute the achievement of control via land ownership solely to military strength. Estates produced food and money as well as men, and these too could be the means to power. Salinguerra ingratiated himself at Ferrara by selling grain there cheaply, a useful support to his military methods. Other lords put communes heavily into their debt before subduing them, one such being Ermanno Monaldeschi, *signore* of Orvieto from 1334, who had loaned to the city more than 5,000 L (in gold) in the previous fifteen years.

The triumph of the Signoria

It remains to discuss the circumstances in which landed power achieved its victories over republicanism. Republican institutions, it has been suggested, rarely achieved stability. In particular the strength of factionalism, both social and political, and the persistence of a violent way of life prevented them from achieving the routine of compromises, conventions and agreements to differ which alone could have given them long life. So long as recourse to violence remained the accepted and conventional way of settling differences – and so long as self-government remained a reality to make local differences substantial ones – the life of the commune was bound to be precarious. Division within the cities and the frequency of external warfare (bound up with the troubled history of the entire peninsula) brought incessant crises and these naturally tended to be both military and fiscal. Warfare between the cities of the north reminded Salimbene of a perpetual game played by children in which there was never a winner: 'they put their hands on one boy's knee and then each in turn puts his hand on top and tries to win by taking away his hand when it is at the bottom.'[4] Territory was lost or threatened, revenue might decline at the very time when more money was needed for troops; these were circumstances recurring frequently in almost every commune. The obvious answer to crisis, so it was felt, was to entrust the fortunes of the city – or a party within it – to a 'strong man'. The particular vices of republicanism, such as slowness in reaching decisions and lack of secrecy concerning them, diplomatic indecisiveness and unpredictability, all these were blamed for the crises. They could be mitigated by granting special powers – perhaps only for a fixed period – to a lord. Moreover this lord was not necessarily merely a strong individual able to offer protection and to overawe opposition. Behind him might lie a formidable diplomatic structure. The Da Romano and Pallavicini *signorie* rose to greatness with Frederick II's alliance in the background and in a similar way, in the last third of the century, Angevin power in Tuscany and north-western Italy did much to undermine republicanism. This tendency showed as early as 1267 when Florence, Lucca and some other Guelf communes in Tuscany made Charles of Anjou their podestà for a term of six years. The intention was not that the king should serve in person, but that he should appoint a trusted man to serve as his vicar. This was a pattern to be followed again and again in Tuscany in the next few decades, but the abnegation of choice shows the mentality of the *signoria* already present. A few years later Brescia and Alessandria went further, naming the king as their podestà for life. In many ways, Angevin favour came to enjoy the role once played by imperialism: when, for example, the Spinola-Doria regime fell at Genoa, it was ousted by the Fieschi family who also relied on Angevin backing.

The route to the *signoria* usually lay through tenure of office, as podestà, captain of the Popolo or captain-general, and then through the prolongation of that office. In the Greek city-states this road to power had been a commonplace and later Machiavelli was to describe the process with his habitual economy: 'When one of the parties begins to favour a single individual, tyranny soon arises. . . . And when a Popolo makes this mistake of building up a man's prestige, to help him oppose those whom it hates, if he is clever he is sure to become tyrant of the city' (*Discorsi*, I xl). It is arguable whether *signorie* arose more frequently through the Popolo having recourse to a lord for protection against the magnates or whether more *signorie* originated through anti-popular leadership. A recent very painstaking count suggested that anti-popular origins were more numerous, but each process, and variations from them, was common and both were compatible with *signori* of feudal origin.

Uberto de Iniquitate, a case of the Popolo 'building up a man's prestige' has been discussed in chapter 6. The conferment on him of the *podesteria* of Piacenza for five years, with provision for his son to succeed, was a typical first step towards the foundation of a *signoria*, though – as often happened – the chain of events snapped before the process had reached full development. A contemporary who gained power in the same way and held it for longer was Giberto da Gente, who in 1253 was chosen by his own city Parma as podestà of the Popolo for five years. Da Gente who was, typically, the master of a bodyguard of 500, was virtually *signore* of Parma and for a time (1253–5) of Reggio; his attempted coup at Modena was unsuccessful. Though he became podestà of the commune also and the first role of his *signoria* was to pacify the parties, his power derived originally from the Popolo.

Another popular regime in the same decade was that of Guglielmo Boccanegra (1257–62) at Genoa. Boccanegra owed his position to a rising, concerning which the chronicler[5] gives a good deal of information. The leaders, 'among whom were some of the most powerful men in the city, shouted: "To arms, to arms! Let us have a Popolo!" They said they wanted a Capitano del Popolo, which pleased some of the *popolani'*. A meeting in the church of San Siro elected Guglielmo Boccanegra, who was himself a *popolano*, as captain, but after thirty-two *anziani* had been chosen and oaths of obedience had been sworn, differences arose over the length of his tenure. Some wanted him to hold office for five years, some for ten, some for life. Such arguments must often have arisen in the early stages of the development of the *signoria*. The decision to make Guglielmo captain for ten years, his brother to succeed him if he died within that period, was no doubt a compromise. In fact he strengthened his hold in 1259, but fell from power three years later. Particularly notable about this 'popular' regime are the ambiguous auspices of its initiation. How genuine was the cry for a Popolo raised by 'some of the most powerful men of the city'? Boccanegra seems a less convincing popular *signore* than Da Gente or than Alberto della Scala, who began his regime at Verona as *Capitaneus generalis populi* before being translated to fuller powers as *totius civitatis Verone capitaneus*. When della Scala was firmly installed in 1277 he had full judicial, legislative and military authority, with the formal right to govern the city 'by his own free will' (*suo libero arbitrio et voluntate*). The podestà, who remained titular head of the commune, was chosen by della Scala. This without doubt deserves to rank as a fully developed *signoria*.

Naturally, people noticed that the expedient of electing to office for a number of years was the commonest prologue to the *signoria*, and defenders of republican institutions constantly devised and repeated statutes forbidding this. Podestà and captains were normally ineligible for re-election; indeed at Padua the penalty for even proposing such a re-election was death. Every conceivable precaution was taken. It was illegal in many communes to elect a podestà from the same city in successive years, while in others no man could serve two years consecutively as an elector to the *podesteria*. In the fourteenth century Parma forbade the election to any office of a man from a city already ruled by a *signore*, thereby greatly limiting its freedom of choice. John of Viterbo, in his book of advice to podestà (*Liber de Regimine Civitatum*), had long before this recommended anyone offered a prolongation of office to refuse; he thought such re-elections rarely successful in their outcome 'nowadays'. The statutes of some cities forbade out of hand the conferment of *regimen* or of any special lordly powers, but it goes without saying that no constitutional defence works could prevail against the might of a party determined to install a *signoria*.

The advent of the *signoria* cannot be understood if it is seen merely as something which 'happened', a development resulting 'inevitably' from the fragility of republican institutions. It was the outcome of human will, of the actions of ambitious men scheming to gain power. Frequently they covered their tracks so carefully and so assiduously substituted mythology for history – their biographers tend to describe the prodigies accompanying the birth of the future *signore* – that one can no longer admire the technique of their coups d'état. One partial exception is the accession to power of Ermanno Monaldeschi at Orvieto in 1334, which no doubt resembles others in its sequence of events. Ermanno was a member of his city's greatest family, wealthy, a frequent office-holder, brother of Orvieto's bishop, and aided by the goodwill of the neighbouring city of Perugia whose territorial ambitions he had supported. On 20 April 1334 he had his principal rival, a distant relative, murdered. The time was well chosen, because at the beginning of May the Capitano del Popolo and podestà, the officials whose task it was to defend the commune, ended their periods of office and were replaced by newcomers. These men had only been in the city a few days when their authority was challenged. On 11 May, in a meeting of the Council of the Popolo, a supporter of Monaldeschi proposed fundamental constitutional reform, including the suspension of thirty-four clauses of the constitution and the appointment of a *balia* of twelve with full powers, able to act even without the presence or consent of the captain. Three days later this *balia* met, together with the seven *anziani*, and resolved to pass on its 'full powers' to Monaldeschi, who was created *Gonfaloniere del Popolo* and *Gonfaloniere di Giustizia* for life. Just over three weeks had passed between the elimination of his rival and the conclusion of his coup. Even this well-documented case does not show whether Ermanno used troops to overawe potential opponents in the council: that he did so seems very probable.

The brief formula whereby Ermanno Monaldeschi became. *Vexillifer populi et Vexillifer iustitie civitatis Urbisveteris toto tempore vite sue* lacks formality compared with the terms of Ferrara's solemn conferment of *signoria* on Obizzo of Este in 1264. It may be worth quoting this document at some length as a conveniently clear definition of seignorial status:

We Pierconte of Carrara, podestà of Ferrara, in a full assembly of all the people of the city of Ferrara in the piazza of the city, gathered in the usual way by the tolling of bells, by the wish, consent and order of the whole commune and population gathered in this assembly, and, together with us, the whole commune and, on behalf of it, those present in the assembly, have decreed as follows, and we wish that it should be inviolably observed, ordering this in perpetuity through our municipal law, for us, our heirs, descendants and successors. The magnificent and illustrious lord Obizzo, grandson and heir of the late magnificent lord Azzo of happy memory, by God's and apostolic grace Marquis of Este and Ancona, is to be Governor and Ruler and General and permanent Lord [*generalis et perpetuus Dominus*] of the City of Ferrara and its district at his own will [*ad sue arbitrium voluntatis*]. He is to possess jurisdiction, power and rule [*imperium*] in the City and outside it and to have the right to increase, do, order, provide and dispose as he shall wish and as shall seem useful to him. And in general he is to have powers and rights as permanent Lord of the City of Ferrara and its district to do and arrange all things in accordance with his wishes and orders, so that the City and district and its present and future inhabitants are to obey lord Obizzo, by the grace of God Marquis of Este and Ancona, with full lordly jurisdiction, as their general and permanent Lord. We wish all the above to apply in perpetuity not only to the lord Obizzo, Marquis of Este and Ancona, for his lifetime, but after his death we wish his heir to be Governor and Ruler and general Lord of the City and district of Ferrara in his place, and to have lordship and rule and power and full jurisdiction, as stated above, in all things as the lord Azzo has . . .

These provisions were to be entered in the statutes of the city, renewed annually and their observance sworn by the city's officials. And

if anyone ever attempts to corrupt or change or infringe them or any part of them they are to be placed under permanent outlawry as violators of the City of Ferrara, all their property is to be confiscated to the commune, they are not to reside in the City or district, nor enter them, but are to remain permanent exiles . . . and if they ever fall into the power of the commune they are to suffer capital punishment.

There follow further clauses confirming these provisions and threatening dire measures against attempts to oppose or alter them[6].

The proceedings of 1264 did not install the first Estense lord of Ferrara, but merely confirmed Obizzo's succession and consolidated and formalised the family's position. The use of the assembly (*arengo*) is a reminder of the fictitious continuation of the commune's outward forms. The commune's posthumous role in the period of the *signoria* was often a lengthy one, the successor securing a formal re-election in each generation, though in practice he had probably been nominated as his heir by his father or whichever relative preceded him. A constitutionally fixed hereditary succession, such as the Ferrarese provided for in 1264, was rare till the later fourteenth century. By that time it was also very common for *signori* to have secured imperial or papal recognition of their status by the grant of vicariate. Matteo Visconti was made his vicar at Milan by Adolf of Nassau in 1294, and from early in the following century this became a conventional way of securing constitutional respectability: by grant from the emperor in imperial territory or from the pope in the State of the Church. It was a certificate of recognition for which *signori* were willing to pay heavily. The logical sequel was the imperial grant of Milan to Giangaleazzo Visconti as a duchy in 1395.

A list of early *signorie* with their dates of origin would make tedious reading, but it is necessary to indicate the chronology of the victory of 'tyranny' over republicanism. The first *signorie* at Ferrara and (under Ezzelino) in the Veneto date from well before the middle of the thirteenth century. Around the mid century a new great lordship (Pallavicini's) came into being and Milan fell to a *signoria*; except for brief periods the most powerful city of Lombardy was never to return to republicanism. The significant title of 'permanent lord' seems first to have been granted at this time, to Buoso da Dovara at Soncino in 1255. By the 1280s the *signoria* had become the normal constitutional form over the entire northern plain, from the sub-Alpine regions in the west (the lands of the marquises of Saluzzo and Montferrat) right across to the Veneto (where the Scaligeri ruled Verona and the Caminesi Treviso) and Romagna. In this province the Polentani were already installed at Ravenna, the Parcitadi and Malatesta disputed control at Rimini. Before the end of the century the *signoria* had won much ground in the next papal province to the south, the March of Ancona. Very approximately, a line drawn along the

Apennine ridge would define the boundary around 1300, republicanism being something of a lost cause to the north-east of this line (there were of course exceptions, notably Venice) though still holding its ground to the south-west of it. Tuscany had as yet seen few experiments in lordship, though Pisa was an exception and had already tried a number of seignorial regimes, notably those of Count Ugolino (1285–8) and of Count Guy of Montefeltro, who was recruited for three years as a war leader in 1289. Dante's melancholy and justified cry that 'the towns of Italy are full of tyrants' (*Purg.*, VI, 124–5) was written about 1313. And by the middle of the fourteenth century a great deal more territory had been lost by republicanism, spasmodically in Tuscany, more permanently in papal Umbria and Latium. Survivals of communes into the fifteenth century are rare.

Some historians have attempted to answer the question of whether the commune or the *signoria* provided better government. It is doubtful if useful generalisations can be made along these lines. The reasons are both quantitative, because so many towns are involved, and qualitative, because 'good government' is a fugitive concept. Unquestionably, political decision-making under the *signoria* was undertaken by a lower proportion of the population and thus it was not a form of regime which could contribute towards preparing Italians for democracy – but, for almost the entire peninsula, any sort of democracy lay very far ahead indeed. As for the city-republic, it gave its citizens a certain 'political education', but the school broke up in disorder and hence one must doubt whether the pupils had learned their lessons. If the school was then transformed into a reformatory, this was at least an enlightened form of captivity in which the institutions of school continued. The *signore* and his party wielded their executive power through the republican forms of the commune. Moreover they were themselves an oligarchy, a narrower one than the 'patrician' oligarchy of the city-republic, yet 'the men of the regime' constituted an important check on the lord and played a role in decision-making as well as in executive action. It is not always easy to draw a firm line between a republic under a tight oligarchy and a *signoria* proper, as may be seen from developments at Florence. There the control of Rinaldo degli Albizzi and his small clique of fellow oligarchs gave way in 1434 to that of the Medici, whom subsequent historians have usually seen as Florence's first real *signori:* in reality no clear distinction can be made between the nature of their control (until their restoration in 1512) and that of the Albizzi. The commune and the *signoria*, in other words, shade into each other and are hard to differentiate, just as it is difficult to pronounce on the republican status of those cities like Ferrara which never achieved emancipation from the strength of their feudal neighbours.

8 The historiography of the City-Republics

The historian himself cannot stand outside the stream of history. Indeed he requires as full a consciousness as he can command of his own position in the 'flux of time' and to achieve this must seek to understand the writings and circumstances which have influenced his own approach to his subject-matter. That is one justification for the addition to this book of a brief essay on the historiography of the Italian communes, written some twenty years after the first edition. The subject has been approached and interpreted in totally contrasted ways over the last two centuries and this fact in itself should serve as a caution and a reminder of the profound truth of Benedetto Croce's dictum that 'all true history is contemporary history'[1]. For what has undergone transformation is not the historical evidence available but rather the understanding of it by successive generations of men.

Before the history of the commune came to be seen as a theme for the historian magnificent collections of material bearing on it were made by antiquarians, many of them activated by the spirit of patriotism and local pride. The accumulation of this material and its accessibility in printed form were perhaps an essential preliminary to the work of interpretation. The last and certainly the greatest figure among the accumulators was the Modenese Lodovico Antonio Muratori (1672–1750). Muratori, who published the text of many medieval chronicles in the 29 volumes of his *Rerum Italicarum Scriptores*, produced a sort of epitome of the labours of earlier antiquaries in his six-volume collection of 'dissertations' which compose the *Antiquitates Italicae Medii Aevi* (1738–42). A number of the essays in the *Antiquitates* are invaluable for the information they incorporate (sometimes comprising entire documents and even one entire chronicle for fourteenth-century Rome) concerning the institutions and life of the medieval Italian cities. But the heart of the matter lies in the sequence of dissertations from nos. XLV to XLVIII, which deal respectively with 'the form of republic taken by many Italian cities and the origin of their liberty', the officials of the cities, their increased power and lordship, and the Lombard League. Impressive as it is as a work of erudition, the *Antiquitates* is a compilation, innocent of those grapplings with causality which, for better or for worse, characterise 'true history'.

Those who were to be concerned (in Lucretius's phrase) 'to know the causes of things' might fall far behind Muratori in learning and in disinterestedness, but they would require a stronger sense of chronological development. The first important historical writer on the medieval Italian cities for whom such a claim can be made was the Swiss J. C. L. S. de Sismondi (1773–1842), author of the vast *Histoire des républiques italiennes du moyenâge* (16 volumes, 1808–18). Sismondi was a passionate Rousseau-ite, who turned to the past to illustrate and confirm his own enthusiasm for liberty. He was concerned that history should 'be explored . . . for instructions in the government of mankind'; as he explained, 'history has no importance but as it contains a moral lesson'. As occurred with all the great Romantic historians, the baby of disinterested erudition was thrown out together with the antiquarian bathwater. Sismondi took as his model the medieval Italians because 'from the moment they formed their own governments, and formed them for the common good, they prospered: while every other nation suffered, they rose in intelligence as well as virtue . . . their experience directed the meditations of some superior minds formed in the government of the Italian republics, who rose from the practice to the theory of civil society, and showed, not only to their own country, but to future nations and ages, the object to which all human associations should tend, and the best means by which to attain it'. In Sismondi's *Études sur les Constitutions des Peuples Libres* (written before the *Histoire* but not published till 1836), medieval history was yet more obviously the teacher of lessons for the contemporary world. 'Every Florentine', he explained, 'even if he was poor and ignorant and was condemned to manual work from dawn to nightfall, felt that he was something in his fatherland ("il était quelque chose dans sa patrie"); he was a participant in political rights and sovereignty as a member of his gild'. And the Lombard League, the subject of one of Muratori's essays, was the federation which humiliated the great Barbarossa and which owed its power of resistance to the foreigner to 'the solidarity of fellow-citizens who know and love one another' ('la solidarité des concitoyens qui se connaissent et qui s'aiment')[2].

It was characteristic of the main lines of development of nineteenth-century thought that history as the history of liberty should be succeeded by history as the history of race. The idea that each nation had its own innate nature and its own destiny, which underlies Mazzini's nationalism, was accompanied and complicated by an overwhelming emphasis on the concept of race. In particular it was an accepted commonplace that there was a Teutonic, a Latin and a Slav race. The German historians Heinrich Leo (*Entwickelung der Verfassung der lombardischen Städte*, first edition 1820) and Karl Hegel (*Geschichte der Städtverfassung von Italien*, 1847) indeed saw the rise of the Milanese in the eleventh century as a triumph for liberty, but for them it was also the successful struggle of the free Germanic valvassors against the power of the Archbishop of Milan. The study and writing of history achieved a new professionalism in the German universities in the first half of the nineteenth century[3], and one aspect of this development was the emphasis given to legal history. The great German legal historians tended to see medieval Italy as a region in which the Teutonic invaders – Ostrogoths, Lombards and Franks – breathed new life into the existing Roman law. It was natural that they should also emphasise the crucial role in the early development of the communes of the oath sworn between equals, or *coniuratio*, an essentially Germanic institution. It would be wrong to imply that the nineteenth-century Germans had nothing to offer but the aphorism of Sidonia in Disraeli's *Tancred* (1847) that 'All is race; there is no other truth'. In fact some of the eighteenth-century virtues were regained and objective scholarly standards were reasserted. Moreover the primacy claimed for law in the study of the medieval period has survived, at least to an important degree. Yet racialism was a pseudo-science, a poisonous as well as a silly one, and it would be cynical to suggest that a false explanation of historical development was an improvement on none at all.

A continuing feature of historical investigation was the need for a causative factor, an 'explanation'. From race as the motive force of history one moves on to class. Obviously race did not disappear from the vocabulary of history, indeed the Italian

Pasquale Villari in his *I primi due secoli della storia di Firenze* (written between 1866 and 1893, first edition 1893) turned Teutonic racial notions on their head by presenting the medieval communes as the triumph of the Latin peoples over the Germanic races. However, class is to be found as a predominant explanatory factor by the middle of the century in the *Révolutions d'Italie* (1848–52) of the Frenchman Edgar Quinet and it was to play the same role in the writings of the Italian 'scuola economico-giuridica'.

The impact of this 'school' on the historiography of the Italian communes is most clearly seen in the *Magnati e popolani in Firenze dal 1280 al 1295* of Gaetano Salvemini (published in 1899). Salvemini was an Apulian who moved to Florence as a student in 1890 and became an enthusiastic socialist under the influence of the *Communist Manifesto* and Marx's other writings. In his book the young Salvemini analysed the politics of a crucial period of Florentine history in terms of a class struggle. Salvemini later turned to modern historical topics and with the advent of Fascism became one of the most illustrious of Italian political exiles. *Magnati e popolani* is a compelling book and perhaps the most generally influential one to have been devoted to the Italian communes. Its publication was soon followed by the appearance of the earliest writings of a yet more gifted historian, Gioacchino Volpe (1876–1971), whose first significant monograph, *Studi sulle istituzioni comunali a Pisa*, appeared in 1902. A series of briefer syntheses and monographs followed, most notably the *Questioni sull'origine e svolgimento dei Comuni italiani* (1904), a brilliant essay which combined innovation with balanced judgement; in a sense this was a summary of the *status questionis* which 'saw off' all the least convincing aspects of nineteenth-century approaches to the subject. Volpe's shorter writings of 1904–10 were collected in his *Medio Evo Italiano*. Thereafter, like Salvemini, Volpe turned to more recent periods of history; his political views were those of a nationalist and he became a prominent supporter of Fascism. A third figure among the economic-juridical historians of the same generation whose contribution must secure a mention is Gino Luzzatto (1878–1964). Luzzatto's publications on the towns of the March of Ancona (notably an essay of 1906 on submissions of feudatories and social classes in some communes and a long article of 1913 on Matelica) averted the danger that studies of the uncharacteristic large cities might so dominate the field that a misleading picture would be given of urban development in Italy generally. After the First World War, however, Luzzatto dedicated most of his energies to the economic history of one of the greater cities, Venice.

The degree to which the various writings of the 'economic-juridical school' were influential in provoking reaction was perhaps in direct proportion to their 'wrongness'. Luzzatto's contributions were the least controversial of those mentioned above. Volpe's work, on the other hand, has stimulated much criticism. It is not easy to analyse Volpe's greatness as a historian, but his strength lay in his almost intuitive ability to provide vivid and convincing connections between economic developments and the political and institutional 'superstructures' of the towns. The mesmerised reader feels that somehow he is not merely observing the urban ant-hill but actually understanding it. Volpe's critics have set to work patiently to examine the detail of his investigation of early Pisan history and have raised many doubts about his theses. Emilio Cristiani's *Nobiltà e popolo nel comune di Pisa* (1962) cannot compete with Volpe for readability or intellectual stimulus, yet it is persuasive in its findings that much in Volpe's view of Pisan development 'does not stand up to deeper analysis' and is vitiated by internal contradictions[4]. Cristiani's painstaking work of criticism has surely helped also to stimulate Marco Tangheroni's volume on a later period (*Politica, commercio, agricoltura a Pisa nel trecento*).

The first and greatest critic of *Magnati e Popolani* was Nicola Ottokar (1884–1957), whose *Il comune di Firenze alla fine del dugento* (1926) is a masterpiece of detailed historical analysis based largely on patient prosopography. Ottokar was a refugee from the USSR and had been a professor at Perm. He had already published (1919) a book in Russian on five northern French towns in the Middle Ages in which the work of the great Henri Pirenne had undergone searching and sceptical examination[5]. The principal propositions of Ottokar's *Il comune di Firenze* are that Salvemini's cut-and-dried model of class warfare would not serve as a satisfactory explanation of Florentine developments in the later thirteenth century, that a homogeneous ruling clique survived the many constitutional changes of the period and that 'magnates' continued to play a leading role in the city's external policy. His main theme was the continuity of a governing class ('ceto dirigente') which was neither composed merely of the 'older' families of wealthy merchants nor of the newer 'popolani' merchants. The reverberations of Ottokar's thesis continue to be felt. Thus the co-operative work of Sergio Raveggi, Massimo Tarassi, Daniela

Medici and Patrizia Parenti entitled *Ghibellini, Guelfi e Popolo Grasso. I detentori del potere politico a Firenze nella seconda metà del dugento* (1978) is a detailed criticism of Ottokar's views; its authors maintain that there was no 'substantial homogeneity of origin or intent among the political leaders whose periods in office alternated in the city' in the later thirteenth century[6].

After mentioning so many titles within the category of the *economico-giuridico* historians and their critics, it would be unfair to make no suggestions about reading. The essay which opens Volpe's *Medio Evo Italiano* still seems to me the most stimulating brief introduction to the subject. And the reader who does not know Ottokar's *Comune di Firenze* is missing a fascinating historical masterpiece. Neither of these works is available in any language other than Italian.

I come now to current attitudes and controversies. As elsewhere in this chapter, treatment must be highly selective. Despite the advent of psycho-history it is evident that, following the ages of liberty and race, we are still in the third age of history, that of class. Beside the continuation of the controversy over the interpretation of Florentine history in terms of a class-struggle, a few topics may be identified within the general category of class considered as a dominant historical factor. The most powerful piece of writing of recent years dealing with the Italian communes is Dr Philip Jones's 'Economia e società nell'Italia medievale: la leggenda della borghesia' (which is not yet available in English)[7]. The principal thrust of Jones's argument is that the dominant element in most towns was at first a group of landed families and that when these were joined by later arrivals the consequence was an ennobled bourgeoisie rather than a democratised nobility. The lasting power in the communes, in their outlook, law and politics, was that of the nobles. As for the 'Renaissance', 'there was no bourgeois culture because there was no bourgeois State'.

A series of conferences organised in Florence by the 'Comitato di studi sulla storia dei ceti dirigenti in Toscana' is typical of recent developments. Several of these meetings on 'governing groups', the proceedings of which have been published, have been concerned with the period of the city-republics[8]. A particular preoccupation within the theme of oligarchy is a crucial question of nomenclature. Contemporary sources, both official and unofficial, refer to 'nobles', 'knights' (*milites*) and 'magnates' in the cities; the significance of these terms has been examined with particular care by Giovanni Tabacco[9]. Closely connected with the debate on the composition of the ruling class in the cities is that on the policy adopted by the communes towards their subject countryside. A favourite field for this debate is the *contado* of Siena, a city favoured by the survival of exceptionally rich source material. The *Communist Manifesto* enshrined the orthodox nineteenth-century view of this matter in the statement that 'the bourgeoisie subjected the country to the rule of the towns'. However, the question becomes a complicated one when it is realised that the very people who possessed the land were often the dominant figures in the towns; hence the continuing debate on the theme[10].

Current historiography on the city-republics is not adequately summarised as a mere continuation – perhaps in subtler terms – of the debate on class as the predominant causative factor. The doctrine that 'everything has a history', the flight from institutional history and even the pursuit of the will-o'-the wisp of 'total history', have all left their mark. Interest in *mentalités* and in visual symbolism is reflected in recent writings which derive also from an earlier concern, civic patriotism. An example is Chiara Frugoni's book *Una lontana città. Sentimenti e immagine nel Medioevo* (1983), on the 'image' of the medieval city, another is Hannelore Zug Tucci's very substantial article on 'Il carroccio nella vita comunale italiana' in *Quellen u. Forschungen a. italienischen Archiven u. Bibliotheken*, vol. 65 (1985). As with the controversy on the *contado*, Siena is a key location for the symbolism of civic patriotism: apart from the burgeoning literature on the Guidoriccio question (see above, p. 116), contributions will soon appear from Quentin Skinner to the debate on the symbolism of Pietro Lorenzetti's Good Government fresco in the Sienese *palazzo*.

Connected in some ways with visual symbolism is the theme of town planning, now the subject of a great deal of work. A prominent contributor is Enrico Guidoni, author of *Arte e urbanistica in Toscana (1000–1315)* (1970) and *La Città dal Medioevo al Rinascimento* (1981) and editor of an excellent collection of essays entitled *Città, contado e feudi nell'urbanistica medievale* (Biblioteca di Storia di Cultura, Multigrafica Editrice, Rome 1974).

From town-planning it seems logical to turn, via archaeology – there is now a flourishing journal of *Archeologia Medievale* – to the recent literature of urban geography. Geographers, placing special emphasis on the history of settlement or occupation, have contributed fruitfully to the history of village and castle sites, less so (hitherto) to that of the medieval cities. The study of deserted villages – and the much less numerous deserted cities – has prospered in Italy as elsewhere (see, for example, T. W. Potter, *The Changing Landscape of Southern Etruria*, 1979). But the principal contributions of the geographical approach to medieval Italian history have lain in the study of new urban foundations by the communes, particularly in Tuscany, of the history of settlement, as in the articles of Alberto Grohmann concerning Umbria, and above all of the history of castles. We are moving still further from the city-republics; for recent work on castles see, above all, A. A. Settia, *Castelli e villaggi nell'Italia padana. Popolamento, potere e sicurezza fra IX e XIII secolo* (1984), and the book by Pierre Toubert mentioned below. In one aspect the history of the development of castles belongs with military history, itself still a curiously neglected field in view of its obvious central role in the institutions of the city-republics. For recent publications on this topic see the articles by Anna Imelde Galletti and the present writer cited in the bibliography to chapter 3. No less central – though its technical nature may have been found daunting by some intending researchers – is the subject of the 'diplomatic' of the communes, the processes whereby their official documentation was generated. Clearly a proper understanding of these processes is crucial to an accurate assessment of their activities and achievement. Some recent work has centred on the role in the early commune of the notaries (for example, G. G. Fissore, *Autonomia notarile e organizzazione cancelleresca nel comune di Asti*, 1977), and by far the most thorough treatment of the 'diplomatic' of a single commune is now to be found in A. Bartoli Langeli's *Codice diplomatico del comune di Perugia, 1139–1254* (2 vols, 1983–85: index not yet published).

Is it proper for a bibliographical review to end with a prophetical paragraph? It is to be hoped that the fashion for large-scale monographic surveys of cities and regions will continue. Already such studies have offered much to Italian urban history, most notably (for the Middle Ages) in Toubert's *Les structures du Latium médiéval* (1,500 pp. in 2 vols, 1973), but also P. Racine's *Plaisance du Xe à la fin du XIIIe siècle* (1,542 pp., 1979) and A. Grohmann's *Città e territorio tra Medioevo e Età moderna (Perugia, secc. XIII–XVI)* (1,178 pp. in 2 vols, and maps, 1981). Finally, it would be strange if much more attention were not again to be given to the origins of communal institutions, despite the scarcity of source material, and to the neglected topics of ecclesiastical institutions and religious feeling within the city-republics.

Notes and references

Introduction

1 *Laws*, v; *Politics*, iii, 17 and vii, 4; *Ethics*, ix, 10.

1 The legacy of power

1 MGH, xx, p. 396: *The Itinerary of Benjamin of Tudela*, ed. M. N. Adler (London, 1907), p. 5.

2 The population

1 P. Jones in *Cambridge Economic History*, i (ed. 2), p. 348.
2 Based on G. Pardi, 'Il catasto d'Orvieto dell'anno 1292' *Bollettino della R. Deputazione di Storia Patria per l'Umbria*, ii (1896). Values are in L of Cortona.
3 *Ann. Bol.*, ii, 2, pp. 304 ff; iii, 2, pp. 5–13: *St. Parma*, ii, pp. 159–60.
4 *St. Viterbo*, pp. 504–5.
5 MGH, xx, p. 397.
6 *Ann. Gen.*, i, pp. 258–9.
7 N. Ottokar, *Il comune di Firenze alla fine del dugento* (Florence, 1926), p. 82; J. K. Hyde, *Padua in the Age of Dante* (Manchester, 1966), pp. 84–5.
8 RIS, o.s., viii, c. 480.
9 *Speculum Perfectionis*, ed. P. Sabatier (Paris, 1898), pp. 10–11 (tr. R. Steele).
10 *ASI*, (1845), p. 622.

11 Quoted in F. Ercole, *Dal comune al principato* (Florence, 1929), p. 30.
12 *Ann. Gen.*, v. p. 151.
13 RIS, n.s., viii, 1, p. 22; *Bollettino dell'Istituto Storico Italiano*, x (1891), pp. 95–6.
14 RIS, o.s., viii, c. 482.

3 Government

1 G. Assandria (ed.), *Il Libro Rosso del comune d'Ivrea* (Pinerolo, 1914), pp. 159–63.
2 MGH, xx, pp. 396–7: tr. C. C. Mierow.
3 See E. Artifoni, 'La "coniunctio et unitas" astigiano-albese del 1223–1224', *Bollettino Storico-Bibliografico Subalpino*, lxxviii (1980).
4 Mainly based on G. Fasoli, *Dalla 'civitas' al comune* (Bologna, 1961), p. 156.
5 MGH, xviii, p. 435.
6 *St. Pisa*, i, pp. 7, 18, 33; *C.D. Crem.*, i, pp. 100 ff.
7 *St. Parma*, i, pp. 44 ff.
8 *St. Pistoia, Pop.*, pp. 204–5; *St. Parma*, ii, pp. 54–5.
9 *Doc. Arezzo*, ii, pp. 462–4.
10 *Ann. Gen.*, ii, p. 36.
11 *St. Modena*, i, pp. 4–7.
12 *St. Viterbo*, p. 455.
13 *Ann. Gen.*, iii, pp. 18–19.
14 *St. Pistoia, Pop.*, p. 24.
15 *St. Modena*, i, 1, pp. 103 ff, 111 ff, 171 ff.
16 *St. Pisa*, i, p. 515.
17 Information on Sienese finance is based on figures given by E. Fiumi in *ASI*, 1959, p. 455; *Libri dell'Entrata e dell' Uscita della rep. di Siena*, vii; Siena, Archivio di Stato, Biccherna, vol. 33 & 43, ff. 24v., 111.
18 *Ann. Gen.*, i, p. 74; ii, p. 131.
19 E. Fiumi (ed.), *Statuti di Volterra (1210–24)* (Florence, 1952), i, pp. 224–5.
20 Quoted in N. Ottokar, *Studi comunali e fiorentini* (Florence, 1948), p. 149n: see the same author's *Il comune di Firenze alla fine del dugento*, pp. 282–3.
21 *C.D. Crem.*, ii, pp. 26 ff.
22 *St. Modena*, i, p. 405; *St. Pisa*, i, p. 260.

23 *Liber Potheris communis civitatis Brixiae* (Turin, 1899), cc. 900–5.
24 Quoted in L. Zdekauer, *La vita privata dei senesi nel dugento* (Siena, 1896), p. 45.
25 Bologna, Archivio di Stato, Rif. e Provv. (series cart.), I, ff. 105v–106, 108v, 117, 162.
26 *Ann. Bol.*, II, 2, pp. 343, 357 ff.
27 Villani, XI, 94.
28 *St. Parma*, II, p. 122, IV, pp. 42, 112.
29 *St. Pisa*, I, pp. 67–8, 95, 98–9, 216, 300–3.
30 C. Pinzi, *Storia di Viterbo* (Rome, 1887–1913), II, p. 70n.
31 *Ann. Gen.*, V, pp. 147 ff.
32 *St. Pisa*, I, pp. 3–15.
33 Based on the analysis in W. Braunfels, *Mittelalterliche Stadtbaukunst in der Toskana* (Berlin, 1953), pp. 38–41.
34 D. Herlihy, *Medieval and Renaissance Pistoia* (New Haven & London, 1967), p. 236.

4 Town and country

1 *Doc. Arezzo*, II, pp. 54–5.
2 *St. Pisa*, pp. 673–6.
3 A. Natalini (ed.), *S. Pier Parenzo. La leggenda scritta dal maestro Giovanni* (Rome, 1936), § 10–11.
4 Paolo da Certaldo, *Libro di Buoni Costumi*, ed. A. Schiaffini, Florence, 1945, p. 87.
5 *Doc. Arezzo*, II, pp. 56–7.
6 *C.D. Crem.*, I, p. 100.
7 *ASI*, VI, pt. 2, pp. 23–4, 28.
8 A. Corna, F. Ercole, A. Tallone (eds.), *Il registrum magnum del comune di Piacenza* (Turin, 1921), I, pp. 310 ff.
9 *Doc. Arezzo*, II, p. 306.
10 *Ann. Bol.*, I, 2, pp. 178 ff, 203, 211.
11 L. Tonini, *Storia civile e sacra riminese* (Rimini, 1848–88), III, pp. 381–2.
12 *Doc. Arezzo*, II, pp. 413–16.
13 D. Velluti, *Cronica domestica* (Florence, 1914), p. 133.
14 L. Zdekauer (ed.), *Il Constituto del comune di Siena dell'anno 1262* (Milan, 1897), p. 417.
15 Quoted by C. M. Cipolla, *Cristofano and the Plague* (London, 1973), p. 23, from G. F. Ingrassia, *Informatione del pestifero et contagioso morbo . . .* (1576).

16 D. Herlihy, *Medieval and Renaissance Pistoia* (New Haven and London, 1967), p. 288.
17 *Discorsi*, ɪ, lv.
18 G. Cherubini, 'Proprietari, contadini e campagne senesi all'inizio del trecento' in *Signori, Contadini, Borghesi* (Florence, 1974), pp. 231–311.
19 G. Chittolini, 'I beni terrieri del Capitolo della Cattedrale di Cremona fra il xɪɪɪ e il xɪv secolo', *Nuova Rivista Storica*, xʟɪx (1965), pp. 213–74.
20 See P. Cammarosano, *La famiglia dei Berardenghi. Contributo alla storia della società senese nei sec. xɪ–xɪɪɪ* (Spoleto, 1974).
21 P. J. Jones in *Papers of the British School at Rome*, xxɪv (1956), p. 205.
22 *Libro di Buoni Costumi*, pp. 114–15.

5 External relations

1 MGH, xx, p. 396.
2 *Doc. Arezzo*, ɪɪ, pp. 52–3, 119, 194 ff.; Bartoli Langeli, *Codice Dipl. del comune di Perugia*, ɪ, pp. 43–6, 147–50.
3 MGH, vɪɪɪ, pp. 18 ff.
4 MGH, Const., ɪ, p. 428.
5 MGH, xɪx, pp. 445 ff.
6 Quoted by R. Caggese, *Roberto d'Angiò e i suoi tempi* (Florence, 1922–30), ɪ, p. 47.
7 *C.D. Crem.*, ɪ, pp. 266–8.
8 S. Angelini, *La diplomazia comunale a Perugia nei sec. xɪɪɪ e xɪv* (Florence, 1965), p. 24.
9 Ottonis et Rahewini, *Gesta Frederici Imperatoris* (Scriptores rerum germanicarum in usum scholarum, ed. G. Waitz, Hanover-Leipzig, 1912), pp. 204, 271; MGH, xɪx, p. 242; Salimbene, ɪ, p. 513; *Ann. Gen.*, ɪɪ, pp. 168 ff.
10 RIS, n.s., xɪ, v, p. 37.
11 Quoted by M. B. Becker in *Mediaeval Studies*, xxvɪɪ (1965), p. 292n.
12 *Ann. Gen.*, ɪɪ, p. 201; ɪɪɪ, p. 27.
13 RIS, o.s., xvɪ, c. 657.
14 Perugia, Archivio di Stato, Rif., v, ff. 31v ff; *Ann. Gen.*, ɪɪɪ, pp. 179–80; ASI, (1867), pt. 2, pp. 3–16.
15 *St. Pistoia, Pot.*, p. 35.
16 ASI, (1845), pp. 272, 420, 448.

17 *Ann. Gen.*, ɪ, pp. 47–8; ᴠ, p. 3.
18 Document cited by Braunfels, *Mittelalterliche Stadtbaukunst in der Toskana*, p. 208n.
19 G. Milanesi, *Documenti per la storia dell'arte senese* (Siena, 1854), ɪ, p. 180.
20 RIS, n.s., xᴠ, ᴠɪ, p. 550.
21 Villani, ɪx, 256–7.
22 Milanesi, op. cit., 1, doc. 12.
23 Quoted in J. White, *Art and Architecture in Italy: 1250 to 1400* (London, 1966), p. 278.
24 See G. Ragionieri, *Simone o non Simone* (Florence, 1985) and the articles by M. Mallory and G. Moran ('New evidence concerning "Guidoriccio"') and A. Martindale ('The Problem of "Guidoriccio"') in *The Burlington Magazine*, ᴄxxᴠɪɪɪ (Apr. 1986), pp. 250–73.

6 Internal divisions

1 MGH, ᴠɪɪɪ, pp. 16, 62; Malispini, chapter 101.
2 Villani, xɪ, 94; *Ann. Gen.*, ɪᴠ, pp. 71–3.
3 G. Tabacco, 'Nobiltà e potere ad Arezzo in età comunale', *Studi Medievali*, s. 3, xᴠ (1974), pp. 1–24. C.D. Crem., ɪ, pp. 215–17; *St. Pistoia, Pop.*, pp. 129–30.
4 F. Patetta, *Nobili e popolani in una piccola città dell'alta Italia* (Siena, 1902), pp. 106–16.
5 The sources concerning the *consorzeria* translated here are all printed in F. Niccolai, *I consorzi nobiliari ed il comune nell'alta e media Italia* (Bologna, 1940), pp. 147–52, 164–9.
6 *Itinerary of Benjamin of Tudela*, p. 5.
7 *Ann. Gen.*, ɪɪ, pp. 44–5; RIS, n.s., xɪ, ᴠ, pp. 11–12.
8 Villani, ᴠɪɪɪ, 68.
9 *Ann. Gen.*, ɪɪɪ, pp. 81–2, 96; *St. Pisa*, ɪ, pp. 369 ff.
10 *St. Spoleto*, p. 35.
11 Galvaneo Fiamma, 'Chronicon Maius' in *Miscellanea di Storia Italiana* (Turin), ᴠɪɪ (1869), p. 745.
12 A. Gloria (ed.), *Statuti del comune di Padova dal sec. xɪɪ all'anno 1285* (Padua, 1873), ɪ, p. 133.
13 *St. Pistoia, Pop.*, p. 38.
14 *St. Spoleto*, pp. 41–2; *Statuta communis Pergami* in *Monumenta Hist. Patriae.* xᴠɪ. pt. 2 (Turin, 1876), cc. 2016–8.
15 MGH, xᴠɪɪɪ, p. 411.

16 Ibid., pp. 499–502.
17 *St. Pistoia, Pop.*, pp. 63–4.
18 *St. Modena*, I, 1, pp. 363–4.
19 *St. Pistoia, Pop.*, pp. LVIII–LX.
20 *Ann. Bol.*, II, 2, p. 464.
21 Cited by G. Fasoli in *L'Archiginnasio*, 28 (Bologna, 1933), pp. 176n–177n.
22 Quoted in J. K. Hyde, *Padua in the Age of Dante*, p. 243.
23 C. Vignati, *Codice Diplomatico Laudense* (Milan, 1879–83), II, pp. 41–2.
24 Salimbene, II, pp. 25–6.
25 Villani, V, 38–9.
26 RIS, o.s., XI, c. 117.
27 MGH, XVIII, pp. 542–3.
28 RIS, n.s., XII, 1, p. 291; RIS, n.s. XVI, IV, p. 8.
29 RIS, n.s., VIII, 1, p. 32: Salimbene, I, p. 272.
30 *St. Parma*, II, pp. 41 ff; Perugia, Archivio di Stato, Rif. VI, f. 310.
31 *St. Pistoia, Pop.*, p. 80; RIS, n.s., VIII, V, p. 10.
32 *Ann. Bol.*, III, 2, pp. 214–21, 233–6.
33 RIS, n.s., VII, 1, pp. 57 ff; RIS, o.s., V, c. 534.
34 Guittone d'Arezzo, *Le Rime* (Bari, 1940), pp. 89–93; *Lettere* (Bologna, 1922), p. 179.

7 The failure of the republics

1 E. Salzer, *Über die Anfänge der Signorie in Oberitalien* (Berlin, 1900), p. 48.
2 Villani, VII, p. 120.
3 RIS, o.s., XI, c. 705; J. Larner, *The Lords of Romagna* (London, 1965), pp. 112–3.
4 Salimbene, II, pp. 844–5.
5 *Ann. Gen.*, IV, pp. 25–8.
6 L. A. Muratori, *Delle Antichità Estensi ed italiane* (Modena, 1717–40), II, pp. 25–7.

8 The Historiography of the City-Republics

1 B. Croce, *Teoria e Storia della Storiografia* (ed. 5, Bari, 1943), p. 4.

2 De Sismondi, *History of the Italian Republics* (Everyman edn, 1907), pp. 1–4 and *Études sur les Constitutions des Peuples Libres* (Brussels, 1838), pp. 82, 295.

3 See H. Butterfield, *Man on his Past* (1955).

4 E. Cristiani, *Nobiltà e Popolo nel comune di Pisa* (Naples, 1962), pp. 13–17.

5 See N. Ottokar, *Le città francesi nel Medio Evo* (Florence, 1927), especially the preface (pp. v–viii). This superb book has remained uninfluential, and indeed almost unknown, for obvious linguistic reasons.

6 S. Raveggi, M. Tarassi, D. Medici, P. Parenti, op. cit., p. xix.

7 The work appeared in 1978 in *Storia d'Italia. Annali 1* (Turin) under this title and in 1980 in P. Jones, *Economia e società nell'Italia medievale* (Turin), with a slightly different title ('il mito della borghesia'). Quotations are from pp. 258 and 291 of *Annali*, I.

8 *Atti* of the 2nd, 3rd and 4th *convegni*, published respectively at Pisa (1982) and Florence (1983, 1982).

9 Notably in two articles in *Studi Medievali* (1974 and 1976). See also his paper in the proceedings of the 1985 conference on medieval Perugia (Deputazione di Storia Patria per l'Umbria).

10 For some recent contributions see D. Waley, 'A commune and its subject territory in the 13th century: law and power in the Sienese *contado*' in *Diritto e Potere. Atti del 40 Congresso int. della Soc. Italiana di Storia del Diritto in onore di B. Paradisi* (Florence, 1982), pp. 303–11 and particularly P. Cammarosano, 'Le campagne senesi dalla fine del sec. XII agli inizi del trecento: dinamica interna e forme del dominio cittadino' in *Contadini e proprietari nella Toscana moderna. Atti del convegno di studi in onore di G. Giorgetti* (Florence, 1979), pp. 153–222.

Abbreviations

The following works are cited in an abbreviated form in the notes:

Ann. Bol. = L. Savioli, *Annali Bolognesi* (Bassano, 1784–95)
Ann. Gen. = *Annali Genovesi di Caffaro e de' suoi continuatori* ed. L. T. Belgrano and C. Imperiale in Fonti per la Storia d'Italia
ASI = *Archivio Storico Italiano* (Florence)

C.D. Crem. = L. Astegiano, *Codice Diplomatico Cremonese* (Turin, 1895–8)

Doc. Arezzo = U. Pasqui, *Documenti per la Storia della Città di Arezzo* (Florence, 1879–1920)

Malispini = Ricordano Malispini, *Storia fiorentina* (Leghorn, 1830)

MGH = Monumenta Germaniae Historica, Scriptores

RIS, n.s. = G. Carducci and V. Fiorini, Rerum Italicarum Scriptores (Città di Castello and Bologna, 1900–)

RIS, o.s., = L. A. Muratori, Rerum Italicarum Scriptores (Milan, 1723–51)

Salimbene = Salimbene de Adam, *Cronica*, ed. F. Bernini (Bari, 1942)

St. Modena = C. Campori, *Statuta Civitatis Mutine* (Parma, 1864)

St. Parma = A. Ronchini, *Statuta Communis Parmae* (Parma, 1856–60)

St. Pisa = F. Bonaini, *Statuti Inediti della Città di Pisa dal XII al XIV secolo* (Florence, 1854–7)

St. Pistoia, Pop. = L. Zdekauer, *Breve et Ordinamenta Populi Pistorii, 1284* (Milan, 1891)

St. Pistoia, Pot. = idem, *Statutum Potestatis Comunis Pistorii, 1296* (Milan 1888)

St. Spoleto = G. Antonelli, *Statuti di Spoleto del 1296* (Florence, 1962)

St. Viterbo = I. Ciampi, Statutum Viterbii, 1251 in *Cronache e Statuti di Viterbo* (Florence, 1872)

Villani = Giovanni Villani, *Cronica*, ed. F. G. Dragomanni (Florence, 1844–5)

Bibliography

General Works

J. K. Hyde, *Society and Politics in Medieval Italy* (London, 1973)

P. Jones, 'Communes and despots; the city state in late-medieval Italy', *Transactions of the Royal Historical Society*, 5th s., xv (1965)

E. Jordan, *L'Allemagne et l'Italie aux xiie et xiie siècles* (Paris, 1939) (best account of the general political background)

N. Ottokar, 'Comuni' in *Enciclopedia Italiana*, vol. xi: reprinted in *Studi comunali e fiorentini* (Florence, 1948)

idem, 'Il Problema della formazione comunale' in *Questioni di Storia Medioevale*, ed. E. Rota (Milan, n.d.) (good bibliography)

C. W. Previté-Orton, 'The Italian Cities till c. 1200' in *Cambridge Medieval History*, vol. v (1926) (good bibliography)

Y. Renouard, *Les Villes d'Italie de la fin du xie siècle au début du xive siècle* (Paris, 1969)

G. Volpe, *Medio Evo Italiano* (Florence, 1928) (especially Chapter 1)

G. Tobacco, *The Struggle for Power in Medieval Italy* (Cambridge, 1990)

J. Larner, *Italy in the Age of Dante and Petrarch 1216–1380* (London, 1980)

P. Jones, 'Economia e società nell'Italia medievale: la leggenda della borghesia' in *Storia d'Italia. Annali I* (Turin, 1978) (also in Jones, *Economia e società nell'Italia medievale* (Turin, 1980))

G. Galasso (ed.), *Storia d'Italia* (Turin) vol. 4 (*Comuni e Signorie: istituzioni, società e lotte per l'egemonia*, 1981); vol. 5 (*Comuni e Signorie nell'Italia settentrionale: il Piemonte e la Liguria*, 1986); vol. 6 (Lombardy, forthcoming); vol. 7 (north-eastern and central Italy, 1987)

R. Bordone, *La Società urbana nell'Italia comunale* (*secc. XI–XIV*) (Turin, 1984) (good bibliography)

For economic background

Cambridge Economic History of Europe, vols I (ed.2), II, III (Cambridge, 1952–66)
P. Jones, 'La storia economica' in *Storia d'Italia*, ed. R. Romano and C. Vivanti, vol. II (Turin, 1974)
R. S. Lopez and I. W. Raymond (eds), *Medieval Trade in the Mediterranean World* (New York and London, 1955)
G. Luzzatto (trs. P. Jones), *An Economic History of Italy* (London 1961)

Some studies of individual cities

Ancona: J. F. Leonhard, *Die Seestadt Ancona* (Tubingen, 1983)
Assisi: *Assisi al tempo di San Francesco* (Soc. Internazionale di studi francescani, Assisi, 1978)
Asti: E. Artifoni, 'Una società di "Popolo": modelli istituzionali, parentele, aggregazioni societarie e territoriali ad Asti nel XIII secolo', *Studi Medievali*, s.3, XXIV (1983)
Bassano: G. Fasoli, 'Un comune veneto nel duecento: Bassano', *Archivio Veneto*, s.5, XV (1934)
Bologna: A. Hessel, *Geschichte der Stadt Bologna v. 1116 bis 1280* (Berlin, 1910: Ital. trans. 1975)
Florence: R. Davidsohn, *Geschichte von Florenz* (Berlin, 1896–1927: also Ital. trans.); F. Schevill, *History of Florence* (London, n.d.); E. Fiumi, 'Fioritura e decadenza dell'economia fiorentina', ASI, 1957–9; the works by G. Salvemini and N. Ottokar cited in Chapter 8
Mantua: P. Torelli, *Un comune cittadino in territorio ad economia agricola* (Mantua, 1930–52)
Milan: *Storia di Milano*, Fondazione Treccani (Milan, 1953–66)
Orvieto: D. Waley, *Mediaeval Orvieto* (Cambridge, 1952)
Padua: J. K. Hyde, *Padua in the Age of Dante* (Manchester and New York. 1966)
Pavia: P. Vaccari, *Profilo storico di Pavia* (Pavia, 1950)
Perugia: A. Grohmann, *Città e territorio tra medioevo e età moderna* (*Perugia secc. XIII–XVI*) (Perugia, 1981); *Società e istituzioni dell'Italia*

comunale: l'esempio di Perugia (secc. XII–XIV) (Deputazione di Storia Patria per l'Umbria, 1988)

Piacenza: P. Racine, Plaisance du XIe à la fin du XIIIe siècle (Paris/Lille, 1979)

Pisa: G. Volpe, Studi sulle istituzioni comunali a Pisa (Pisa, 1902 repr. Florence 1970); E. Cristiani, Nobiltà e Popolo nel comune di Pisa (Naples, 1962); D. Herlihy, Pisa in the early Renaissance (New Haven, 1958); M. Tangheroni, Politica, commercio, agricoltura a Pisa nel trecento (Pisa, 1973); C. Violante, Economia società istituzioni a Pisa nel medioevo (Bari, 1980)

Pistoia: D. Herlihy, Medieval and Renaissance Pistoia (New Haven and London, 1967)

Rome: R. Brentano, Rome before Avignon (London, 1974)

San Gimignano: E. Fiumi, Storia economica e sociale di S. Gimignano (Florence, 1961)

Siena: F. Schevill, Siena (London, 1909; repr. New York and London, 1964); W. M. Bowsky, The Finance of the Commune of Siena, 1287–1355 (Oxford, 1970); idem, A Medieval Italian Commune: Siena under the Nine, 1287–1355 (Berkeley, L. A. and London, 1981); D. Balestracci and G. Piccinni, Siena nel trecento. Assetto urbano e strutture edilizie (Florence, 1977).

Venice: F. C. Lane, Venice: a Maritime Republic (Baltimore and London, 1973); G. Luzzatto, Studi di storia economica veneziana (Padua, 1954); idem, Storia economica di Venezia (Venice, 1961)

Verona: Verona e il suo territorio, vol. II (Verona medioevale), (Ist. per gli studi stor. veronesi, Verona, 1964)

1 The legacy of power

G. Fasoli, Dalla 'civitas' al comune (Bologna, 1961, 1969)

C. Violante, La società milanese nell'età precomunale (Bari, 1974)

G. Dilcher, Die Entstehung der lombardischen Stadtcommune (Aalen, 1967)

H. Keller, Adelsherrschaft und städtische Gesellschaft in Oberitalien (9–12 Jahrh.) (Tübingen, 1979)

2 The population

R. S. Lopez, 'Aux origines du capitalisme génois', Annales, IX (1937)

G. Luzzatto, 'Le sottomissioni dei feudatari e le classi sociali in alcuni comuni marchigiani' in *Dai servi della gleba agli albori del capitalismo* (Bari, 1966)

Y. Renouard, *Les hommes d'affaires italiens du moyen âge* (Paris, 1949)

J. K. Hyde, *Padua in the Age of Dante*; idem, 'Italian social chronicles in the Middle Ages', *Bulletin of the John Rylands Library*, 49 (1966)

Famille et Parenté dans l'Occident Médiéval, Part III (École française de Rome, 1977)

3 Government

M. A. Zorzi, 'L'ordinamento comunale padovano nella seconda metà del sec. XIII', *Miscellanea di Storia Veneta*, vol. V, 3 (1931)

E. Ruffini Avondo, *I Sistemi di deliberazione collettiva nel medioevo italiano* (Turin, 1927)

G. Hanauer, 'Das Berufspodestat in dreizehnten Jahrh.', *Mittheilungen d. Inst. f. oest. Geschichtsforschung*. XXIII (1902)

V. Franchini, *Saggio di ricerche sull'istituto del podestà nei comuni medievali* (Bologna, 1912)

Manuals for podestà: 'Oculus Pastoralis' in L. A. Muratori, *Antiquitates*, diss. XLVI (and ed. D. Franceschi in *Mem. dell'Accad. d. Sc. di Torino: cl. di sc. morali, storiche e filologiche*, s.4, XI, 1966): Johannes Viterbensis, *Liber de Regimine Civitatum* in Bibl. Iurid. M. Aevi, III (Bologna, 1901)

Syndication of officials: V. Crescenzi, 'Il sindacato degli ufficiali nei comuni medievali italiani' in *L'Educazione Giuridica*, IV; *Il pubblico funzionario: modelli storici e comparativi*, Tomo 1 (Perugia, 1981)

Armies: D. Waley, 'The Army of the Florentine Republic from the 12th to the 14th cent.' in N. Rubinstein (ed.), *Florentine Studies* (London, 1968); idem, '*Condotte* and *condottieri* in the 13th. century', *Proceedings of the British Academy*. LXI (1976); A. I. Galletti, 'La società comunale di fronte alla guerra nelle fonti perugine del 1282', *Bollettino d. Deputazione di Storia Patria p. l'Umbria*, LXXI (1974); A. A. Settia, 'L'esercito comunale vercellese del sec. XIII: armamento e techniche di combattimento nell'Italia occidentale', *Congresso Storico Vercellese, 2–3 ott. 1982*

Finance and Taxation: G. Biscaro, 'Gli estimi del comune di Milano nel sec. XIII', *Archivio stor. lombardo*, LV (1928); E. Fiumi,

'L'imposta diretta nei comuni medioevali della Toscana', in *Studi in onore di A. Sapori*, I Milan, 1962); W. M. Bowsky, *The Finance of the Comune of Siena*, (see above: with review of this work in *Rivista Stor. Italiana*, LXXXV, 1973); A. I. Pini, 'Gli estimi cittadini di Bologna dal 1296 al 1329. . .', *Studi Medievali*, s.3, XVIII (1977: with further bibliography)

Church: G. Volpe, *Medio Evo Italiano*, ch. 7; G. Salvemini, *Studi Storici* (Florence, 1901), ch. 2; R. Brentano, *Two Churches* (Princeton, 1968)

Grain: H. C. Peyer, *Zur Getreidepolitik oberitalienischer Städte im 13 Jahrh.* (Vienna, 1950); G. Pinto, 'Appunti sulla politica annonaria in Italia fra XIII e XV secc.' in *Aspetti della vita economica medievale, Atti del Convegno . . . Melis . . . 10–14 marzo 1984*, Florence, 1985

Citizenship: D. Bizzari, 'Ricerche sul diritto di cittadinanza nella costituzione comunale', *Studi senesi*, XXXII (1916); W. M. Bowsky, 'Medieval citizenship: the individual and the state in the Commune of Siena, 1287–1355', *Studies in Medieval and Renaissance History*, IV (1969); A. I. Pini, 'Un aspetto dei rapporti tra città e territorio nel medioevo: la politica 'ad elastico' di Bologna fra il XII e il XIV sec.' in *Studi in Memoria di F. Melis* (Naples, 1978)

4 Town and country

G. Luzzatto, 'Città e campagna in Italia nell'età dei comuni' in *Dai Servi della gleba agli albori del capitalismo*

E. Fiumi, 'Sui rapporti economici tra città e contado nell'età comunale', *Archivio Storico Italiano*, CXIV (1955)

G. De Vergottini, 'Origine e sviluppo storico della comitatinanza', *Studi Senesi*, XLIII (1929)

G. Cherubini, *Signori, Contadini, Borghesi* (Florence, 1974)

P. Jones, 'From manor to mezzadria' in N. Rubinstein (ed.), *Florentine Studies*; idem, chapter in *Cambridge Economic History of Europe*, vol. 1 (ed.2)

P. Vaccari, *L'affrancazione dei servi della gleba nell'Emilia e nella Toscana* (Bologna, 1926)

Structures féodales et féodalisme dans l'occident méditerranéen (Xe–XIIIe s.) (École française de Rome, 1980); Part 3 (La Ville et la Féodalité)

P. Cammarosano, 'Le campagne senesi dalla fine del sec. XII agli

inizi del trecento: dinamica interna e forme del dominio cittadino' in *Contadini e proprietari nella Toscana moderna. Atti del
convegno di studi in onore di G. Giorgetti* (Florence, 1979)

D. Waley, 'A commune and its subject territory in the 13th
century: law and power in the Sienese *contado*' in *Diritto e
Potere. Atti del 4o Convegno int. della Soc. Italiana di Storia del
Diritto in onore di B. Paradisi*

E. Carpentier, *Orvieto à la fin du xiiie s. Ville et Campagne dans le
Cadastre de 1292* (Paris, 1986)

O. Redon, *Uomini e comunità del contado senese nel duecento* (Siena,
1982)

5 External relations

E. Jordan, *L'Allemagne et l'Italie aux xiie et xiiie siècles*; idem, *Les
Origines des la domination angevine en Italie* (Paris, 1909; repr.
N. Y., 1960), Introduction (on Frederick ii)

G. Fasoli, 'La lega lombarda: antecedenti, formazione, struttura'
in eadem, *Scritti di Storia Medievale* (Bologna, 1974)

Relations with Empire: P. Brezzi, 'Le relazioni tra i comuni italiani
e l'Impero' in *Questioni di Storia Medioevali* (v. sup.) and revised
In *Nuove Questioni di Storia Medioevale* (Milan, 1964)

Relations with Papacy: D. Waley, *The Papal State in the 13th.
Century* (London and New York, 1961)

Diplomacy: S. Angelini, *La diplomazia comunale a Perugia nei secoli
xiii e xiv* (Florence, 1965)

Patriotism: *La coscienza cittadina nei comuni italiani del duecento*,
Convegni del Centro di Studi sulla spiritualità medievale xi
(Todi, 1972); J. K. Hyde, 'Medieval descriptions of cities', (*Bull-
etin of the John Rylands Library*, 48 (1966); Hannelore Zug
Tucci, 'Il Carroccio nella vita comunale italiana', *Quellen u.
Forschungen a. italienischen Archiven u. Bibliotheken*, 65 (1985).
Characteristic descriptions are Bonvicino's of Milan in *Bollettino
dell'Istituto Storico Italiano*, xx (1898) (also ed. M. Corti, Milan,
1974); Opicino's of Pavia in RIS, n.s., xi, 1; and that of Bergamo
in RIS, o.s., v (new edn in *Studi Medievali*, 1970).

Town planning: W. Braunfels, *Mittelalterliche Stadtbaukunst in der
Toskana* (Berlin, 1953): E. Guidoni, *Arte e urbanistica in Toscana
(1000–1315)* (Rome, 1970: see also Chapter 8)

Civic spirit and the visual arts: H. Wieruszowski, 'Art and the
Commune in the time of Dante', *Speculum*, xix (1944); N.
Rubinstein, 'Political ideas in Sienese art', *Journal of the Warburg*

and Courtauld Institutes, XXI (1958) (see also Q. Skinner, 'Ambrogio Lorenzetti: the artist as political philosopher; *Proceedings of the British Academy,* LXXII (1986); J. Paul, *Die mittelalterlichen Kommunalpaläste in Italien* (Cologne, 1963); on the *Opera* see N. Ottokar, *Studi comunali e fiorentini,* ch. 5

6 Internal divisions

J. Heers, *Le clan familial au Moyen Age* (Paris, 1974)

J. K. Hyde, 'Contemporary views on faction and civil strife in 13th and 14th century Italy' in L. Martines (ed.), *Violence and Civil Disorder in Italian Cities, 1200–1500* (Berkeley, L. A. and London, 1972)

Consorzerie: F. Niccolai, *I Consorzi nobiliari ed il Comune nell'alta e media Italia* (Bologna, 1940)

Popolo: G. De Vergottini, *Arte e Popolo nella prima metà del sec. XIII* (Milan, 1943), and the same author's articles on the Popolo of Modena (in *Volume in onore del prof. P. Rossi,* Siena, 1931) and that of Vicenza (*Studi Senesi,* XLVIII (1934)). Both articles are reprinted in his *Scritti di Storia del Diritto Italiano,* I (Milan, 1977)); G. Fasoli, 'La legislazione antimagnatizia a Bologna', *Rivista di Storia d. Diritto Italiano,* VI (1933) and 'Ricerche sulla legislazione antimagnatizia nei comuni dell'alta e media Italia', *ibid.,* XII (1939); U. G. Mondolfo, *Il Populus a Siena* (Genoa, 1911); U. Gualazzini, 'Il "Populus cremonese" e l'autonomia del comune', *Riv. di Storia d. Diritto Italiano,* XI–XII (1938–9); N. Rubinstein, *La lotta contro i magnati a Firenze* (Florence, 1939); E. Artifoni, 'La Società del "Popolo" di Asti fra circolazione istituzionale e strategie familiari', *Quaderni Storici,* 51 (1982)

Bolognese *compagnie delle armi*: G. Fasoli in *L'Arciginnasio,* 28 (1933)

Guelfs and Ghibellines: R. Davidsohn, *Quellen zur Geschichte v. Florenz* (Berlin, 1896–1908), IV, pp. 29–67; G. A. Brucker, *Florentine Politics and Society, 1343–78* (Princeton, 1962); some of the titles given under Chapter 5 are also relevant

7 The failure of the republics

E. Salzer, *Über die Anfänge der Signorie in Oberitalien* (Berlin, 1900; repr. Vaduz. 1965)

E. Sestan, 'Le origini delle signorie cittadine: un problema esaurito?', *Boll. dell'Ist. stor. Ital.,* LXXIII (1961)

F. Ercole, *Dal comune al principato* (Florence, 1929)

Studi Ezzeliniani (Ist. Stor. Ital. per il Medio Evo, Rome, 1963)

J. Laurent, 'The Signory and its supporters: the Este of Ferrara', *Journal of Medieval History*, 3 (1977); eadem, 'Feudalismo e Signora', *Archivio Storico Italiano*, 1979: see also A. Castagnetti, *Società e politica a Ferrara* (Bologna, 1985)

Historical Gazetteer

Alessandria came into being through its formal foundation in 1168 by the Lombard League. As *Civitas nova* (it had other temporary names) its fortifications were built on the banks of the Tanaro in 1164–7. The marquises of Montferrat enjoyed some overlordship from 1178, though in 1183–98 the city was again imperialist, as 'Cesaria'.

Control was exercised by William VII of Montferrat, as captain (1260–2, 1278–90) and for a time by Charles of Anjou (from 1268, and from 1270 as 'perpetual' *dominus* and *rector*). Later Alessandria fell to the Visconti (1295), to Robert of Anjou and again (1315) to the Visconti and later the Sforza.

Ancona was, theoretically at least, under Byzantine overlordship (as part of the Pentapolis) till the twelfth century. It underwent several imperialist sieges (1137, 1167, 1174), then passed at the end of the century from imperialist overlordship (Markward of Anweiler) to that of the Estensi, via papal suzerainty. By 1199 there was a colony of Ancona merchants at Constantinople.

The earliest surviving reference to consuls is 1128, the first to a podestà is from 1199. There is no evidence of a 'popular' pressure-group at Ancona. The city remained under papal rule (confirmed by Albornoz in the mid-fourteenth century) and was an important source of income to the papacy. A very brief Malatesta overlordship was the only form of local *signoria*.

Arezzo had consuls (and 40 *boni homines*) by 1098. In 1153 there was a single *rector et gubernator*; after a gap there were podestà again in 1193, 1203, 1205 and often thereafter. There was a *societas populi* by 1256. The bishops continued to exert great influence in the commune, among them Guglielmino Obertini (killed at Campaldino, 1289) and, in the early fourteenth century, Guido Tarlati. There was a considerable *dominio* (Cortona submitted in 1258), but Arezzo itself was ceded in *signoria* to Florence for five years by a local faction (1337) for money. Independence was regained spasmodically but in 1384 the city was again sold to Florence (by Enguerrand de Coucy) and this time the domination was enduring.

Assisi came under imperialist rule (within the Duchy of Spoleto) in the second half of the twelfth century, but passed to the papacy in 1197. There were consuls by 1184, a (local) podestà by 1204 (and no consuls again after 1212). A series of compromises between *maiores* and *minores* (or *homines populi*) marked the early commune (1203, 1210).

Authority over the city in the fourteenth century was disputed between papal rectors (e.g. Albornoz, 1367), local *signori* (e.g. the Trinci of Foligno, 1327–30) and the commune of Perugia (the main dominating power between 1321 and 1367). A similar series of external rulers (including the Visconti in 1400, the Montefeltro from 1408, Francesco Sforza in 1434–42) controlled Assisi in the fifteenth century.

Asti had consuls by 1095, comital power there having been granted by Henry IV in the previous year to the bishop (though it was occasionally shared by a lay count). Frederick I captured the city (1154) but recognised its commune and appointed a podestà (1159). Asti joined the Lombard League (1168), but was again defeated by Frederick I (1174).

Later Asti resisted successfully the Count of Savoy (1255) and Charles of Anjou (1275). The first clear evidence of the existence of a unified popular organisation is 1257; there was a *potestas populi* (1257–63) and in the 1270s the *societas* or *societates populi* had alternately a captain and rectors.

In the early fourteenth century Asti fell under the lordship of King Robert (of Anjou), then that of the Counts of Savoy and later of the marquises of Montferrat and the Visconti of Milan. In 1387 it was the dowry of Valentina bride of Louis d'Orléans (hence the later French claim) but from 1422 returned in practice to the Visconti.

Bergamo had consuls by 1112 and a (local) podestà before 1175. The city was a member of the Lombard League (1167 – and also of the revived League of 1226).

The city was allied to Pallavicino but he fell out with the Torriani of Milan over control (1265). This development led to an alliance with the Torriani and Charles of Anjou (also with papal legates), but in 1269 Bergamo resisted an Angevin *signoria*. From 1315 it fell to the Visconti and remained under Milanese domination except for the episode of John of Bohemia's lordship in 1331–3.

Bologna had a commune by 1114 and it received an imperial privilege in 1116. Its territorial gains start in 1131 (Nonantola) and the city refused to admit the Emperor Lothar in 1132. Guido da Sasso was *Bononensium rector et potestas* in 1151–4. Consuls are recorded by 1156 but presumably existed earlier. The first clear constitutional gains for the Popolo date from 1228; further gains were achieved in 1255, from which year there was an 'outsider' as Capitano del Popolo.

The city passed from imperial to papal overlordship in 1274. The commune was dominated by the Pepoli family in 1337–50, then by the Visconti (1350–60). Papal control was restored, but diminished after 1376. The Bentivoglio enjoyed ascendancy in 1401–2 and 1435–1507.

Brescia had conducted negotiations in 945 and 1038, but the earliest surviving reference to consuls dates from 1127. The commune was involved in opposition to Frederick I (1159–61 and 1167) and adhered to the Lombard League (1177). It continued to be involved in anti-imperialist alliances (1198, 1226, 1231, 1238, 1252). Factional organisation is attested by an alliance between Brescia's *societas militum* and Cremona (1200, 1202–8).

Ezzelino was a powerful influence from 1256 and *signore* from 1258–9 (in a joint regime with Pallavicino, who was himself *signore* from 1262–4). There followed a succession of *signorie*: Buoso da Dovara, Bernardo Maggi bishop of Brescia, and later (after the city's capture by Henry VII in 1311) the Scaligeri and then Visconti.

Cremona developed municipal institutions precociously. A *conspiratio populi* is reported in 924, an imperialist grant to the 'citizens' – later quashed – in 996, and a *domus civitatis* in 998. There was a commune by 1098 (invested with lands by the Countess Matilda) and consuls by 1112. Disputes with the bishops played an important part in these developments. Imperial privileges (1157, 1162, 1164, 1176 and 1226) were connected with

Cremona's longstanding enmity with Milan, yet Cremona was a member of the Lombard League in 1167–76.

There was a Popolo by 1210. After an alliance, Pallavicino became *perpetualis dominus et potestas* (1254–66), to be dispossessed by his own local ally Buoso da Dovara. After a brief Angevin interlude and a period of imperial control (1311), authority passed to the Visconti (1313 and, for an enduring lordship, 1344).

Fermo was in imperial territory (the 'March of Fermo' until the early twelfth century, then the March of Ancona) which passed to the papacy in 1198, then as a fief to the Estensi (held of Otto IV in 1210, of the popes from 1212). The bishops had a considerable 'liberty' in the region. However, the city had a podestà by 1164 and consuls are recorded by 1199 (they probably preceded the podestà). Fermo was held at various periods by the Hohenstaufen (1242–7; 1250; privileged by Manfred 1258). From the fourteenth century it fell under the series of *signorie*, some of them short-lived. Notable among the *signori* were Mercenario da Monteverde (1331–40), Gentile da Mogliano (1348–55), Giovanni Visconti da Oleggio (1360–6), Lodovico Migliorati (1406–28) and Francesco Sforza (1433–46).

Ferrara passed (from the Exarchate) to the popes in 774 but jurisdiction lay in practice with the archbishops of Ravenna (or in 1101 with Countess Matilda). The 'population' received an imperial privilege in 1055.

Control came to be contested between the Adelardi (or Marcheselli) and Salinguerra (Torelli). After a period of imperial authority (1158–64), Ferrara entered the Lombard League (1167–84). The early podestà (1195–) were all Salinguerra or Estensi. Control passed from Guglielmo III degli Adelardi to his nephew by marriage, Azzo VI of Este. There followed joint government by Azzo VII and Salinguerra II (1213–22), after which the latter was sole *signore* (1222–40). For Obizzo's succession in 1264 see above, p. 169. From 1292 the *signore* could choose his own successor. A big dominion was built up, including Modena. Despite the challenges of Venice and the papacy, Este lordship was recognised by a vicariate (1332) and eventually (1471) the grant of a duchy.

Florence became a centre of margravial administration in 1057. Though the first campaigns by the Florentines date from 1107 (Fiesole was captured in 1125 and Siena fought in 1129), the earliest reference to a 'commune' is later. There were consuls by

1138. An imperial privilege was received in 1187. Florence had a *consul mercatorum* in 1192 and a podestà (a Florentine) in 1193. The first *societas populi* dated from 1250.

The city made great territorial gains in Tuscany from the mid-thirteenth century. Thereafter the main landmarks are: 1260–7 (Ghibelline regime); 1282– (regime of 6 priors); 1293, Ordinances of Justice; Ghibelline wars followed by Charles Duke of Calabria's protectorate, 1325–8; 1342–3, the Angevin-linked Duke of Athens in control as Capitano di Guerra; 1378, Ciompi rising, followed by oligarchical regime, with Albizzi and Niccolo da Uzzano as leading figures; 1434–94 and 1512–27, Medicean domination, resumed 1530 (Alessandro becomes Duke of Florence 1532, Cosimo Grand Duke of Tuscany 1569).

Forlì was in the 'Exarchate'. By 1138 (at the time of an alliance with Ravenna) there was a commune (consisting of *capitanei*, *valvassores* and *populus*) with a *rector*. The first clearly dated reference to consuls is in 1153, but the institution was not then a new one. In 1194 there was a podestà.

Forlì passed to papal overlordship, with the rest of Romagna, in 1278. The local family of Ordelaffi gained control as *signori* soon after this (though there was a brief period under Mainardo da Susinana in 1298–1301). From about 1315 the Ordelaffi *signoria* was asserted in a durable fashion (apart from a brief episode of direct papal control in 1404–6).

Genoa as a city received privileges in 958 and 1056 and fought campaigns against Islamic powers in 1015 and 1088. The first reference to consuls is in 1099, to the 'Compagna' (a sort of voluntary commune) in 1143. In 1162 an imperial charter granted the Genoese wide powers, including that of choosing their own consuls. The first external podestà held office in 1191; the podesteria alternated with consuls till 1218. A single Capitano del Popolo (Guglielmo Boccanegra) held office 1257–62.

Genoa held an extensive empire in the Levant and closer at hand. After 1299 all Corsica (partially Pisan before) became Genoese, but Sardinia was lost to Aragon in the fourteenth century.

From 1306 there were Doria–Spinola, then Spinola, regimes. After brief control by Henry VII, Guelf nobles (Fieschi and Grimaldi) took over, then King Robert of Naples (1318–34). Simone Boccanegra was doge and *signore* 'for life' (1339 and 1356–63). After many brief interludes, there were periods of

French (1396–1409) and Monferrat (1409–13) rule, till the Visconti (1421–36) and Sforza (1463–6, etc.) intervened up to the time of the French invasion of 1494.

Gubbio possessed consuls by 1163 (they are mentioned in an imperial privilege) and a podestà by 1203. The early commune was for a time submitted to Perugia (1183), but also secured the temporary submission of Cagli (1190). Some of Gubbio's *contado* was awarded by the pope to Perugia in 1257, as an outcome of its pro-imperialist history. The first Capitano del Popolo is recorded in 1258.

The first half of the fourteenth century was a time of Perugian predominance in Umbria, but Gubbio experienced a brief local *signoria* under Giovanni di Cantuccio dei Gabrielli (1350–4) before coming under direct papal authority. The first firm *signoria* was that of Antonio da Montefeltro, Count of Urbino, and the city remained under the Counts (later Dukes) of Urbino till it passed into the papal dominions in 1631.

Lucca was the recipient of a promise from Henry IV that no imperial palace should be built in the city and no castle within 6 miles (1081). There were consuls by 1142 and a single *dominus civitatis* around the middle of the twelfth century.

There were brief periods of Hohenstaufen (1260) and Angevin (1266–72) domination, but the earliest *signoria* was that of Uguccione della Faggiuola (1314–16), followed by Castruccio Castracane (1320–8). Control passed through many hands; Pisa was dominant from 1342–69, the Guinigi (a local family) from 1392 to 1430. Lucca remained a republic up to the time of the Napoleonic principate (1805–13), then became a Bourbon duchy before passing (1847) to the Grand Duchy of Tuscany.

Mantua was involved in an agreement with Brescia and Verona before 945 and received its first imperial privilege in 1014. There were consuls by 1126 and a council of 40 by 1164. The bishop was podestà in 1184–6 and occasionally later; marquises of Este were podestà in 1207–8, 1210–11 and 1212–13. The city was a member of the Lombard League (1167).

The Count of S. Bonifacio and Marquis Azzo of Este were captains of the Popolo in 1257 and again in the 1260s. From the later 1260s the local family of Bonaccolsi were gaining control; Pinamonte was made Capitano del Popolo for life in 1276–7, as was his son in 1291, and in 1308 Guido was recognised as hereditary *signore*. In 1328 the Gonzaga gained authority and retained their position, after 1433 as marquises. After 1707 Mantua passed to the Empire (and to a united Italy in 1866).

Milan had been a great city in the classical period and 'Dark Ages' and was at one time the residence of the western Emperor. There is evidence of quasi-independent diplomatic activity by the Milanese in 894. For the struggle for authority between the archbishop, 'captains', valvassors and *cives* from 979 see above, pp. 9–10. There were sworn associations of captains and valvassors by 1035–7 and a war (led by the archbishop) was fought against Pavia in 1059. Milan had consuls by 1097, a podestà in 1186, and a 'popular' organisation by 1225.

The earliest signs of a seignorial authority go back to 1241 (Della Torre), but the first clear *de facto signore* was Archbishop Ottone Visconti (1277). Control alternated between these two families up to the time of Matteo Visconti (1311). After being *domini generales* (1330–), the Visconti became Dukes of Milan (1395–1447). In 1450 the duchy passed to the Sforza family.

Modena was the scene of a *conspiratio populi* against the bishop in 891, but the earliest surviving reference to consuls dates from 1135. There was a *rector* in 1151, 1156 and 1177. By 1182 there was a *consul mercatorum* but the first constitutional gains for the Popolo date from 1229; by 1249 a *societas populi* was firmly established.

The earliest *signoria* was that of Obizzo d'Este (lord of Ferrara) from 1288–1306 followed by Passerino Bonaccolsi of Mantua (1312–18, 1319–27). Various short-lived regimes were succeeded by Estense control from 1336 onwards (Borso d'Este becoming Duke of Modena and Reggio in 1452). After the Napoleonic period the rule of the Austrian Estensi lasted till 1859.

Orvieto had a commune by 1137, consuls (who took an oath to the pope) in 1157, and the subjugation of a *dominio* had begun by 1168. There was a *civitatis rector* in 1171, a podestà (normally) after 1200. A Popolo existed as a single organisation by 1244 and had a captain after 1250.

The first *signore* was the local Ermanno Monaldeschi (1334) and this family retained control, with some interruptions, up to 1352. Thereafter papal authority was stronger and lasted (with brief episodes of control by the Orsini and others) till the unification of Italy.

Padua was an ally of Vicenza by 1117 and had 17 consuls in 1138. The city was in the anti-imperial alliance of 1164 which became the Lombard League. There was a single podestà in 1174. The early history of the *comunanza* (Popolo) is obscure, but it had come into existence by 1256.

The city was briefly under the control of Azzo VII of Este (1236–7), then that of Ezzelino (1237–56). The Della Scala family provided *de facto signori* (1318–37), to be followed by the Carraresi (formally *signori* from 1339). The Visconti superseded them in 1389 but from 1405 (with brief interludes) authority passed to the Venetian republic.

Parma had *cives* by 1081 and there is a reference *toto parmensi populo* in 1092; there were consuls before 1150. The city joined the Lombard League (1167) and had a podestà pre-1175. There was a Capitano del Popolo 1244 (and the 'party of the Empire' had its own Capitano in 1247).

Giberto da Gente was virtually *signore* 1253–9 (as podestà of the Popolo and later the commune) as was Pallavicino 1263–9, and Ghiberto di Correggio (as *protector et gubernator* etc.) 1303–8 and 1309–16. The long period of Visconti control after 1346 suffered only brief (Scaligeri and Estensi) interruptions. Sforza domination (1449–99) was followed by the Farnese duchy of Parma and Piacenza (1545–1731), then Bourbon and Austrian rule up to 1860.

Pavia was a Lombard capital. There is an indication of independent action by its people in 894 and in 1024 they destroyed the royal palace. A war was fought against Milan in 1059. There were consuls by 1112 (and 'judicial consuls' in 1145). Pavia fought with Frederick I against Milan in 1162 and received an imperial grant of privileges (higher judicial powers and the right to appoint consuls) in 1164. There was a podestà in 1179 (but not thereafter till – perhaps – 1225).

The 'popular' *societas* of S. Siro had consuls by 1208, the Popolo (and also the nobles) a podestà in 1253 (and a captain by 1278).

Pallavicino controlled the city from 1254–68, becoming 'perpetual' podestà and *dominus*. The Visconti asserted authority from 1315, this lasting (with some brief interruptions) up to 1447. It was followed by Sforza (to 1535), and then Spanish–Austrian, rule.

Perugia achieved its first gain in its *contado* in 1139; the document recording this contains the earliest surviving reference to the city's *populus* and consuls. There were podestà in 1177 (an imperial official), 1183 and 1195. An important imperial privilege of 1186 conferred the right to elect consuls. A *comunitas* is mentioned in 1193, a *commune* not till 1201. There were disputes between *populares* and *milites* in 1212–14 and 1221–3, but no important popular constitutional gains till 1255–6.

The terms of papal overlordship were defined in 1210, but Perugia remained quasi-independent, dominating much of the surrounding zone in the fourteenth century. Exceptions to this situation were the brief periods of domination of Giangaleazzo Visconti (1400–02), King Ladislas of Naples (1408–14) and Braccio da Montone (1416–24). Papal overlordship was more strongly asserted from that time, though the local family of Baglioni were predominant in the city (but not its *signori*) in 1488–1540.

Piacenza had consuls by 1126, but there were some twelfth-century experiments with podestà (including imperial ones, 1162–4). The Popolo had its own podestà (as did the *milites*) by 1220 and from 1222 it won an agreed share of offices. It was reformed in 1250 with Uberto de Iniquitate chosen as its podestà for a five-year period.

Pallavicino gained control and was named *dominus perpetuus* (1254–7, 1261–5). Alberto Scotti became *signore* (as *anzianus perpetuus* and *defensor et rector mercadandie*) in 1290, but his family lost power in 1304. A period of Visconti domination lasted 1313–1447, with interruptions in 1322–5 and 1402–18. Sforza possession (also interrupted) lasted from 1450 to 1521. Pope Paul III created the duchy of Parma and Piacenza (1545–1731), which was followed by Bourbon and Austrian rule up to 1860.

Pisa led a campaign against Muslim Sicily in 1063. In 1081 the first major imperial grant relinquished jurisdiction within the city. There were consuls by 1085 (and a council of 'senators' and six representatives per quarter by 1164). There were podestà in the 1190s (possibly earlier) and consuls are not mentioned after 1217.

A Popolo had its own statutes and officials by 1237. By 1254 it had a captain and had gained much authority.

Early *signorie* were short-lasting (Count Ugolino della Gherardesca, 1285–8; Count Guy of Montefeltro, 1289–92; Uguccione della Faggiuola, 1314–16).

Of Pisa's maritime empire, Corsica was lost to the Genoese in 1299 and much of Sardinia to the Aragonese in 1324.

A further series of rather brief *signorie* between 1365 and 1402

(Giovanni dell'Agnello, Pietro Gambacorta, Giacopo d'Appiano, Giangaleazzo Visconti) terminated with the loss of independence to Florence (1406). Thereafter Pisa was ruled from Florence with the exception of the years 1494–1509, when Pisa regained autonomy.

Pistoia had consuls as early as 1105. In 1158 there was a single *dominus civitatis* and a series of podestà from 1188 (though an unbroken series of 'outside' podestà begins only in 1219). A Popolo existed by 1236 and had its own captain in 1263 (there was a *potestas militum* in 1237).

Domination by Florence was the norm after 1296, but was several times interrupted (e.g. by the Tedici in 1322–5 and Castruccio Castracane in 1325–8). In 1351 independence was finally lost to the Florentines.

Ravenna was an important classical city. Part of the Exarchate, it tended to be under the dominance of its own archbishop up to the thirteenth century (it passed to papal overlordship, with the rest of Romagna, in 1278).

The 'citizens' of Ravenna rose against Conrad II in 1026 and attacked Faenza in 1080 (Forlì became an ally in 1138). The first reference to consuls dates from 1109, to a podestà from 1181.

The local family of Traversari were in a position of power from the end of the twelfth century to 1240, the Polenta (who became papal vicars) from 1275 up to 1441. Thereafter Venetian influence – already dominant in the port – secured submission to the republic (as a papal vicariate) from 1449 to 1509. Thereafter Ravenna reverted to papal rule.

Rimini was in the (Byzantine) Pentapolis, then within the Lombard and Frankish zones of authority. Its people made a treaty with Ravenna in 1111, had consuls (probably) by 1158 and a podestà by 1195. Gilds and *contrade* were represented in a council by 1232 and there were *capitanei populi et ordinum* in 1254.

The local family of Malatesta was prominent by 1248. Expelled in 1288, they became *signori de facto* in 1295 and formally in 1334. From 1355 they held a papal vicariate (Rimini having passed to the papacy in 1278) and retained control till 1500, with brief reappearances in 1503, 1522–3 and 1527–8. Venice was in control from 1503–9, after which the city reverted to papal domination.

Rome's medieval development does not fit easily into the normal mould of medieval city-republics, owing in particular to its peculiar papal and imperial status and the heritage of its classical past. Nevertheless some features of its history – particularly the theme of power in the surrounding baronially controlled *dominio* and that of the senatorship as an occasional quasi-Popolo – relate to developments elsewhere.

A senate was set up by Arnold of Brescia (1144–55) and at this time (1151) a commercial agreement was negotiated with Pisa. The emperor asserted control over the senatorship in 1167, but from 1188 this was normally regulated by agreement with the papacy. There was usually one senator after 1205, two after 1238, often from leading families of Rome and the Campagna. 'Popular' trends show in the senatorships (combined with captaincy of the Popolo) of the Bolognese Brancaleone degli Andalò from 1252–5 and his uncle in 1258. King Charles of Anjou was 'life' senator from 1263–7. The later senatorships, reflecting power in the city, cannot be recorded here, but Cola di Rienzo's demagogic regime (1343–7, 1354) deserves mention.

Siena had *boni homines* by 1124 and by the following year consuls. There may have been no podestà till 1199; from 1211 the post was always held by a non-Sienese.

By 1212 there was a *societas populi*; this had a captain by c. 1235 and made important gains in constitutional authority in 1256–62.

Though there were institutional and diplomatic changes, the commune of Siena maintained a continuous and independent political life into the sixteenth century (broken only by Visconti suzerainty in 1399–1402). The local Petrucci family held a position of predominance between 1487 and 1524, but from about 1516 increasing Florentine and imperialist pressure made itself felt. In 1557 the city was forced to become part of the Duchy of Florence.

Spoleto, an old but never a powerful city, was destroyed by Frederick I in 1155. There had probably been a commune before this, but the earliest surviving reference to one dates from 1173. There was a (local) podestà by 1201. A popular faction was in dispute with the nobles in 1251 and had its own captain from 1274.

In the fourteenth century Spoleto, an increasingly insignificant place, fell at times under Perugian domination (1324–7), at times under that of the Prefetti (di Vico) and the Manenti. Papal overlordship, dating from 1198, was asserted in the 1350s (Albornoz's fortress) and maintained thereafter despite brief interruptions; Spoleto received Lucrezia Borgia as governor from 1499–1500.

Venice resembled Rome in that it was *sui generis*. The doges (dukes) date from c. 687 and were originally Byzantine officials; *de facto* independence of Byzantium was a gradual achievement. The Venetians defeated neighbouring Comacchio in 886, won control of the Gulf of Venice in the tenth century and a leading position in the trade of the Adriatic in the eleventh.

References to a Venetian 'commune' date from the mid-twelfth century and there was a conciliar structure by the 1170s. The membership of the Great Council, then numbering some 1,100, was 'closed' in 1297.

The republic's Mediterranean empire was greatly increased by the acquisition of three-eighths of the territory of Byzantium (1204). Gains on the mainland (including Padua, Vicenza and Verona) began in 1404–6. Venice retained its independence as a republic until 1797.

Verona was party to an agreement (concerning currency) with Brescia and Mantua pre-945 and to a treaty with Venice in 1107. There were consuls by 1136 and the Count of S. Bonifacio was podestà in 1169. The commune was a member of the Lombard League (1164). It expanded its territory greatly by the acquisition of Garda and the surrounding region (1193). Marquis Azzo of Este was podestà from 1206–8. Ezzelino was podestà in 1226 and retained his hold (though he was never *dominus*) from 1236 to 1259. Mastino della Scala was podestà del Popolo in 1259, Capitano del Popolo in 1262, and this family retained control up to 1387, the *de facto signoria* being passed on through successive generations (with an imperial vicariate from 1317). The Visconti gained authority from 1387–1403. In 1405 Verona passed to Venice and remained Venetian till 1797.

Vicenza made a treaty with Padua in 1115 and had consuls by 1122. It was in the Lombard League (1164) and gained the submission of Bassano (1175, in which year there was a podestà, Vazone of Cremona). The Popolo chose its own podestà in 1206 and won the right to one-third of the offices in 1222. Ezzelino (II) was podestà from 1210– c. 1213. Azzo of Este was podestà in 1236, in which year Ezzelino (III) became *signore*, until 1259.

Vicenza fell under Paduan control from 1266–1311, then under the Scaligeri from 1311–87 and the Visconti from 1387–1404. After 1404 it remained Venetian with the exception of a brief imperialist regime in 1509–15.

Viterbo was included in the Frankish donations to the papacy. From the twelfth century it was often threatened by the aggrandising policies of the city of Rome. It had consuls by 1148 (but probably as early as 1099). The first known podestà dates from 1197, but Marquis Conrad of Monferrat had been *Viterbensium dominus* c. 1176–7. The city received an imperial privilege in the latter year and was often under imperial control in the second half of the twelfth century (also in 1240–3 and 1247–51).

'Popular' institutions may date from the 1250s, but *anziani* of the Popolo or *reformatores* appear only in 1281.

From the fourteenth century direct papal rule alternated with periods of control by the Prefetti di Vico (before 1435) and another family of the region, the Gatti. After the early sixteenth century papal authority became the principal factor.

Index

DATE DUE
